War In
Peace

Volume 7

War In Peace

The Marshall Cavendish Illustrated Encyclopedia of Postwar Conflict.

Editor-in-Chief
Ashley Brown

Editorial Board
Brig-Gen. James Collins Jr (USA Retd.)
Vice-Admiral Sir Louis Le Bailly KBE CB
Ian V Hogg; David Floyd
Professor Laurence Martin
Air-Vice Marshal SWB Menaul CB CBE DFC AFC

MARSHALL CAVENDISH
NEW YORK, LONDON, TORONTO

Reference Edition Published 1985

Published by Marshall Cavendish Corporation
147 West Merrick Road
Freeport, Long Island
N.Y. 11520

Printed and Bound in Italy by L.E.G.O. S.p.a. Vicenza.

British Library Cataloguing in Publication Data

Brown, Ashley
    War in peace : the Marshall Cavendish
    illustrated encyclopaedia of post-war conflict.
    1. History, Modern—1945-   2. War—History
    —20th century
    I. Title   II. Dartford, Mark
    909.82   D842

    ISBN 0-86307-293-3
          0 86307 300 X   vol. 7

Library of Congress Cataloging in Publication Data

Main entry under title:

War in peace.

    Includes bibliographies and index.
    1. Military history, Modern—20th century.   2. Military
art and science—History—20th century.   3. World politics—1945-
I. Marshall Cavendish Corporation.
U42.W373 1984   355'.009'04   84-19386
ISBN 0-86307-293-3
          0 86307 300 X   vol. 7

Editorial Staff

Editor	Ashley Brown
Editorial Director	Brian Innes
Editorial Manager	Clare Byatt
Editorial Editors	Sam Elder
	Adrian Gilbert
Sub Editors	Sue Leonard
	Simon Innes
Artwork Editor	Jonathan Reed
Artwork Buyer	Jean Morley
Picture Editor	Carina Dvorak
Picture Consultant	Robert Hunt
Design	EDC

Reference Edition Staff

Editor	Mark Dartford
Designer	Graham Beehag
Consultant	Robert Paulley
Indexers	F & K Gill
Creation	DPM Services

Editorial Board

Contributors

David Blue served with the CIA in various countries of Southeast Asia, including Laos, and is a writer on and a student of small wars.

Gordon Brook-Shepherd spent 15 years in Vienna, first as lieutenant-colonel on the staff of the British High Commission and then as a foreign correspondent for the *Daily Telegraph*. A graduate in history from Cambridge, he is currently Chief Assistant Editor of the *Sunday Telegraph*.

Jeffrey J. Clarke is an expert on recent military history, particularly the Vietnam War, and has written for the American Center of Military History.

Major-General Richard Clutterbuck OBE has been Senior Lecturer in politics at Exeter University since his retirement from the army in 1972. His works include *Protest and the Urban Guerrilla, Guerrillas and Terrorists* and *Kidnap and Ransom*.

Alexander S. Cochran Jr is a historian whose area of research is modern Indochinese affairs with particular reference to the war in Vietnam since 1945. He is at present working in the Southeast Asia Branch of the Center of Military History, Department of the Army.

Colonel Peter M. Dunn is a serving officer in the USAF. His doctoral thesis is on the history of Indochina during the mid-1940s.

John B. Dwyer served both with the infantry and with armoured units in Vietnam. He was editor and publisher of the Vietnam veteran's newsletter *Perimeter* and has been a writer and correspondent for *National Vietnam Veteran's Review* for the past few years. His particular interest are Special Forces and Special Operations.

Brenda Ralph Lewis has specialised in political and military history since 1964. She s a regular contributor to military and historical magazines in both Britain and the United States.

Hugh Lunghi served in Moscow in the British Military Mission and the British Embassy for six years during and after World War II. He was interpreter for the British Chiefs of Staff at the Teheran, Yalta and Potsdam conferences, and also interpreted for Churchill and Anthony Eden. He subsequently worked in the BBC External Services and is a former editor of *Index on Censorship*.

Charles Messenger retired from the army in 1980 to become a fulltime military writer after 21 years service in the Royal Tank Regiment. Over the past 10 years he has written several books on 20th century warfare, as well as contributing articles to a number of defence and historical journals. He is currently a Research Associate at the Royal United Services Institute for Defence Studies in London.

Billy C. Mossman is a well-known American writer and historian. He is currently working on a volume on the Korean War for the US Army Center of Military History.

Bryan Perrett served in the Royal Armoured Corps from 1952 to 1971. He contributes regularly to a number of established military journals and acted as Defence Correspondent to the *Liverpool Echo* during the Falklands War. His recent books include *Weapons of the Falklands Conflict* and *A History of Blitzkrieg*.

Chapman Pincher is one of England's leading authorities on international espionage and counter-intelligence. He is the author of political novels and books on spying, the most recent of which is *Their Trade is Treachery*, which deals with the penetration of Britain's secret services by the Russian secret police.

Yehoshua Porath is a noted scholar at the Hebrew University in Jerusalem. He has made a special study of the Palestinian problem and is the author of two books on the subject, the most recent of which is *The Palestinian Arab National Movement 1929—39*, which was published in Britain in 1977.

Contributors

Antony Preston is Naval Editor of the military magazine *Defence* and author of numerous publications including *Battleships, Aircraft Carriers* and *Submarines.*

Brigadier-General Edwin H. Simmons, US Marine Corps, Retired, is the Director of Marine Corps History and Museums. At the time of the Inchon operation and the Chosin Reservoir campaign, he, as a major, commanded Weapons Company, 3rd Battalion, 1st Marines. Widely published, he is the author of *The United States Marines.*

Ronald Spector is an expert on Vietnam and has recently completed a book on that subject for the Center of Military History in the United States.

Andres Suarez served in the Cuban ministry of education from 1948–1951, took part in the Cuban revolution, and served in the ministry of housing from 1959. From 1965, he has been Professor of Latin American Studies at the University of Florida. Other publications include *Cuba and the Sino—Soviet Rift.*

Sir Robert Thompson KBE, CMG, DSO, MC is a world authority on guerrilla warfare, on which he has written extensively. He was directly involved in the Emergency in Malaya in the 1950s and rose to become permanent Secretary for Defence. From 1961 to 1965 he headed the British Advisory Mission to Vietnam and since then has advised several governments, including the United States, on counter-insurgency operations Sir Robert Thompson is a Council member of the Institute for the Study of Conflict, London. His books include *Defeating Communist Insurgency and Revolutionary War in World Strategy, 1945—69.*

Patrick Turnbull commanded 'D' Force, Burma during World War II. His 29 published works include a history of the Foreign Legion.

Contents of Volume

Taking to the streets

The development of urban guerrilla warfare in Latin America

Latin America has long exhibited two apparently contradictory characteristics: a marked social stability and resistance to change combined with a penchant for violence as part of the political process. In the 1960s its mushrooming cities provided an ideal site for the evolution of urban guerrilla warfare as a new form of revolutionary struggle with its own clearly articulated strategy and tactics.

Of course, the idea of politically inspired campaigns of violence in urban areas in the pursuit of revolutionary or nationalist objectives was neither new nor Latin American in origin. Latin American guerrillas themselves referred to the Jewish campaign in Palestine (1944–48) and the FLN campaign in Algeria (1954–62) as examples and sources of inspiration. Nevertheless, it was in Latin America that ideas of urban guerrilla warfare were first formulated and applied in a coherent and systematic manner, with all the implications that this entailed for the future conduct of operations by insurgents and counter-insurgents alike.

The theory of urban guerrilla action had its roots in the Spanish anarchist tradition, transferred to Latin America by theoreticians such as Abraham Guillen, a Spaniard associated with urban guerrillas in Uruguay, and in the ideas of violence as a social and personal cleansing force that were being expounded in the 1960s by such writers as Herbert Marcuse and Franz Fanon. In Latin America, the individual widely regarded as the father-figure of urban guerrilla warfare was the Brazilian, Carlos Marighela. His writings were banned in many countries and thereby acquired the status of holy writ, despite their lack of real coherence. Like Che Guevara, Marighela achieved revolutionary canonisation after an early death in heroic failure.

According to the theory, the aim of urban guerrilla warfare was to provoke a political and social crisis within the state that the revolutionary cause would then be able to exploit. A small number of lightly armed fighters, protected by the anonymity of the modern city, would be able to humiliate the authorities and undermine the sense of stability and legitimacy on which government pow-

er rests. The theory appealed especially to disaffected members of middle-class youth – it provided the immediate possibility of spectacular action, very different from the painstaking organisation and patient long-term planning typical of the communists and other traditional revolutionary groups. But two problems posed by the urban guerrilla theory were never effectively tackled in practice: Marighela was adamant that the urban campaign could only succeed in cooperation with rural insurgency and with the eventual support of mass action by the urban population. Cut off by their clandestine methods from any contact with a mass

Below: Bleeding profusely from a head wound, a Peruvian guerrilla of the Maoist 'Sendero Luminoso' group is displayed by his comrades after being shot and killed by the Guardia Civil.
Bottom: Venezuelan politicians display part of a captured guerrilla arms cache supposedly supplied by Cuba.

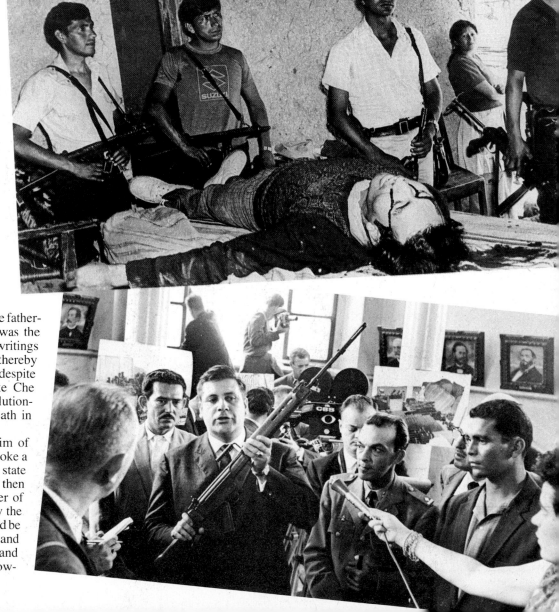

organisation and unable to link up with rural insurgents, the urban guerrillas remained isolated and even at their most successful and popular were far from any possibility of eventual victory.

The choice of the urban battlefield was natural in some Latin American countries – in Uruguay, for example, over half the population lived in the capital city, Montevideo, and the rural terrain offered poor cover for guerrilla action, while in Argentina over 70 per cent of the population lived in urban areas. But the turn to urban action was encouraged by the disastrous failure of rural insurgency in Latin America from the time of the Cuban revolution to 1967.

In fact, the Cuban campaign of 1956-59 had been characterised by a consistently high level of urban violence that proved crucial in polarising Cuban society against the government of General Fulgencio Batista, providing the rural insurgency movement of Fidel Castro with a constant source of manpower, supplies and money, and sapping the will of the security forces for the struggle in the countryside. But

Castro deliberately played down the urban contribution to his victory and his would-be emulators in Central and South America dedicated themselves to rural campaigns. The decisive defeat of the small rural guerrilla bands, culminating in the death of the legendary Che Guevara in Bolivia in 1967, encouraged the growth of the urban guerrilla movements, most notably in Venezuela, Uruguay, Argentina, Brazil and Guatemala. In some countries rural guerrilla warfare carried on – notably Peru, where unrest among the Indian population was constant throughout the 1970s – while in Colombia insurgency in the countryside was accompanied by small-scale guerrilla actions in the streets of the capital, Bogota. But after 1967 the major revolutionary movements operated in towns.

In Venezuela and Uruguay, urban guerrillas fought against democratic regimes. The Uruguayan movement was the Movimiento de Liberación Nacional – popularly known as the Tupamaros – while in Venezuela the main threat to the authorities was posed by

Below: Drenched in cow's blood, a member of a crack Peruvian anti-terrorist squad brandishes a knife during a psychological training programme.

The long shadow of Uncle Sam

Latin American urban guerrillas regarded US officials and businesses as prime targets for attack, while the Americans in their turn were dedicated to preventing guerrilla victories. From 1959 onwards US governments pursued a twin policy of financing economic and social development to obviate the root causes of discontent in Latin America and providing training and equipment to improve the counter-insurgency capability of the Latin American military. In the course of the 1960s several thousand officers from most Latin American countries underwent training each year in various US installations, such as the School of the Americas in Panama. Police forces also received equipment and training – between 1966 and 1970 more than 3500 Latin American police officers were trained by US Agency for International Development (AID) personnel and the FBI.

Under President Kennedy in the early 1960s, US support for Latin American governments was allied to the promotion of democracy in the region, but from 1964, with Johnson as president, the US shifted towards backing for military regimes – immediately after the military take-over in Brazil in April 1964 President Johnson sent the new leaders a telegram of congratulations. It was made clear to governments that they had carte blanche to carry out whatever measures they might feel necessary to guarantee internal security. Murder, torture and other violations of human rights would not lose a regime American financial and technical backing. Without US support, many regimes might have crumbled in the face of determined guerrilla attacks.

The culmination of this policy came under President Nixon when the US played a significant role in bringing to power the brutal military government of General Pinochet in Chile in 1973. Support for military regimes and extreme methods of repression was certainly effective in keeping the enemies of the US out of power, but US governments could not avoid criticism on moral grounds for their policies.

the Fuerzas Armadas de Liberación Nacional (FALN). The FALN flourished (and was largely defeated) in 1963, before the theory of urban guerrilla conflict had evolved. The democratically-elected Venezuelan government succeeded in beating down the challenge to its authority while in general maintaining the rule of law and democratic practice. In this it was unique. By contrast, in Uruguay the Tupamaros campaign resulted in the destruction of a long-established democratic tradition, but not to their advantage. Founded in the early 1960s, the Tupamaros were probably the first revolutionary movement to reject Castro's ideas and assert that rural insurgency had limited relevance in a society which was predominantly urban. They were well organised and their

The United States were particularly concerned over the political atmosphere throughout Latin America and were keen to deny left-wing militants a foothold. While Castro (right, during a visit to Chile) was the great example for revolutionaries, the US was more than willing to offer support to threatened administrations (above, the Venezuelan President, Romulo Betancourt, left, meets with US President Kennedy at the White House).

activities between 1968 and 1970 contained a very attractive public relations element that invited imitation. Increasingly committed to the struggle from 1971, however, the armed forces effectively destroyed the Tupamaros in the course of 1972 by the suspension of civil rights and ruthless interrogation, and the next year the military took over government.

In Brazil and Guatemala counter-terror was also practised, with much the same result. In Brazil a wave of social discontent followed in the wake of the 1964 military coup that removed the moderately reformist government of João Goulart. In the years that followed, the hard-line monetarist policies of Marshal Castelo Branco were matched by mass arrests, torture and murder by the security forces as they broke what little power was wielded by the guerrilla organisations, which were plagued by constant fragmentation along ideological lines that sapped their strength and vitality. Exactly the same situation prevailed in Guatemala where successive attempts to wage revolutionary warfare were wrecked by counter-terrorism of a savagery unparalleled anywhere in Latin America, and by the weaknesses within the divided revolutionary movement. Just as the death of Carlos Marighela in a gun battle with police in São Paulo in November 1969 broke the effectiveness of his Accão Libertadora Nacional party in Brazil, so the most powerful of the Guatemalan groups, the Trotskyist Movimiento Revolucionario 13 Noviembre (MR-13) never recovered from the loss of their leader, Yon Sosa, in May 1970. Neither MR-13 nor the other major Guatemalan insurgent force of the 1960s, the Fuerzas Armadas Rebeldes, was able to soldier on into the 1970s.

Brutality and death

In Argentina, the Peronist Montoneros and the Trotskyist Ejército Revolucionario del Pueblo began operations in 1970 against the Lanussa military junta and helped bring about its fall in 1973, but under the succeeding Peronist regime their actions only increased in ferocity. The return to military rule in 1976 was welcomed by many Argentinians as the only means of stopping a slide to full-scale civil war, but the regime of General Jorge Videla proved exceptionally brutal. The military regarded its operations as 'directed against a minority whom we do not consider Argentinians', a type of logic which offered a free hand to right-wing vigilantes and the security services to detain, torture and murder at will. Between 1976 and 1982, perhaps 10,000 people 'disappeared'. This counter-terrorism broke the urban guerrilla movements, but it made a return to civilian rule unthinkable because the military dared not put itself in the position of having to account for its actions. It took the 1982 Falklands War to bring back civilian government.

The ultimate failure of urban guerrilla warfare in the 1960s and early 1970s was the result of a combination of factors. The urban masses were too disorganised and divided to provide a radical base for social upheaval, and the guerrilla movements themselves were almost without exception divided and unable to cooperate against the security forces. But the prime cause of their failure was the readiness of the police, the army and the death-squads to use the most extreme and indiscriminate measures to ensure the maintenance of the status quo. Whether such counter-terrorism offers any real prospect for future stability in Latin America must be doubtful. **R. G. Grant**

Maxims from Marighela's Minimanual

As a theoretician, Carlos Marighela stuck close to the practicalities of urban guerrilla warfare, steering clear of ideological questions:

'Experience has shown that the basic arm of the urban guerrilla is the sub-machine gun. This arm, in addition to being efficient and easy to shoot in an urban area, has the advantage of being greatly respected by the enemy...

'The ideal machine gun for the urban guerrilla is the INA .45 calibre ... Each firing group of urban guerrillas must have a machine gun managed by a good marksman. The other components of the group must be armed with .38 revolvers, our standard arm....

'In order to function, the urban guerrillas must be organised in small groups. A group of no more than four or five is called the firing group.... The old-type hierarchy, the style of the traditional left, doesn't exist in our organisation. This means that, except for the priority of objectives set by the strategic command, any firing group can decide to assault a bank, to kidnap or to execute an agent of the dictatorship, a figure identified with the reaction, or a North American spy, and

Above: Carlos Marighela

can carry out any kind of propaganda or war of nerves against the enemy without the need to consult the general command....

'The organisation is an indestructible network of firing groups...that functions simply and practically with a general command that also participates in the attacks; an organisation that exists for no other purpose than pure and simple revolutionary action.'

Carlos Marighela writing in his Urban Guerrilla Minimanual.

Heroes or villains?

The Tupamaros in Uruguay

The Tupamaros, founded in 1963 by Raúl Sendic Antanaccio (above left), quickly gained notoriety with a spectacular series of bank raids and terrorist acts, often leaving their distinctive sign (above right). The success of the Tupamaros in destroying democratic government, however, gave the military a free hand to embark upon a programme of ruthless interrogation which led to many informers exposing the whereabouts of known Tupamaros (left, a Tupamaros leader is arrested by police).

The Tupamaros were the most famous of all the urban guerrilla movements that operated in South America. Officially named the Movimiento de Liberación Nacional (MLN), the guerrilla organisation survived in the streets of Uruguay for a decade from 1963 to 1973, grabbing the headlines with a spectacular sequence of bank raids, kidnappings, terrorist acts and publicity stunts. In their early years they showed an unfailing sense of public relations, as when, on Christmas Eve 1963, they hijacked truckloads of Christmas food and distributed it in the slums of Uruguay's capital, Montevideo. Small gestures became famous – when a bystander fainted during a Tupamaros bank raid, a guerrilla stopped to give her first aid. But this 'Robin Hood' image of the Tupamaros faded in the later years as their conflict with the police, the army and right-wing death squads grew in bitterness, and the guerrillas found themselves with blood on their hands.

The Tupamaros are generally credited with the destruction of democratic government in Uruguay, but the movement was the product, not the cause, of a deepening political, economic and social crisis within Uruguay that would have come to a head at some time, with or without the urban guerrillas. Uruguay was a country with an enviable record of stable government, democratic practice and advanced social legislation that set her apart from every other country in South America, but in the 1960s the bill for this record was presented, and dishonoured. The economy could no longer sustain high living standards, fund the welfare system, and service a growing debt. With the country unable to pay its way, inflation was rampant – the cost of living index rose by 6457 per cent between 1962 and 1972. As early as 1965 civil rights guaranteed under the constitution were suspended in order to deal with labour unrest, and the period 1965–72 as a whole witnessed a series of increasingly bitter disputes between unionised workers and the government. Uruguay's two-party system was conservative, too weak to govern (still less to reform), but too strong to be superseded by a radical alternative. In short, by the mid-1960s Uruguay's economic performance could not match national expectations, and her political system could neither lead nor govern.

Revolutionary consciousness

Such was the background to the formation of the MLN by Raúl Sendic Antanaccio, a former union activist, in early 1963. Perhaps somewhat surprisingly in view of its assertion 'that revolutionary action in itself... generates revolutionary consciousness, organisation and conditions', the MLN did not begin its main campaign until five years later, in 1968. In 1965, for example, it carried out only four operations of any significance, all of them bombings of institutions. One of these bombings (the 9 August 1965 attack on the Bayer chemical company which was supplying the Americans in Vietnam) was the occasion of the MLN announcing itself as the Tupamaros. The period 1963–68 was one of careful organisation and a deliberate avoidance of any premature action that could alienate potential support and provoke a police response that the Tupamaros would be as yet too weak to resist. During this time they created the military infrastructure that would be the basis of future armed action, adopting the cell – equivalent to the Provisional IRA active service unit – as the basic unit of organisation. Each cell had between five and ten members and was grouped with the other cells into 'columns'. Cells were supposedly self-contained, self-supporting and, if necessary, capable of reconstituting themselves if ravaged by police operations. By this policy of decentralisation the Tupamaros sought to ensure security against infiltration and guarantee survival as they set about securing support from individuals at every level of society. As with everything the Tupamaros did, these efforts were successful up to a point.

The movement had few working-class activists and commanded only limited support in the unions. The guerrillas were overwhelmingly drawn from the intellectual and professional classes. The Tupamaros never had a precise ideology, so they avoided the damaging fragmentation so common to the revolutionary left and did not antagonise people on ideological grounds. But the movement lacked a coherent political programme, although it did proclaim itself to be socialist, in favour of workers' control, and for revolutionary solidarity with the rest of Latin America. Such causes held only limited attraction for most Uruguayans when the going got tough, although many were amused, impressed and even sympathetic to individual Tupamaros acts (an opinion poll in 1970

Prisoner of the Tupamaros

Above: Geoffrey Jackson, British ambassador, in his 'people's prison'.

On 8 January 1971 the British ambassador, Geoffrey Jackson, was kidnapped by the Tupamaros. After his eight-month ordeal in captivity, he wrote this account of his abduction:

'It was a beautiful morning, and the way we took to the Rambla was very quiet; the president had just left on a seaside holiday, taking with him many of the usual security forces. As always, I was relieved when we turned in from the open corniche into the narrow and crowded side-streets leading to my office, and I was joking with my driver as we edged slowly along the single lane left by the vehicles parked on either side. We were at a point where virtually every day we had to wait for delivery-trucks to finish unloading at one or other of the wayside stores, so I did not pay especial attention to a large red van – certainly of three, possibly of five tons – until it edged out from the kerb as we drew level. There was little room for my driver to swerve, but ample time for the truck-driver to realise and correct his mistake. I knew however that frequently they did not do so till after impact, and was not really surprised when, despite my driver's signals, he bored relentlessly into our left front wing. With a philosophical shrug, and obvious resignation to a coachwork job and some ineffectual insurance activity, Hugo opened his door to climb out and take particulars.

'Instead, as the cab-door opened and the truck-driver leapt down, a young man stepped from nowhere and struck Hugo savagely over the head. Simultaneously there was a violent rattle of automatic weapons which continued for what to me seemed an endless time; one of its main constituents originated from a sub-machine gun concealed in a basket of fruit carried by an apparently innocuous bystander – my captors were very proud of this refinement, of which I was told repeatedly afterwards.

'The driver of the truck climbed into my chauffeur's seat, and opened the opposite door for a second young man. A third put his arm round the door-pillar and expertly unlocked the back door from the inside, while a fourth, stationed next to me by the right-hand rear door... danced a dance like a semi-despondent fury, making frantic and furious signals at me, presumably to encourage me to open the door for him. This was done for him by the third young man, who had meanwhile climbed into the rear compartment by the now open door, on which Operative Number Four came in shooting – quite inexplicably, if my capture was the aim, because he nearly killed me, to quote him as he sat across my knee with his smoking automatic after two holes, in apparent slow motion, had appeared in the seat next to my leg and in the roof above my head. "Almost I killed you, Old Man," he yelled accusingly as he proceeded to hammer away at my head....'

revealed 20 per cent public support for the guerrillas).

The upsurge of guerrilla activity in 1968 coincided with rising trade union and student unrest. The Tupamaros concentrated first on operations designed to humiliate the authorities and keep the movement supplied with money and arms; bloodshed was avoided where possible. The guerrilla organisation was expensive to run and the Tupamaros operated on the principle that the capitalists should finance it. Bank raids became commonplace – in one week in May 1969 there were nine successful robberies – although the biggest haul was not from a bank, but from a raid on General Motors at Penarol which yielded 500 million pesos in June 1969. Other operations secured penicillin, wigs from a Montevideo beauty parlour and radios and transmitters (the Tupamaros operated a clandestine radio station). Arms and ammunition were obtained through the temporary occupation of police stations and military installations: for instance, on 29 May 1970 the Tupamaros raided, and for several hours occupied, the Navy Training Center in Montevideo, escaping with nearly 500 weapons and 60,000 rounds of ammunition. On 8 October 1969 the guerrillas even occupied the whole town of Pondo. When Tupamaros were captured, daring raids were carried out to liberate them.

Abductions of important personalities were used to reveal the inability of the government to protect its supporters in the most humiliating way possible. Another major embarrassment for the government came as a result of a raid on a finance house, Financiera Monty, on 14 February 1969. The Tupamaros made public documents captured in the raid which revealed widespread corruption on the part of many closely associated with the regime. The inability of

the authorities to stop the Tupamaros put intense strain on a political system already under attack from strikes and demonstrations.

Around 1970, however, the nature of the conflict began to change. When the Tupamaros started their activities, they opposed a society which had been at peace for 60 years and a police force that was not trained for counter-insurgency. The police soon became demoralised by their inability to deal with the guerrillas. But by 1970 the military were taking an ever increasing role in the fight against the guerrillas. 1970 also saw the emergence of right-wing death squads, dedicated to violence against the Tupamaros and other left-wingers.

The Tupamaros' activities also changed. In 15

Above: Angry street scenes as well protected policemen search a block in Montevideo looking for Tupamaros sympathisers.
Below: Despite the oppressive measures instigated by the government, the Tupamaros continued to proclaim their existence by daubing graffiti on walls and buildings.
Right: Government troops and police surround a wounded guerrilla.

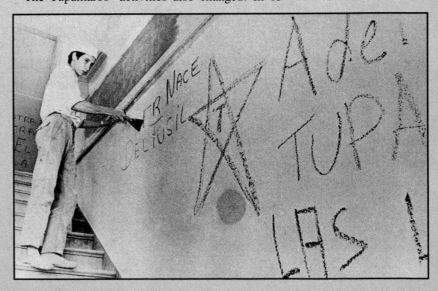

November 1969 they carried out their first assassination. In early 1970 a Brazilian diplomat, a US agronomist and a US adviser to the police were abducted and kept in clandestine 'people's prisons'. On 7 August, as negotiations for the release of these foreign hostages in return for Tupamaros prisoners were proceeding, nine members of the Tupamaros leadership, including Raúl Sendic, were arrested. In reply, on 9 August, the US police adviser Dan Mitrione was killed. The following January the British ambassador, Geoffrey Jackson, was kidnapped; he was not released until September 1971. A house-to-house search of Montevideo and the most extensive security measures had failed to discover his 'people's prison'. Jackson's kidnapping was used as propaganda by the Tupamaros, who allowed him to be interviewed and photographed by journalists and made the maximum effort to publicise their success in holding him for so long, until they finally released him.

But the tide was turning against the Tupamaros. They knew that ultimate success would elude them unless they waged a 'combined struggle', an amalgam of urban and rural guerrilla warfare and mass political action. They developed a mass support organisation (the Comités de Apoyo Tupamaro) and tried to diversify operations into the countryside, but in these efforts they failed. In effect, the Tupamaros lacked the technique to grow from an elitist group that owed its success to secrecy and anonymity into a mass organisation. The Tupamaros gave critical support to a broad left-wing coalition, the Frente Ampla, in the presidential elections of November 1971, but this grouping obtained only 18 per cent of the vote. The elections brought a hard-line conservative, Juan María Bordaberry, to the presidency.

On 14 April 1972 the Tupamaros killed four members of death squads and, in response, the government declared a state of 'internal war'. A series of attacks by death squads, the police and the army ravaged the Tupamaros and other left-wing organisations. Between April and July 1972 the authorities claimed to have killed 100 Tupamaros and arrested 600 more. The guerrillas had breached their own security by their attempt to move into rural areas and to build up a mass organisation, and the authorities were increasingly unscrupulous in their methods. The Tupamaros had sought to polarise society and promote confrontation by their actions, but now they were no match for army terror tactics of torture and murder.

The intensifying anti-guerrilla campaign had effectively given the military control of the country. In February 1973 the army and air force began to move against civilian rule; by June President Bordaberry had been reduced to a mere figurehead and congress was suspended. Uninhibited by the restraints of a democratic government, the military were able to use mass arrests and ruthless interrogation to break the Tupamaros for good, as well as crushing all other opposition.

The Tupamaros were the product of a democracy that was in decline and which they destroyed. They proved too weak, however, to take advantage of this success, and the inheritance passed to their enemies. In the words of one observer, 'the Tupamaros dug the grave of democracy and fell into it themselves'.

Graham Brewer

Attack on the Navy Training Center

In the early hours of the morning of 29 May 1970, the Tupamaros raided the Navy Training Center in the heart of the Uruguayan capital, Montevideo. The following account, translated from a South American newspaper report, conveys the spirit of skill and daring that characterised so many Tupamaros actions at this time, winning the admiration of Latin American radicals and humiliating government forces incapable even of defending their own installations.

Guerrilla raid

❝ Fernando Garin takes off his helment and puts it on again. It is 1.45 on the morning of 29 May 1970, and everything has been planned. Garin is an orderly of the guard, so the sentry standing at the entrance of the Uruguayan Navy Training Center pays no attention to this unimportant gesture.

The three men in the car which has just taken off down Washington Street toward the center know with certainty that the man who removed his helmet and put it on again is Fernando Garin, 23 years old, a native of the town of Juan Iacase, and son of one of the founders of the textile syndicate.

Next to the car rises the strongwall of the military center. A hundred metres away the traffic in Montevideo's seaside avenue is heavy in spite of the hour. On the roof of the entrance gate, there is another sentry. Around 60 persons – officers and sailors – sleep inside the old building. Another guard stands in back, facing the street called Lindolfo Cuestas, and, in the surroundings of the garrison, 19 commandos belonging to the Tupamaros await a signal.

Now everything depends on the three revolutionaries who are in the car and, above all, on Fernando Garin's steady nerves. When the car stops in front of the gate, the guards become worried. Two Tupamaros get out of the automobile. 'We're from the police, we need to see the officer on duty,' they command with an authoritarian voice. The guard calls the orderly. Garin comes out frowning, pretending suspicion. He goes to one side and inspects the papers of the alleged police agents. He asks them to go in.

The scene is carefully watched by other members of the Tupamaros who are hiding in the darkness of the street a hundred metres away. Before crossing the entrance-gate one of the men looks rapidly above: on the roof, four metres above the ground, the sentry, now at ease, puts down his AR-15.

The garrison fortress is in a dock neighbourhood on the corner of Washington and Guarani Streets, only two blocks away from Buenos Aires Street. Twelve blocks away stands the Plaza de la Independencia and the Presidential Palace.

An enamoured couple wanders down Washington Street. As they pass by the garrison's high grey wall, one of the newly arrived 'policemen' halts them.

'Identification.' he demands.

(Nervous hands, signs of weakness, the boy searches in his pockets, the girl in her purse.)

'We don't have any,' they say in a low voice. 'We're students from the Institute Vazquez Acevedo. We can prove it.'

'We'll see,' answers the policeman and orders them to go into the garrison.

Meanwhile, on the garrison roof, Garin walks up to the sentry and tells him he's come to substitute for him. There seems to be too much activity this morning, though, and the sentry feels that something is not working right; it can be observed in his indecision. But Garin strikes the guard in the stomach with his Colt .45 and takes the rifle.

By now, the 'policemen' and the two 'students' have surrounded the sentry at the entrance gate. From above, Garin is pointing a rifle at him.

When Garin and the two Tupamaros disguised as policemen enter the military establishment, the corporal calls the officer on duty. He doesn't suspect anything and it doesn't occur to him to ring the alarm which would go off in the dormitories. The officer and the corporal are quickly overpowered and tied up.

Uruguayan sailors wear a special poncho which can easily be exchanged; two Tupamaros slip into the ponchos and take over the guard. From outside, the Navy Training Center looks just the same as any other night.

Seventeen more Tupamaro commandos are let into the garrison courtyard. They take over the building in which 30 sailors are sleeping – and the infirmary, the dining room, the recruiting office, the officers' rooms, the artillery section . . . .

The startled sailors are lined up in the central patio, most of them still in underclothes. There is tension among the Tupamaros because the keys to the cells don't show up. Twenty minutes later the cells are opened and the sailors are locked up.

A truck enters through the entrance gate and parks in the middle of the patio. The commandos empty the arsenal and gather up the arms left in the dormitories. A total of 300 rifles, two .30 calibre machine guns, 60,000 bullets, 150 Colt .45 calibre pistols, several sub-machine guns, and six AR-15 rifles used by the Americans in Vietnam plus 75 powerful grenades also used in Indochina.

Just at this moment, two sailors belonging to the garrison arrive at the entrance, greet the disguised Tupamaros, and go on in. But the commandos have prepared for this kind of an emergency, and a special trap controls them as they enter.

At 3.30 am, the truck carrying the arsenal and the commandos pulls out of the garrison unnoticed, leaving six Tupamaros behind. All the telephone wires have been cut from the beginning. The garrison is completely quiet; only the traffic on the nearby avenue can be heard.

One of the remaining commandos quietly raises the Tupamaro flag, takes photographs of the jailed officers and sailors, of the flag, and of the revolutionary slogans written on the walls. Garin leaves a letter explaining how he could no longer endure seeing the tortures inflicted on the workers of 'Usinas y Telefonos del Estado' who were arrested during a strike. At 4.15, the remaining Tupamaros depart from the garrison and drive out of the area in a number of cars left parked in the vicinity.

Quite some time passes before a group of navy officers manage to open up their locks, and run to warn the Army Intelligence Service, located two blocks away. Agents and navy forces begin to mobilise, but only the Tupamaro flag remains in the morning of the 29th, when the president, the minister of defense, and high military chiefs begin an emergency meeting. 99

Far left: Shortly after the successful Tupamaros raid on the Uruguayan Navy Training Center, military police stop and search a passing bus at a city roadblock. Below: The prison of Punta Carretas, guarded by an M3 light tank, from which over 106 Tupamaros escaped *en masse* in 1971.

Theorists and gunmen

Brazilian revolutionaries from the 1960s

The Brazilian authorities had the unique distinction of beginning their counter-insurgency crackdown before guerrilla warfare started. This was a consequence of the Brazilian armed forces' conviction that a good part of the legitimate business of the military was to act specifically as the leader and ruler of the nation. The Brazilian Superior War College had long run courses on political and economic affairs as well as on military matters and indoctrinated officers with the notion that Brazilian economic expansion was vital to achieve their goal of turning the nation into a global superpower. As nothing was to be allowed to stand in the way of this objective, the armed forces toppled the reformist President João Goulart in April 1964. After their coup, the forces tried to establish various sub-democratic forms for the election of the president but in reality Brazil had a military government.

The military regime was paranoiacally concerned with a guerrilla uprising. Castroite imitators were springing up all over Latin America but, in Brazil itself, the radical opposition had been caught off guard by the military coup and was incapable of mounting armed opposition. Rural guerrillas raised their heads briefly in 1967 but were swiftly destroyed. The real opposition problem was one of schism and faction-fighting. The communists held that armed revolt was wrong because the situation was not ripe for it and, while this was incontestably true, the more fiery spirits could not tolerate inaction but split into a complex maze of extremist groups and military formations.

In its way the Brazilian government constructed its own guerrilla opposition. When student protests and demonstrations against the regime gathered force in 1968, the military insisted that they were communist-inspired (when there was good evidence that they were not) and suppressed them with unnecessary brutality. It is true that there were some inept attempts at a bombing campaign but, in the main, the opposition of 1968 consisted of middle-class students who were bemused to have tanks and heavily armed gendarmes deployed against them and horrified to find that they were possible targets for a fully-fledged right-wing death squad, the Comando Caça Comunista (CCC – Commando for Hunting Communists). Protest had become too dangerous and the movement declined after October 1968, but its more determined supporters probably decided then on guerrilla action.

Resistance movements

The violent opposition that already existed was too ramshackle to be taken seriously and it had not achieved much. A Maoist wing of the Brazilian Communist Party had been advocating armed resistance since 1962 and there was a Brazilian nationalist radical group, the Movimento Nacionalista Revolucionário (MNR), which was formed fairly soon after the coup. There were also the Movimento Armado Revolucionário (MAR – Armed Revolutionary Movement) and the Movimento Revolucionário do Julho 26 (MR-26 – the 26 July Revolutionary Movement). Indeed the profusion of groups affords a certain grim commentary on the confusion of the guerrillas. A typical example might be POLOP (Workers' Politics) which split into the Vanguarda Popular Revolucionária (VPR – Popular Revolutionary Vanguard), which later allied to the MNR, and the COLINA (Commando of National Liberation) which turned into the VAR-Palmares (Armed Revolutionary Vanguard). The remaining POLOP members allied with a Communist Party splinter group to become the POC (Workers' Communist Party) but later split with it and readopted the name POLOP. Of all these guerrilla groups the most important were to be the Acção Libertadora Nacional (ALN – National Liberation Action) led by Carlos Marighela and the VPR led by Carlos Lamarca, a renegade army captain.

The intensive phase of urban guerrilla activity occurred between 1969 and 1971, but at no stage did the guerrillas look like winning. In January 1969 Lamarca defected from the army with automatic weapons and the incidence of bank raids and attacks on government installations increased. In August the ALN seized Radio São Paulo and Marighela broadcast a speech while, on 4 September, the US ambassador C. Burke Elbrick was kidnapped. This marked

Top left: Large areas of urban squalor illustrate the conditions in which revolution and dissent bred rapidly.
Above: Well armed Brazilian miners reflect the fear of attack from both government and rebel forces. Right: In response to the military domination of their country, Brazilian terrorists struck back with a series of attacks against military personnel. Here, Admiral Nelson Fernandez lies dying after an attack which also killed General Artur Costa e Silva, the presidential candidate for the army.

the high water mark of guerrilla success. On 4 November Marighela was shot dead and the authorities let it be known that he had been betrayed under torture by two Dominican friars, which led to coolness between the revolutionaries and their supporters in the church. There were other kidnappings: the Japanese consul and the German and Swiss ambassadors were taken but the government always struck back fiercely. In April and October 1970 the ALN lost de Brito and Ferreira who had succeeded Marighela as leader. With the ALN decapitated, the other guerrilla groups were steadily culled. The last act in the most violent stage of the drama came in August 1971 when the important VPR activist Jose Raimundo Costa was shot dead and, shortly afterwards, his chief, Carlos Lamarca, was betrayed by a fellow revolutionary under torture and killed.

In more stable political worlds – in Western Europe, for example – urban guerrillas were opposed by methods that usually respected basic human rights.

But in Brazil, as in Argentina, the insecure military government was unrestrained in its reaction, and took the opportunity to destroy many political opponents, not merely the guerrillas.

There were dozens of torture centres all over the country often seeming to compete with one another: São Paulo alone had an establishment at Rua Tutoia 921, the infamous Tiradentes prison and the Operations Centre for Internal Defence headquarters, not to mention a similar institution run by the Division of Internal Operations and yet another centre run by the Department of Political and Social Order. There were further death squad organisations (notably the Operação Bandeirantes – OBAN) which competed with the CCC. The sheer weight of torture and murder that fell on the urban guerrilla movement was too much for it to cope with and it was rapidly snuffed out. Guerrilla attacks tailed off markedly in 1971 and most of the remaining dissident leaders admitted in 1973 that their campaign had been defeated. **P.J. Banyard**

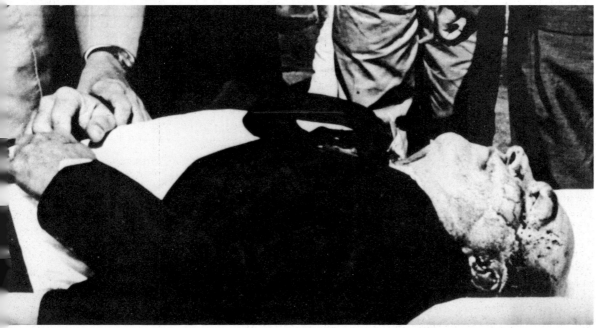

Under the premise that it was the military's duty to act specifically as the leader and ruler of the Brazilian nation, the armed forces removed President João Goulart (above left) from power and replaced him with a military administration under Marshal Humberto de Alencar Castelo Branco (above right) in April 1964.

From pampas to plaza
The Argentinian urban guerrillas

In the mid-1960s when rural guerrilla movements were springing up all over Latin America, Argentina was not much affected. It was the accepted opinion among radicals (endorsed by the famous Argentinian-born revolutionary Che Guevara) that Argentinian society was too hopelessly bourgeois to support a guerrilla movement. The point seemed proved in early 1964 when the Argentinian gendarmerie discovered a guerrilla band in the northwest of the country and destroyed it in a series of clashes which cost the life of a single gendarme for the death of 15 or so guerrillas and the capture of some two dozen more. All the guerrillas identified who were Argentine citizens were distinctly middle class: students and office workers without a single peasant in their number. On the other hand it was clear enough that, if the peasantry was not a radical influence, there were classes in the towns who made up for the apathetic showing of the countryside with their revolutionary fervour. In the capital, Buenos Aires, there was a proliferation of extreme left-wing groups and publications and these urban organisations often supported guerrilla movements in other countries.

Throughout the 1960s and 1970s Argentina suffered from a long-drawn-out political and economic crisis which effectively provided these urban radicals with the right situation for guerrilla action. These difficulties were the legacy of the deposition of the popular President Juan Perón by the armed forces in September 1955. Perón was no ordinary figure in Argentine politics but the founder of 'Peronism', a genuine mass movement with a quasi left-wing political stance which, in fact, owed as much to fascism as to socialism. After 1955 Perón was exiled but the Peronistas were still very much a force for opposition in the country as military or military-approved governments tried to combat the economic chaos inherited from Perón. The endless deflationary squeeze of the 1960s produced much hardship which ended in a rising in Cordoba – the *Cordobazo* – in May 1969. This proved to be the watershed that provoked urban guerrilla action on the one hand and instilled uncertainty in the government on the other.

In July 1970 the Trotskyite Revolucionario de los Trabajadores (Workers Revolutionary Party) set up an armed wing called the Ejército Revolucionario del Pueblo (ERP – People's Revolutionary Army) which was to be the most active guerrilla organisation in the first years of the struggle. The ERP was hostile to the orthodox Communist Party of Argentina and to its Maoist wing which, in turn, had its own armed group the Fuerzas Armadas de Liberacion (FAL – Armed Forces of Liberation). None of the Communist groups were on good terms with the two Peronist groups which were the Montoneros and the Fuerzas Armadas Revolucionarias (FAR – Revolutionary Armed

Above: Hooded terrorists in Argentina called a press conference in 1971 to announce a new plan of action. Above right: General Videla who assumed power after Isabel Perón was deposed and whose military government mounted unscrupulous attacks against the terrorists.

Right: Government anti-guerrilla commandos break camp and prepare to move onto the offensive against a Montoneros base. From 1973 onwards, the guerrillas expanded their operations to include rural warfare as well as the established urban operations.

Forces). The confusion was to be slightly lessened in October 1973 when the two Peronist groups joined forces.

At first the violence was limited to the selective assassination of army officers, police officers and government officials. To finance their campaigns the guerrillas started a successful and ruthless policy of kidnapping the owners or representatives of major businesses. The ransoms demanded were very large indeed (above $14,000,000 in one case) and they were usually paid because those victims who were not ransomed were promptly murdered. In response to this the authorities substituted one unsatisfactory general for another in power and agreed to presidential elections in May 1973. These elections were won by Perón's nominee, Hector Cámpora, and in June, when Perón returned to Argentina in triumph amid public jubilation, Cámpora stood down and Perón was elected president while his wife Isabel became vice-president.

Attacking military targets

It might have been supposed that the Peronist terrorist groups would become inactive once Perón was returned to power but this did not prove to be so. While the institutions of the previous regime (such as the bureaucracy and the armed forces) still existed, the Montoneros felt quite at liberty to attack them. In fact they had moved far to the left of Perón's position and would be unsatisfied with any reforms he might make. There was also the matter of the increasing power of the Trotskyite ERP; the Montoneros were uneasy at being outshone by the ERP who had expanded their activities to include rural guerrilla warfare in 1973 and were ready to begin a new and intensive phase of their insurrection by using large bands of guerrillas to attack military targets. In January 1974 70 men attacked the barracks at Azul, killing the commanding officer of the garrison and his family and capturing a colonel. This trick did not work twice. In August an assault on the barracks at Catamarca by 90 guerrillas was beaten off and they lost 19 dead and 15 captured. In December 1975 a force of some 500 ERP men attacked the Monte Chingolo arsenal outside Buenos Aires but lost 160 dead.

By this time Perón's death had to some extent unshackled the Montoneros. Perón died in July 1974 and was replaced as president by his wife. The loyalty of the Peronists to Isabel was rather patchy and labour unrest began to add an endless series of strikes to the deteriorating security situation. Señora Perón became increasingly isolated and appeared to rely utterly on the advice of Lopez Rega who had been her husband's secretary. Accusations of corruption and a lack of confidence in the regime led the Argentine Congress to propose impeachment of Señora Perón but she forestalled this move by suspending Congress. From that moment on the government's claim to legitimacy and a democratic mandate looked shaky.

All the while the breakdown in law and order grew worse. By summer 1975 the ERP rural guerrillas were operating on such a scale in Tucuman province that the army deployed its entire 5th Infantry Brigade in a major counter-insurgency operation. By the first months of 1976 the 5th Brigade had achieved a series of successes and claimed to have killed 174 terrorists but, in other ways, 1975 had gone very badly for the security forces. The guerrillas had begun to shoot

down aircraft; their most successful effort in this direction was in January 1975 when they destroyed an aircraft carrying a number of members of the Army General Staff. Attacks on military installations grew ever more daring and, in August, a frigate that was being built in the Rio Santiago naval shipyard was blown up and sunk. At other times civilian aircraft were hijacked and senior officers fell victim to the assassination campaign. All this occurred against a background of economic chaos and labour unrest that darkened the picture still further and eventually persuaded the armed forces to take action. In March 1976 Isabel Perón was deposed and a military junta under General Jorge Videla took power.

For some time before this coup, right-wing death squads of the Alianza Anticommunista Argentina (AAA) had been active. It has always been assumed that the AAA was largely composed of off-duty police officers and that it had the tacit backing of the armed forces as it murdered left-wingers and those suspected of terrorism or complicity in terrorism. Despite the AAA campaign and the fact that the new military government adopted a totally unscrupulous approach to the security problem, matters continued to worsen for a time. After the coup, the Montoneros seemed to be more active than the ERP and they tended to concentrate on attacking the police (perhaps in recognition of the fact that killing army conscripts was unlikely to make them broadly popular). In 1976 there was a successful series of Montoneros bomb attacks

in which the general commanding the police was killed as well as numerous police officers in the Police Headquarters in Buenos Aires and in La Plata, on a police bus in Rosario and in an area police station in Buenos Aires. While conscripts were a counter-productive target their officers were not and many were injured in an attack on a Buenos Aires officers' club. General Videla himself narrowly escaped three assassination attempts between February 1976 and April 1977.

Despite the apparent successes of the guerrillas, the unrestrained violence of the authorities and the efforts of the AAA were proving to be an effective counter-insurgency weapon. As the campaign progressed, torture became more or less institutionalised and was not merely intended to gain information; the aim was quite clearly to terrorise the population into avoiding contact with the guerrillas, and to this end all those suspected of even sympathising with the revolutionaries were treated with great barbarity. Besides this the authorities did not rely on the AAA for all the killing but routinely murdered suspects in various prisons and holding centres. The authorities' counter-terror chilled support for the guerrillas. During 1977 the level of revolutionary violence decreased quite dramatically and, at the end of 1978, the crisis was past. By the end of the decade it was obvious that not only the guerrillas were dead or imprisoned but the majority of their potential supporters as well.

P.J. Banyard

Above: The 'mothers of the Plaza de Mayo' protest against the disappearance of their sons under the oppressive military regime which ruthlessly eliminated those suspected of opposing the government.

G3 ASSAULT RIFLE

The West German Gewehr-3 (G3) assault rifle presently equips the armed forces of some 40 countries throughout the world, from South America and the Middle East to Africa and Southeast Asia. Its popularity as a weapon, especially in those countries with limited defence budgets and no arms-manufacturing facilities, results from its position as the centre pin of a versatile family of weapons designed to fulfil a variety of combat roles. The weapons-family concept has the advantages of drastically reducing the complexity of training involved in the use of infantry company weapons, from individual smallarm to unit-support machine gun, and simplifying the logistical process of supplying units in the field. A great many of the components are interchangeable between the weapons designed for the various roles, easing the pressure on parts replacement, especially on the battlefield. A further major attraction of the system is that it is manufactured in three different calibres to accommodate not only the standard Nato 7.62 × 51mm round, but also the lighter intermediate 5.56 × 45mm and the Soviet 7.62 × 39mm cartridges; this can be an important factor when potential clients are considering future sources and availability of ammunition.

The initial concept and early development of what was to become the G3 took place in Germany towards the end of World War II at the Mauser works at Oberndorf am Neckar. The product of this research was the StG 45M assault rifle which featured an unusual delayed-blowback mechanism based on a two-piece bolt with a twin-roller locking mechanism. It weighed 3.7kg (8.18lb) and was fed from a 30-round detachable box magazine. Constructed from metal stampings, the StG 45M was a simple, well-balanced weapon but the design was never fully developed before the close of the war. Research along the same lines, however, continued. After the war, Ludwig Volgrimmler, one of the original Mauser engineers who had worked on the StG 45M, went first to the French arms centre at Mulhouse, where he designed two further delayed-blowback breech mechanisms for the US 7.62 × 33mm carbine car-

tridge, and then on to the Centro de Estudios Tecnicos de Materials Especiales (CETME), the Spanish government weapons research establishment. At CETME Volgrimmler, with a number of other German and Spanish designers, produced the prototype of the CETME automatic rifle which was ready for trials in 1952. The original CETME rifle was chambered for a special CETME short-cased lightweight round, designed for high velocity, but further tests led to the adoption of a reduced-power version of the

standard Nato 7.62mm round. Research continued and, in 1954, the German firm of Heckler and Koch was assigned the licence to develop the CETME rifle. Over the next three years they modified the weapon into the G3, capable of firing the full-power Nato cartridge. By 1959 the G3 had been accepted as the Bundeswehr standard assault rifle, replacing the German G1-designated Belgian FN FAL, and since then a range of weapons has appeared from Heckler and Koch based on the G3's delayed-blowback mechan-

Previous page: With his G3A3 at the ready, a nervous El Salvadorian government militiaman stands point at a street corner while (above) surrounded by spent cartridge cases, an El Salvadorian regular engages guerrillas with his G3 on sustained fire.

Above: The Spanish 7.62mm CETME assault rifle which features a roller-delay locking mechanism and was the forerunner for the design of the Heckler and Koch G3 series. Below: The standard Heckler and Koch G3A3 assault rifle, issued to the German Bundeswehr.

ism. The current standard G3 model is the G3A3, although there are several other G3 marks which incorporate minor modifications. The G3A1 is fitted with a folding stock and flip-over backsight, the G3A2 has a rotating backsight, and the G3A4, designed for use by paratroopers and AFV crews, has a retractable stock to provide a more compact version of the basic weapon. A sniping version, the G3A3ZF, is also available.

One of the basic design problems of all blowback, as opposed to gas-operated, weapons is that at the moment of firing of a high-power cartridge, the internal pressure forces the cartridge case hard against the walls of the chamber. Unless some kind of delay mechanism is built in, the case head can be torn off as the mechanism tries to eject the spent case and the weapon will jam. The G3 overcomes this problem by means of a two-piece bolt and the provision of locking rollers in the barrel extension. When the trigger is pulled, the hammer strikes the firing pin which fires the cartridge. The gases released by the firing drive the bullet down the barrel and the locking rollers, which have been forced outwards into the recesses in

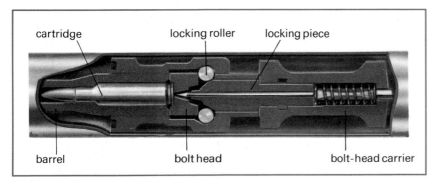

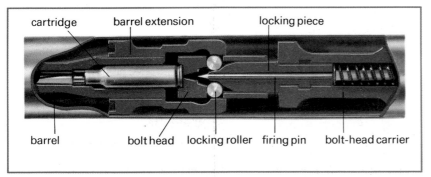

the barrel extension by the forward movement of the locking piece and bolt head carrier, prevent the immediate unrestricted recoilling of the bolt. As the expanding gases force the bolt head back, pressure is applied to the locking rollers which in turn force the locking piece and bolt head carrier backwards. The bolt head and spent cartridge case are now free to recoil and the case is ejected. In effect, this arrangement keeps the breech closed until the bullet leaves the muzzle and the pressure drops to a safe level before ejection takes place. Initial extraction of the cartridge case is aided by 12 flutes cut into the chamber which allow the propellant gases to leak forwards along the cartridge and float the mouth of the case away from the front of the chamber. The recoiling of the bolt then compresses the return spring which drives the bolt forward to repeat the cycle.

Most automatic rifles, such as the M16, operate by a gas port and piston system, but on the G3 neither are necessary and problems with blockage are eliminated. The G3 system provides a cyclic rate of fire of between 500 and 600 rounds per minute and is said to be capable of accepting virtually any brand of ammunition supplied by Nato countries or acquired elsewhere in time of war.

Above (top to bottom): An export version of the G3, field stripped to show its main components; the G3AZF sniper version; two diagrams showing the G3's delay mechanism. In the top diagram the bolt is locked while below, after the bullet has left the muzzle, the bolt is free to recoil. Right: The G3 has seen action in a number of African countries with both colonial and guerrilla forces, and can be seen here as part of a motley selection of smallarms fielded by a ragged unit of FNLA guerrillas in Angola.

The G3 is constructed mainly from metal stampings, making it a cheap and easy weapon to manufacture. Like the M16 and the FN FAL, it is fitted with a tough plastic stock and forward handguard. It is easy to strip down and maintain in the field and can be fitted with a range of accessories. Rifle grenades can be fired without the addition of a muzzle attachment and the standard flash suppressor doubles as a guide for the fitting of grenades. An infra-red night sight is also available. For training purposes, the G3 can be fitted with a blank-firing adaptor for both semi-automatic and automatic fire.

In the 7.62 × 51mm calibre group, two further weapon variants are available which are closely related to the parent G3A3. The HK11 light machine gun is constructed from the same group of components as the assault rifle and can be fed by either a 20-round box or an 80-round double-drum magazine. A front-mounted bipod is available for use with the box, while a centre-mounted bipod is fitted when using the larger drum magazine. Similar in many ways to the HK11 is the HK21 machine gun. The HK21, however, is considerably heavier and is usually fed from a metal-link belt, although it can, by means of a special adaptor, accommodate a box magazine. Designed specially for sustained fire, the HK21 has a cyclic rate of fire of some 850-900 rounds per minute and is equipped with a quick-change barrel. A bipod can be fitted in both the front and centre positions, as on the HK11, but for heavy sustained usage a tripod mounting is also available. A Swedish variant of the HK21, the HK21A, differs in that the feed tray is hinged rather than removeable.

In 1963 Heckler and Koch began work on a new, scaled-down version of the G3, chambered for the less powerful 5.56 × 45mm cartridge. After five years, and a number of modifications, it was put into production as the HK33 assault rifle. While maintaining the same method of operation as the G3, the HK33 weighed less, and the lower-powered intermediate

Above top: The HK11 light machine gun version of the G3, fitted with a bipod and 30-round box magazine. Above centre: The 7.62mm HK21A1 metal-link belt-fed machine gun. Above: The scaled-down version of the G3, the HK33, which is chambered for the 5.56 × 45mm intermediate round.

Left: A unit of Portuguese infantry awaits further orders during a search and destroy operation in Mozambique. The G3 is the standard infantry weapon of the Portuguese armed forces and the soldier in the foreground has the belt-fed machine gun version, the HK21.

round considerably improved its accuracy on automatic fire. The HK33 also had a much higher muzzle velocity than the G3 and a slightly improved cyclic rate of fire. Feed is provided by a 20-, 25-, 30- or 40-round box magazine and the weapon can be fitted with bayonet, blank-firing attachment, rifle grenades, bipod and telescopic sight. Variants on the HK33 include the HK33K, a carbine version with shorter barrel and retractable stock, and the HK53, also a reduced-barrel version with retractable stock, designed for use in the sub-machine gun role. In keeping with the Heckler and Koch weapon-family concept, the HK33 is also manufactured as the HK13 light machine gun, fed by a 100-round dual-drum or 25-round box magazine. The 5.56 × 45mm group further includes the HK21 machine gun version and the HK23, a lighter version of the HK21A.

With an eye open to a market in those nations which receive smallarms from the Soviet Union, Heckler and Koch have also manufactured the G3-based series as the HK32 assault rifle, the HK12 light machine gun and the HK21 machine gun, all chambered for the Soviet M1943 7.62 × 39mm cartridge. The HK32 is fed from a 30-round box magazine but, although identical in dimension and operation to the HK33, it has a considerably reduced muzzle velocity and degree of accuracy. An HK32K carbine version has also been produced.

Since the early 1950s, the original concept and research behind the delayed-blowback mechanism has been thoroughly exploited with a view to supplying armed forces the world over. Heckler and Koch continuously update their systems and have produced A1, A2 and A3 versions. In the early 1980s, a number of E-designated variants appeared featuring a 3-round burst facility in addition to the single shot and continuous fire modes. Apart from German manufacture, the G3 has been built under licence in Brazil, Pakistan, Portugal, Iran, Norway, Sweden and Spain. Manufacture has also been subcontracted

to both the French SAV-CIE arms factory and the British Royal Small Arms Factory at Enfield. It has seen action in a number of countries including El Salvador and Iran and was put to extensive use by the Portuguese in Angola, Mozambique and Guinea. Its versatility as a family of weapons is undeniable, especially when used by armed forces lacking the high standard of training demanded by many modern and sophisticated weapon systems, and it is ideally suited to the conditions of small-unit action.

Below: Like the G3, the HK33 is also manufactured in a retractable-stock carbine version, the HK33K. The weapon illustrated is an HK33KA1. Centre: Another shortened version of the HK33 is the 5.56mm HK53 sub-machine gun which weighs only 3.05kg (6.72lb) unloaded.

Left: A black South African infantryman stationed near the border with Angola, proudly shows off his G3A3 for the photographer.

Right: Keeping a tight hold on his G3 rifle and an eye open for any signs of enemy movement, an El Salvadorian soldier crawls through undergrowth during an anti-guerrilla operation in El Salvador's countryside.

G3 Assault Rifle

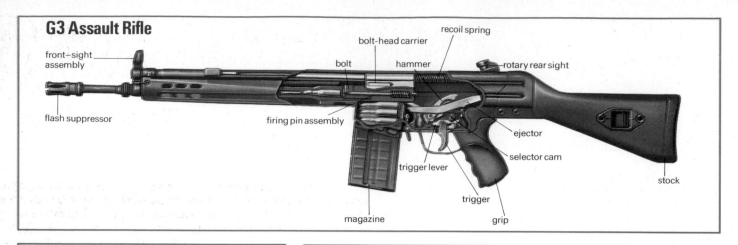

- front-sight assembly
- flash suppressor
- firing pin assembly
- bolt
- bolt-head carrier
- hammer
- recoil spring
- rotary rear sight
- ejector
- selector cam
- trigger lever
- trigger
- grip
- magazine
- stock

G3A3 Assault Rifle

Calibre 7.62mm
Length (fixed stock) 102.5cm (40.38in)
Weight (loaded with 20-round box magazine) 5kg (11lb)
Rate of fire Cyclic 500-600rpm; practical automatic 100rpm; practical single-shot 40rpm
Maximum effective range 400m (440yds)
Magazine 20-round box
Cartridge 7.62 × 51mm Nato
Muzzle velocity 780-800mps (2458-2624fps)

Above: The 5.56 × 45mm calibre group of Heckler and Koch infantry weapons also includes the HK13 light machine gun. The model shown here is the HK13E. Although usually fed from a box magazine, the HK13E can be converted to belt feed by fitting a magazine adaptor and a different bolt. The HK13E also features the 3-round burst mode of fire in addition to the usual single-shot and continuous modes.

Left: A unit of Portuguese troops, armed with an HK21 machine gun, move through a village in Guinea Bissau in search of guerrillas.

Riding high

The 1st Cavalry Division in Vietnam

Of all the many tactical innovations that took place during the war in Vietnam, the most significant was the widespread use of the helicopter. Although the Americans' reliance on the helicopter has remained a controversial subject, there can be little doubt that when employed correctly it proved itself a highly effective battlefield weapon in Vietnam. It was not the use of helicopters as such that was important, but rather their use in large airmobile units that made such an impact on the ground fighting; and this American enthusiasm for autonomous airmobile formations found its first concrete expression in the creation of the 1st Cavalry Division (Airmobile) in 1965.

During the early 1960s the idea of having units of up to battalion strength that could be air transported both in and out of a battle area became feasible in reality as a consequence of advances made in helicopter design. At this time, however, inter-service rivalries between the army and air force hindered developments; the army wanted its own autonomous air units, while the air force was disdainful of army efforts and ever keen to keep control of all that was airborne. Nonetheless the go-ahead was given to the army to form a large air transportable formation and the 11th Air Assault Division (Test) came into being, pioneering techniques for carrying large bodies of men and their weapons and equipment around the skies.

By 1965 the war in Vietnam was growing in intensity: US Army and Marine units were being committed on the ground, and it became inevitable that the army should try out its new airmobile units in this war where mobility and firepower – the strength of airborne formations – were placed at a premium. Drawing on the expertise built up by the 11th Air Assault Division, and taking large numbers of personnel from the 2nd Infantry Division, the 1st Cavalry Division (Airmobile) came into being in July 1965. The first advance units arrived in Vietnam in August, shortly followed by the rest of the division.

The 1st Cavalry Division was just under 16,000 men strong and equipped with over 400 aircraft and 1600 ground vehicles; it was organised along the lines of an infantry division but with the ability to be airlifted into combat. The division aviation group was responsible for air transport and comprised one medium and two light helicopter battalions, plus a general support company. The infantry component stood at eight battalions, of which three could have an airborne capability. Artillery seemed in the first stages to be something of a problem. If the 1st Cavalry was to operate effectively in the field as a division its own organic artillery was essential, and yet the sheer weight and volume of artillery pieces and ammunition militated against the 'lean and mean' concept advocated by the airmobile school. Initially only lightweight 105mm howitzers were employed, being transportable by the Chinook helicopter, but once in Vietnam a battalion of 155mm howitzers was

Above: While ground patrols of the 1st Cavalry Division (Airmobile) move out from their landing zone, door gunners, aboard Bell UH-1H helicopters, adopt fire cover positions to protect both their aircraft and the patrols from possible enemy attacks.

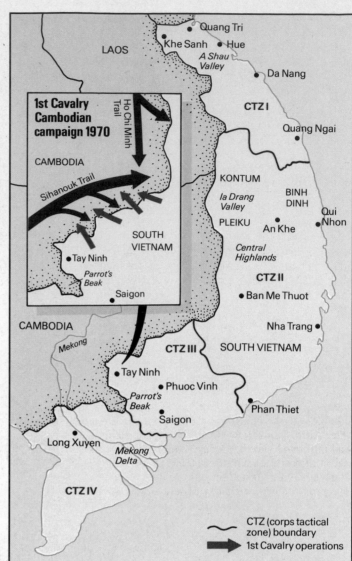

1st Cavalry Cambodian campaign 1970

LAOS

Quang Tri
Khe Sanh
Hue
A Shau Valley
Da Nang

CTZ I

Quang Ngai

Ho Chi Minh Trail

CAMBODIA

KONTUM

Ia Drang Valley
PLEIKU
An Khe
Qui Nhon

BINH DINH

Sihanouk Trail

SOUTH VIETNAM

Central Highlands

CTZ II

Ban Me Thuot

Tay Ninh

Parrot's Beak

Saigon

Nha Trang

CAMBODIA

Mekong

CTZ III

SOUTH VIETNAM

Tay Ninh
Phuoc Vinh

Parrot's Beak

Saigon

Phan Thiet

Long Xuyen

Mekong Delta

CTZ IV

⌇ CTZ (corps tactical zone) boundary
➔ 1st Cavalry operations

Top left: A portable forward command post is loaded aboard a Chinook helicopter. Centre left: A Sikorsky 'Flying Crane' delivering collapsible fuel drums. Left: US troops deploy into a battle zone scattered with spent shells.

attached to the division when it was found that the guns could be air-carried by the CH-54 Sky Crane.

A highly novel way of ensuring mobility and firepower was the formation of an aerial artillery battalion which consisted of three batteries, each with 12 helicopters armed with 2.75in aerial rockets. When used *en masse* the aerial artillery element could be highly effective, able to pour a devastating barrage of firepower on highly specific targets outside the capability of conventional tubed artillery; and, in addition, its effect on morale – on friend and foe alike – could be decisive. Ground commanders became so impressed with the rocket-firing helicopter that they had to be regularly reminded to use conventional artillery support rather than automatically call for an aerial rocket strike.

Reconnaissance was provided by a helicopter-borne air cavalry squadron, invariably the first troops into combat, whose ability to provide divisional HQ with details of enemy movements was a vital tool in finding the elusive Viet Cong. Like any other formation in a modern army, the 1st Cavalry's support services were considerable, especially as the 400-plus helicopters needed round-the-clock attention under battle conditions.

Once in Vietnam, An Khe was selected as the base for the 1st Cavalry, acting as a maintenance and supply centre for the division. Hardly had the base been established when the 1st Cavalry was flung into combat, its role being to interdict a strong force of three North Vietnamese Army (NVA) regiments that had infiltrated into the Central Highlands. The fight became known as the Battle of the Ia Drang Valley, an engagement that tested the 1st Cavalry to the limits but from which it emerged with new-won honours.

Face to face with the cavalry

The battle began with forward units pinning the NVA down or advancing into known enemy areas to draw fire upon themselves in order for support units to locate and engage the now exposed NVA. Fearful of the weight of US artillery and aerial support fire the NVA attempted to get in close to the 1st Cavalry ground positions, so that many of the actions were characterised by fierce hand-to-hand fighting. One platoon leader was found dead with five NVA bodies in and around his command foxhole, and one of his troopers was discovered killed with his hand locked around the throat of a dead enemy soldier.

The determination of the 1st Cavalry to break up the NVA advance began to work: by mid-November the North Vietnamese attack had lost its momentum and in the face of growing casualties they slipped back into Cambodia. Although 59 of the 1st Cavalry aircraft were hit by enemy fire only four were shot down, while the NVA lost an estimated 1800 men. The ability of the 1st Cavalry to throw men and firepower into the combat zone with the utmost speed and actually catch the enemy before he had time to melt into jungle proved the validity of the army's airmobile concept beyond doubt. More than this, the 1st Cavalry's success in their first important operation gave them a confidence and *esprit de corps* which, combined with their developing professional air combat skills, ensured them a reputation second to none in Vietnam.

After Ia Drang and throughout 1966 the 1st Cavalry was engaged in suppressing enemy activity in Binh Dinh Province, as well as conducting strike opera-

Above: A US Army Chinook transport helicopter hovers over triple-canopy jungle in Cambodia while a combat patrol of the 1st Cavalry Division, wearing light webbing, descends an aerial ladder.

tions into the neighbouring Central Highlands provinces of Pleiku and Kontum. A series of sweeps was instigated in Binh Dinh to wear away the Viet Cong hold over the province. Although large hauls of enemy weapons and equipment were located the Viet Cong proved impossible to root out.

During 1967 the 1st Cavalry extended its range of operations, supporting the Marines in the northern provinces of South Vietnam. The mobile firepower element was something the Marines lacked and the 1st Cavalry was able to fly Marines in and out of the battle area at will and provide much needed on-the-spot firepower. This was especially true by the end of 1967 when the 1st Cavalry began to receive its first Huey Cobra gunships which replaced the makeshift UH-1C models. Fast, agile and comparatively well armoured, the Cobra packed a fearsome punch, its armaments including a 40mm grenade launcher, multi-barrelled minigun, 2.75in rockets and TOW air-to-surface missiles. Able to roam over the jungle terrain of South Vietnam at will, the Cobra possessed an awesome ground-fire suppression capability.

The outbreak of the Tet offensive early in 1968 placed the 1st Cavalry's quick-response capability at a premium; helicopter units were rushed to trouble spots as they occurred. The first big 1st Cavalry operation of the offensive was the destruction of a strong communist force in the provincial capital of Quang Tri City. A short while later elements of the division were engaged in carrying out interdiction raids around the battle-torn city of Hue. Denied reinforcements by the 1st Cavalry's roving gunship patrols the communist troops in the centre of Hue were surrounded by US and Army of the Republic of Vietnam (ARVN) forces and, despite fierce resist-

ance, were eventually destroyed.

In March preparations were undertaken for the relief of Khe Sanh, where a beleaguered Marine garrison had been encircled by a strong NVA force. The 1st Cavalry was chosen to lead the relief attack, supplemented by units of Marines and ARVN airborne and Ranger battalions, altogether over 30,000 men. Detailed planning was instigated to coordinate the various services involved, so that once Operation Pegasus went into effect, the assault against the NVA

Left: Men of the 7th Cavalry, 1st Cavalry Division, fire an M55 anti-aircraft gun. This weapon, which mounts four 0.5in Browning machine guns, has a semi-armoured shield and, having wheels, is easily transportable.

Below: While units approach a village during a sweep and search operation (Operation Pershing, May 1967), a flank gunner takes a break from sighting his M60 machine gun. Note the smoke grenade in the immediate foreground.

would be conducted with the utmost speed and surprise. D-Day was 1 April 1968: the Marine battalions attacked westward on the ground while the 2nd and 3rd Brigades of the 1st Cavalry were airlifted behind enemy lines to set up landing zones which formed the springboard for air operations around Khe Sanh.

Despite bad weather the attack was prosecuted with the utmost determination and by D-Day+6 the NVA were fighting their way back into Laos in order to avoid complete envelopment. On 6 April Khe Sanh was formally relieved by the 3rd Brigade of the 1st Cavalry, and following limited clearing-up sorties Operation Pegasus was terminated on 15 April. For the first time the division had been committed in its entirety to a single operation, with all the manoeuvre battalions flown into combat by helicopter.

No sooner was the operation over than the 1st Cavalry was redirected to launch an assault on the NVA stronghold in the A Shau Valley. Bad weather again posed problems for the helicopters which were forced to fly low over the mountains around A Shau. Enemy anti-aircraft defences were heavy and 21 helicopters were shot down, but the US forces were able to penetrate enemy positions uncovering extensive supply depots.

The gunships go in

Towards the end of 1968 the 1st Cavalry was transferred from the north to operate in the III Corps Tactical Zone, the divisional HQ located at Phuoc Vinh. As the process of 'Vietnamization' gathered momentum in 1969 the 1st Cavalry's major role was to act in support of ARVN operations, of which the most important was the invasion of Cambodia the following year. The object of the operation was to destroy the extensive sanctuary bases of the NVA and Viet Cong, the 1st Cavalry spearheading the invasion on behalf of the ARVN.

On 1 May 1970, following B-52 air strikes, the 1st Cavalry flew over the border to establish landing zones and firebases within Cambodia. Surprised by the speed of the offensive, NVA units were caught in the open and shot up by the assaulting gunships. Forced to flee into the interior, the communists abandoned many of their supply dumps which fell into US and ARVN hands. At the close of the operation on 29 June the 1st Cavalry had killed 2500 NVA and Viet Cong and had captured 2244 tons of rice and over ten million rounds of ammunition. Such heavy losses represented a decisive logistics defeat for the communist forces.

The Cambodian invasion marked the high point of the 1st Cavalry's operation in Vietnam, and as the US Army accelerated its withdrawal from Vietnam the 1st Cavalry Division became a part of that withdrawal. Although in many ways an unhappy chapter for the US Army, Vietnam was the major testing ground for the deployment of a large airmobile formation, and in the hands of the 1st Cavalry the airmobile concept was proved a great success. Contrary to the predictions of critics, the helicopter showed itself able to withstand relatively heavy ground fire, and organised on a divisional basis sufficient numbers could be flown into combat to decide the outcome of a battle with the utmost speed. The 1st Cavalry's ability to envelop an enemy position rather than merely penetrate the enemy frontline was the key to its success in bringing the elusive Vietnamese communist forces to battle and defeating them. **Ed Trowbridge**

Helicopters in Vietnam

AH-1G Huey Cobra

Length 13.54m (44ft 5in); **Main-rotor diameter** 13.41m (44ft); **Cruising speed at maximum take-off weight** 309km/h (192mph); **Range** 573km (357 miles); **Crew** 2; **Passengers** 0; **Armament combination** 7.62mm miniguns (turret or underwing), 40mm grenade launchers (turret), 6-barrel cannon (turret), 2.75in air-to-surface rockets (underwing)

With its formidable range of armament, the Cobra gunship's main function was to provide close and direct fire support where its speed and low-level agility proved invaluable. Secondary roles included armed reconnaissance and escort duty.

UH-1D Iroquois

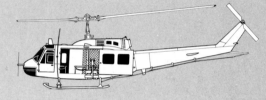

Length 12.78m (41ft 11¼in); **Main-rotor diameter** 14.63m (48ft); **Maximum cruising speed** 283km/h (176mph); **Mission radius** 400km (248 miles); **Crew** 2-4; **Passengers** 11; **Armament** One or two door-mounted 7.62mm M60 machine guns

The UH-1D was mainly deployed as a first-wave troop transport for heliborne assaults, as a supply and equipment mover, and as an airborne command post fitted with additional radio equipment. Until the AH-1G's arrival in Vietnam in 1967, it was also used as a makeshift gunship.

OH-6A Cayuse

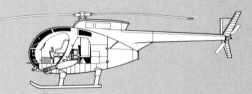

Length 7.01m (23ft); **Main-rotor diameter** 8.03m (26ft 4in); **Maximum cruising speed at sea level** 230km/h (143mph); **Range** 665km (413 miles); **Crew** 2 (pilot and observer); **Passengers** 0-2; **Armament** One externally-mounted 7.62mm minigun pod

The OH-6A's primary function was low-level observation and reconnaissance. Paired with an AH-1G escort gunship (the 'Pink Team') it was able to cover large areas quickly and effectively while relaying information for heliborne-troop deployment.

CH-47C Chinook

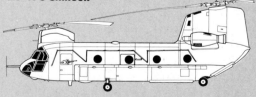

Length 15.54m (51ft); **Main-rotor diameter** (each) 18.29m (60ft); **Maximum speed** at 3110m (10,200ft) 290km/h (180mph); **Mission radius** 185km (115 miles); **Payload** Up to 12,700kg (28,000lb) load on external cargo hook; **Crew** 3; **Passengers** Maximum 33-44; **Armament** One door-mounted 7.62mm M60 machine gun

The CH-47 was the main workhorse helicopter for the US forces in Vietnam. Apart from its role as a troop transport, it was extensively used to move heavy artillery, ammunition and other front-line equipment in and out of fire bases.

Ice-cream and ammunition

US logistics in Southeast Asia

In the early 1970s, when the North Vietnamese were conducting conventional military operations in South Vietnam, it is estimated that they needed about 500,000 tons of supplies a year – transported down the Ho Chi Minh Trail – to sustain their war effort. By contrast, the American Army in Vietnam needed over 10 million tons of supplies a year, shipped from the United States. The American war machine was designed for a heavy use of firepower and technical equipment. Also, the American soldier, product of a consumer society, expected a good standard of food and living conditions – there was no way he was going to live off the country or adapt significantly to local conditions. Sustaining the American way of life and the American way of war in Vietnam demanded a massive logistics effort which strained even US resources of money, organisation and industrial production.

The Vietnam War did not fit the concepts upon which the US Army had evolved its logistical doctrine. It contrasted strongly with both World War II and Korea in that it was essentially a war fought by small units constantly pursuing an elusive enemy and was characterised by small isolated actions involving ground and air assaults mounted from numerous base camps deep in-country. Within South Vietnam there were no secure depots, ports, supply routes, storage facilities or supply areas. Attacks on logistics facilities and operations were frequent and placed support troops in the front line of combat.

When the US administration decided to commit combat troops to Vietnam in the spring of 1965, they posed army logistical planners an awesome problem. Only a skeletal supply network had been developed up to that point to maintain Special Forces advisers in the field, operating out of Nha Trang. The country itself was undeveloped with few all-weather roads, very limited warehousing and storage facilities, little industrial capacity, and only one effective deep-water harbour (at Saigon). No definite plan had been made regarding a full-scale military intervention with ground forces and consequently there were no contingency plans for the organisation of supplies to support such a rapid build-up of forces. Within a short time of President Johnson setting in motion the deployment of US combat troops in Vietnam, the logistical build-up trailed far behind the combat build-up.

On 1 April 1965, to take on the logistical problems facing US forces, 1st Logistical Command, Vietnam (1st LCV) was established in Saigon under Colonel Robert Duke. It assumed responsibility for logistical support in Vietnam, except in areas that were peculiar to the air force or navy. The theatre of war was some 16,000km (10,000 miles) from the source of supply in the United States, and although there was no military threat to this line of communications, the sheer distance posed problems. The US Army control centre at Okinawa provided the Americans with a forward support base – similar to the British use of Ascension Island during the Falklands War – from which US supplies could be taken to Vietnam. The chain of command went from 1st LCV to Okinawa where requirements were either filled or passed to US Army Pacific. From US Army Pacific, requirements could then go to Army Materiel Command (in the US). This chain in fact proved so inefficient that it was responsible for the loss of over 40 per cent of requisitions during the initial build-up period.

Even before a proper supply operation could get under way, the first US combat troops arrived from Okinawa (173rd Airborne Brigade) on 21 April 1965 and immediately put reserve stocks under strain. The infant logistics system was extremely hard pushed to find supplies for the new arrivals. Even with the most necessary commodity for sustaining a war, ammunition, there were supply problems.

In March 1965, just before the US build-up began, the only ammunition stocks in Vietnam were those belonging to the 5th Special Forces units at Nha Trang and armed helicopter units at Tan Son Nhut. The former was a mix of modern, World War II and foreign munitions resupplied monthly from Okinawa; the latter was made up of 7.62mm rounds, 40mm grenades, 2.75in rockets and various signal and smoke flares. They amounted to a total of 1500 tons of munitions, though there were small reserve stocks at Okinawa, Japan, Korea, Hawaii and Thailand. When the 173rd Airborne Brigade arrived in Vietnam, the 1st LCV requested a 15-day supplementary supply of ammunition from Okinawa. The request was refused in the belief that the standard supply would be adequate. The troops deployed and immediately began offensive operations. Within five days they had exhausted a 30-day supply as well as finding much of their munitions obsolete or inadequate for the job. The 1st LCV once again urgently requested resupply from Okinawa. The requisition was approved, the supply request doubled in error and ammunition promptly arrived at Tan Son Nhut, dangerously overloading the ammunition storage site and tying up all available aircraft in the area for a seven-day period. What little system existed was completely disorganised. Indeed, in the early stages of the build-up supplies frequently arrived before units, or units were diverted from their scheduled debarkation points where their ammunition was off-loaded.

Bullets, boots and guns

At the time of the arrival of troops in Vietnam, the army was changing its basic smallarm from the old M1 and M14 to the new M16A1 rifle. Arranging for delivery of the new rifle involved reams of paperwork and requisition orders, and it was often months before the soldier in the field received his new weapon – though plenty of ammunition was in evidence for the unavailable rifle. Even in the case of an issue of tropical boots per capita, the supplies could not meet the demand. Right up until August 1967, troops were being posted to Vietnam without tropical uniforms. Indeed, the situation became so urgent that uniforms and boots were shipped straight to Vietnam without even waiting for requisition orders to arrive.

Work to overcome the initial chaos was relentlessly sustained, and slowly but surely improvements began to emerge. The first job for 1st LCV was to develop a supply system that could begin to handle the huge quantities of war material that were required for the incoming troops. The initial plan provided for a basic network comprising two major base depots at Saigon and Cam Ranh Bay, and five support commands at Can Tho, Vung Tau, Nha Trang, Qui Nhon and Da Nang. Two major changes were made during the execution of the plan: the Saigon base depot was moved outside the city to Long Binh in order to avoid over-congestion, and the support command at Can Tho was not activated. Also, at Da Nang logistics were entrusted to navy rather than 1st LCV control until 1968. Each support command was to have a

Left: A CH-54 Chinook helicopter transports an airmobile artillery firing platform to a fire support base. The fluid nature of the Vietnam War required combat versatility and the ability to deploy artillery into a battle zone at speed was paramount. Below: Supplies are airdropped into the besieged fire base at Khe Sanh. Paradrops often compensated for the inflexibility of a ground-based logistics network. Bottom: An M113 APC flanks a bridgelayer. Despite constant Viet Cong bridge-destroying actions, US forces quickly replaced them using such equipment.

15-day stockage to supply its area and the major depots would have a 45-day supply.

All combat supplies from the US were taken from West Coast depots by ship to Okinawa and then on to Vietnam – only troops and priority cargo were airlifted. Thus port development was an immediate priority. Using special prefabricated piers, the two-berth port at Cam Ranh Bay was quickly transformed into a four-berth harbour. A 120m (400ft) jetty was also constructed, along with a 245m (800ft) rock causeway to aid the unloading of fuels. Similarly, Saigon was upgraded – a complete new port facility was designed and constructed, primarily by civilian contractors. By late 1967 the US was operating seven deep-water harbours and three shallow-draught harbours in South Vietnam.

Air terminals were built in each port complex. In a two-year period from mid-1965, US Army engineers installed or rehabilitated more than 80 airfields. Although the development of road systems lagged far behind that of water and air facilities, a plan was drawn up for the development of some 4106km (3038 miles) of roadway and by 1970 over 40 per cent of this had been completed by more than 11,000 men working full time. Some 250 new road bridges were also built.

With the logistical system under such severe strain, it was important that control be established over the living standards of the troops, to prevent unnecessary goods clogging the supply channels. But in the early days in Vietnam commanders were able to demand – and get – more or less what they wanted for their units. As the official Department of the Army study states: 'Commanders desiring to give their personnel the very highest possible levels of comfort and quality of food, requisitioned air conditioning and refrigeration equipment far in excess of that authorized . . . .' Even at fire support bases ice-cream and fresh eggs were a

standard part of the US soldier's diet. This contributed to a very high electricity consumption – two kilowatts per hour (kWh) of electricity per soldier per day in Vietnam, compared with 0.5kWh per day for each GI in World War II. Shortage of electricity supply became a major problem. One improvised solution was the mooring of obsolete oil tankers fitted out with electricity generating equipment at selected points off the Vietnam coast; eventually, large and small fixed generating plants were installed through most of the country.

Forward support

To cope with the unconventional nature of the war that US combat troops were forced to wage, involving the use of small units well forward of their main base, 1st LCV developed the concept of the Forward Support Activity (FSA). This was a provisional organisation to support a tactical unit constantly engaging enemy troops and, consequently, with very substantial requirements for resupply. The FSA gave the US logistics system a greater flexibility than it had previously enjoyed on the conventional battlefield.

The logistics system was greatly enhanced by the innovative use of aerial resupply to advancing or mobile combat units. In one such operation, Task Force Remagen was maintained in the field for 47 days using this method. The task force, an armoured battalion and a mechanised infantry battalion, was operating at distances between 40km and 60km (25 miles and 37 miles) from its base, the US Marine Corps Vandergrift Combat Base. During the operation, all requests for supplies and repair parts were forwarded to the Forward Support Element who in turn forwarded requests to the 75th Support Battalion Logistics Operations Center at Quang Tri. The requested supplies would be assembled overnight and either flown or sent by convoy the next morning to the

Above: Mixed loads of 227kg (500lb) and 318kg (700lb) bombs await shipment from the dockside at Guam Island to Anderson airbase where they will be loaded onto B-52 bombers. The US logistic system relied heavily upon Pacific island forward supply bases, such as Guam and Okinawa.

Left: US helicopters, on board a refitting vessel in Saigon harbour, await repair. As part of the closed loop system, the refit and repair of aircraft at a local level enhanced the flying life of the machines and substantially reduced both costs and time out of commission. Below: ARVN security guards board an armoured rail carriage to protect a supply train on its run from Saigon to a forward replenishment base.

Forward Support Element which would then send on the supplies to the task force by air. Both the task force battalions maintained combat trains consisting of tracked maintenance and resupply vehicles. All replacement parts were flown to the units in their field locations, exchanged for the defective part and installed on the spot. Defective parts were then returned to the support element for repair. During the entire operation the task force received over 1000 tons of cargo with an average of 13 helicopter sorties per day.

It was operations such as this that began to break the logistic stalemate that had developed in Vietnam. Another innovation was the closed loop support system which was designed to control the flow of serviceable equipment to Vietnam and the return of unserviceable equipment to repair facilities, thus ensuring a timely response to the needs of operational units. The closed loop system was particularly useful in maintaining and extending the service lifetime of first-line aircraft from 2200 hours to 3300 hours.

By the time US troop numbers reached their peak in 1968, the army's logisticians had the problems under control. They had developed a computerised system for the management of the flow of supplies which effectively delivered goods where they were needed in good time. Engineering and construction work had transformed much of South Vietnam, establishing the transport network and power supply that the US war machine required. The logistic planners had also evolved the new concepts and organisation to cope with a war that had no front line and needed exceptional flexibility and speed of response. Over 100,000 tons of ammunition were being delivered and distributed every month. Having decided to fight a high-technology war under conditions which did not favour it, the Americans proved that they could cope with the self-imposed problems this involved.

Alexander McNair-Wilson

The US Marines defend Khe Sanh

On 2 January 1968, a Marine patrol sent out from the base at Khe Sanh in northeast South Vietnam encountered a North Vietnamese Army (NVA) reconnaissance party. The Marines killed five of its six members, and learned that they had bagged a regimental commander and key members of his staff. This was the clinching piece of information to add to the mounting pile of intelligence reports pointing towards a major North Vietnamese offensive in the northern provinces. On 5 January, therefore, General William C. Westmoreland, Commander, US Military Assistance Command, Vietnam (MACV), put his staff to work planning for a massive aerial bombardment to counter the enemy threat in the north. He named the plan 'Niagara', to invoke, as he said, 'an image of cascading shells and bombs'. Indeed, the area around Khe Sanh base would soon have the unenviable distinction of being the most bombed place on earth.

The US Green Berets had established a Civilian Irregular Defense Group (CIDG) at Khe Sanh, which is more of a small plateau than a valley, in 1962. In October 1966 a Marine battalion moved into the base and the CIDG camp was relocated to Lang Vei, some 9km (5 miles) to the west. In April 1967 a regimental-size battle (known as the 'Hill Fights') was fought for command of the hills around Khe Sanh. After that the area was quiescent, until evidence of an enemy build-up began to mount late in 1967.

The decision to defend Khe Sanh against an attacking force which eventually numbered between 15,000 and 20,000 was later criticised, but there were sound reasons for Westmoreland's decision to do so. One was that if the communists were preparing a general offensive in South Vietnam (as seemed likely) then the presence of Khe Sanh would be a block on the strategically important Route 9; another was that the US did not wish to be seen to evacuate areas under communist pressure; and there was also the feeling that the position was very tenable, and the attacks would cost the NVA dear.

'None of us was blind to the possibility that the North Vietnamese might make of Khe Sanh another Dien Bien Phu,' Westmoreland has stated, 'yet we were aware of marked differences in the two situations and were convinced we could hold Khe Sanh with a relatively small ground force if augmented by tremendous firepower.'

In charge at Khe Sanh was Colonel David E. Lownds, commanding officer, 26th Marines Regiment. Lownds had his regimental headquarters and two of his infantry battalions, the 1st and the 3rd, at the combat base. In support he had an artillery battalion, the 1st Battalion, 13th Marines. On 16 January the 2nd Battalion, 26th Marines, joined the garrison, making Lownds' regiment complete. The 26th was part of Major-General Rathvon Tompkins' 3rd Marine Division, strung out in a series of combat bases and strong points west from the mouth of the Cua Viet River along the general line of war-worn Route 9 almost to Laos.

Two North Vietnamese divisions were known to be in the narrow strip between Route 9 and the DMZ. The 324B Division was above Dong Ha and the 325C Division was to the west, threatening Khe Sanh. By mid-January it was confirmed that the 304th Division had come in from Laos to join the 325C Division. Just to the east the 320th Division was identified, apparently poised for an attack against the fire support bases at Camp Carroll and the 'Rock Pile', important because here were the 18 long-barrelled, long-range 175mm guns of the army's 2nd Battalion, 94th Artillery, that were essential to the defence of Khe Sanh.

Tompkins and Lownds were well aware that the French had lost Dien Bien Phu in 1954 because they

iege warfare

had not been able to control the high ground surrounding their valley position. Lownds used most of his infantry strength to outpost the hills. On 20 January a company from his 3rd Battalion went forward from Hill 881 South (881S) towards Hill 881 North (the numbers indicate the height of the hills in metres) and ran into a North Vietnamese battalion. On orders from Lownds the company fell back to Hill 881S, leaving behind 103 counted enemy dead. The North Vietnamese now surrounded Hill 881S, cutting off from the main base (except by helicopter) the two Marine companies that held it. Marines on this hill, and on Hills 861, 558 and 950, were to be critical to the survival of the base.

That same day, 20 January, a North Vietnamese first-lieutenant walked into the combat base, surrendered, and willingly gave a wealth of information. He said there would be an attack against Hill 861 that night. The attack came as predicted and was beaten off by the company that held the hill. But at 0530 hours the following morning several hundred 122mm rockets came crashing down on the main base followed by a thunderous artillery and mortar bombardment. Khe Sanh's principal ammunition dump and much of its fuel blew up. The siege, which was to last over 70 days, had begun in earnest.

In Saigon, Westmoreland moved 'Niagara' from the planning phase to the strike phase. Marine, air force and navy tactical air support formed a ring around Khe Sanh. Farther out B-52s from Strategic Air Command would be used with Westmoreland personally deciding where they would strike. He slept on a cot in his Combat Operations Center so as to 'be immediately at hand for any decision that had to be made on targets or troop deployments.' He was also hastening some of the US Army's best troops to I Corps, the five northern provinces. On 21 January, the same day as the battle for Khe Sanh can be said to have begun, Major-General John J. Tolson opened the command post for his 1st Air Cavalry Division (Airmobile) at Phu Bai, the big Marine base south of Hue, and on 25 January he began planning for an airmobile relief of Khe Sanh. Also on 25 January, Westmoreland decided that he would open a MACV forward command post at Phu Bai so as to take more direct charge of the battle, and his deputy, General Creighton W. Abrams, took up residence there in February.

Meanwhile, at Khe Sanh itself, the North Vietnamese continued to hammer the base and Hill 881S on 22 January. Tompkins gave Lownds another battalion, the 1st Battalion, 9th Marines, which was put into position a mile southwest of the base. For political, if not military, reasons, it was desirable to get some South Vietnamese defenders into the base at Khe Sanh and on 27 January the 37th Rangers, lightly armed and a third the size of a US battalion, arrived and was put in on the eastern side of the perimeter so that there were about 6000 troops holding the position.

By now, the battle was in full swing. The Marines had dug deep bunkers, and ringed their positions with barbed wire. The sensors gave advance warning of major NVA attacking concentrations, which were hit regularly by artillery and aircraft. In return the NVA put down a barrage from artillery dug into the hills. On some days, 1000 rounds would be fired at the base.

Hell in the trenches

Life for the Marines was hell; it was rapidly found that their underground bunkers needed reinforcing with extra timber to make them safe from the endless bombardment, and NVA snipers made movement above ground very risky. Yet morale kept high during the siege, and was perhaps exemplified by the two Marine companies on Hill 881S, who suffered nearly 50 per cent casualties, but each morning sent the Stars and Stripes up on an improvised flag pole, and each evening brought it down, accompanied by the correct bugle call.

If the morale of the defenders stayed high, the politicians back in Washington were very worried. President Johnson was particularly concerned that it should not become another Dien Bien Phu; he had a scale-model of the Khe Sanh area built in the basement of the White House and demanded a formal promise ('signed in blood' is said to have been his phrase) that the base would not fall. These anxieties were compounded by the Tet offensive, that broke throughout South Vietnam on 31 January.

Left: US Marines rush a casevac towards a medical post. The padre accompanying the group (rear left) is probably an indication of the seriousness of the wound. In all, the Marines at Khe Sanh lost 199 men killed.

Left: Ignited ammunition streaks skyward above the main flame of an explosion after Viet Cong rockets score a direct hit on a US ammunition dump at Khe Sanh.

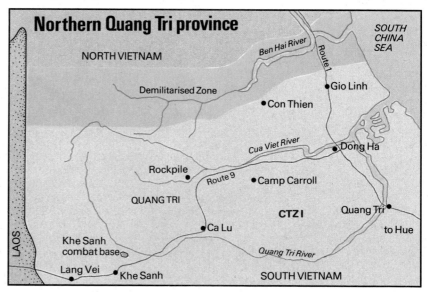

Northern Quang Tri province

- NORTH VIETNAM
- Ben Hai River
- Route 1
- SOUTH CHINA SEA
- Demilitarised Zone
- Gio Linh
- Con Thien
- Cua Viet River
- Dong Ha
- Rockpile
- Route 9
- Camp Carroll
- QUANG TRI
- CTZ I
- Quang Tri
- Ca Lu
- to Hue
- LAOS
- Khe Sanh combat base
- Quang Tri River
- Lang Vei
- Khe Sanh
- SOUTH VIETNAM

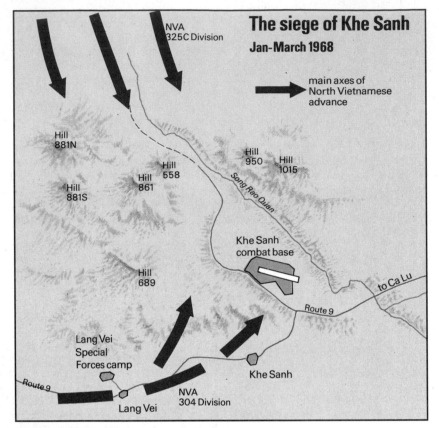

The siege of Khe Sanh
Jan–March 1968

→ main axes of North Vietnamese advance

NVA 325C Division

Hill 881N

Hill 881S

Hill 861

Hill 558

Hill 950

Hill 1015

Song Rao Quan

Khe Sanh combat base

Hill 689

to Ca Lu

Route 9

Lang Vei Special Forces camp

Route 9

Lang Vei

Khe Sanh

NVA 304 Division

Left: Members of the 11th Engineers repair and rebuild the runway at Khe Sanh. The engineers were constantly active throughout Vietnam in the construction of runways and in a two-year period constructed or rehabilitated more than 80 landing strips. Below: A US Skyraider streaks upward away from enemy ground fire, after releasing its bomb load against a Viet Cong artillery piece which had been deployed perilously close to the camp perimeter.

Even though the Tet offensive was quickly suppressed (except in Hue) there was more bad news to come. On 5 February, the North Vietnamese failed to take Hill 881S, leaving 109 dead behind them from the intense air and artillery barrage, but on the next night, not only Khe Sanh but the Special Forces camp at Lang Vei to the west was subjected to mortar and artillery bombardment. Lang Vei's garrison consisted of some 500 irregulars and 24 US Green Berets. Under cover of the artillery barrage, the NVA stormed the camp, using tanks (Soviet PT-76 amphibious models) for the first time in South Vietnam. Only 14 Americans and 60 irregulars managed to get out.

Throughout February North Vietnamese rockets, artillery and mortars continued to pound the Marines at Khe Sanh. The NVA's siege tactics against the base itself were classic: trenches, zig-zag approaches, and parallels. Sometimes the NVA would dig 300m (1000ft) of trenches in a night – and the next day Skyhawks would swoop down and drench them with napalm. Inside the perimeter rumours were rife of tunnels and mining, but none came to anything.

As at Dien Bien Phu, the crucial question was whether resupply and support from the air could cope. The land main supply route – Route 9 – was considered too open to ambush, and in any case the northeast monsoon had made stretches of it almost impassable. At first supplies and reinforcements came into the airstrip by C-130 and C-123 transports with helicopters taking the men and material from there up to the hill outposts. The outposts received the infantry assaults but the base camp was hit hardest by the shelling. By mid-February the landing and take-off of fixed-wing transports had become too costly, so they stopped landing and began making their deliveries by procedures known as LAPES and GPES. Under LAPES (Low Altitude Parachute Extraction System) the aircraft made a low-level approach and a parachute dragged the cargo across rollers out the rear doors. Under GPES (Ground Parachute Extraction System) the aircraft came in low to snag an arresting line which in turn yanked the cargo out of the rear.

The bulk of the helicopter lift burden fell on Marine helicopter squadron HMM-262 flying CH-46s. By the end of February they had lost half their helicopters and had to be reinforced by HMM-364. Supplies for

Above: US Marines take cover as incoming Viet Cong fire increases in intensity. The Marines, who claimed 'never to dig in', quickly learned that pride could not overcome firepower.

North Vietnamese at three points around the base. During the early evening of 29 February sensors warned of an advance from the east. A battalion of the 304th Division got through the air and artillery barrage and assaulted the South Vietnamese 37th Rangers just before midnight. The Rangers held, and although two more assaults were made before dawn they all failed after hard fighting. The base perimeter was never again seriously threatened.

Bombing round the clock

Westmoreland's Operation Niagara was now dropping unprecedented tonnages of explosive around Khe Sanh. Intelligence was recommending at least 150 targets a day, and one of the most lucrative targets, an ammunition storage area 20km (12 miles) southwest of Khe Sanh at Co Roc mountain, was pounded for 24 hours on 15 February and yielded up over 1000 secondary explosions and fires.

By mid-March the monsoon had run its course and the dense clouds that had hampered air support began to disperse. At the same time, the North Vietnamese 325C Division began to withdraw from the battle-zone towards the Laotian border.

As early as mid-February, General Abrams at the MACV forward command post at Phu Bai had fixed 1 April as D-Day for the relief of Khe Sanh. On 10 March the MACV forward command post was redesignated Provisional Corps, Vietnam (later XXIV Corps). Command was given to Lieutenant-General William B. Rosson and Abrams returned to Saigon. Rosson's new corps included the 101st Airborne Division, the 1st Air Cavalry Division, and the 3rd Marine Division.

Operation Pegasus, the plan for the relief of Khe Sanh, was to be a show-piece of airmobility. The 'flying horses' would be the troopers of the 1st Air Cavalry. They were to leapfrog forward in helicopter-borne air assaults while the 1st Marine Regiment moved more mundanely along the axis of Route 9. Ca Lu was designated as the starting point, and General 'Jack' Tolson of the 1st Air Cavalry would be in overall command. Westmoreland ordered that Pegasus should take maximum toll of enemy personnel and equipment.

On 28 March the South Vietnamese made an airborne task force of three battalions available for Operation Pegasus. Altogether Tolson now had over 30,000 men under his command, and Pegasus began at 0700 hours, 1 April, on schedule. The first day the 3rd Brigade, 1st Air Cavalry, under Colonel Hubert S. Campbell, established a fire support base 8km (5 miles) east of Khe Sanh. The 1st Marines, under Colonel Stanley S. Hughes (who had commanded the Marines in the just-ended battle for Hue), moved out on Route 9 covering the work of the 11th Marine Engineer Battalion.

On 4 April the 1st Battalion, 9th Marines, attacked southeast from Khe Sanh taking Hill 471. Next morning the North Vietnamese 7th Battalion, 66th Regiment, attempted a counterattack against the Marines on Hill 471 and were slaughtered. 6 April was a day of fighting and of meetings: the 2nd Battalion, 7th Cavalry, fought a day-long battle at a loop in the road, while the 2nd Battalion, 12th Cavalry, reached the 1st Battalion, 9th Marines, on Hill 471. Westmoreland, called back to Washington for consultations, had the pleasure of announcing the link-up to the press on the White House lawn.

the outposts were no longer staged at Khe Sanh but at Dong Ha, 32 km (20 miles) away. Three deliveries a day would be made – at 0900, 1300 and 1700 hours – by 'super gaggles' of 12 CH-46s with a standard load of 1360kg (3000lbs) escorted by two UH-1E gunships, controlled by two UH-1E 'slicks', and preceded by four to 12 strike aircraft, usually Marine A-4s from Chu Lai, who would suppress enemy fire while the helicopters made their deliveries and picked up any medevacs or other passengers.

Enemy shelling reached a peak on 23 February when 1307 projectiles hit Khe Sanh; this coincided with intelligence reports indicating the massing of

Khe Sanh combat base
Quang Tri province

drop zone

RED SECTOR

to Khe Sanh village

forward operating base 3

155mm howitzer battery

4.2in mortar battery

105mm howitzer battery

fuel dispensing centre

BLUE SECTOR

air support radar team

GREY SECTOR

Marine air traffic control unit

fire support coordination centre and 26 Marine command post

control tower

direct air support centre

water point

ground controlled approach

airstrip

105mm howitzer batteries

main ammo dump

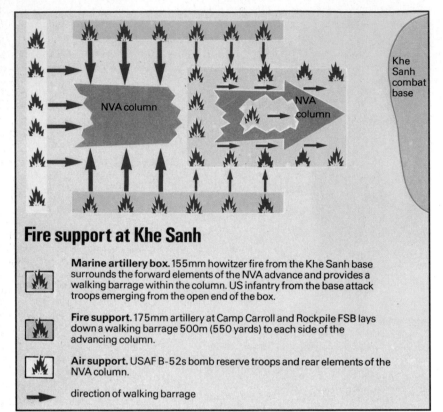

Fire support at Khe Sanh

Marine artillery box. 155mm howitzer fire from the Khe Sanh base surrounds the forward elements of the NVA advance and provides a walking barrage within the column. US infantry from the base attack troops emerging from the open end of the box.

Fire support. 175mm artillery at Camp Carroll and Rockpile FSB lays down a walking barrage 500m (550 yards) to each side of the advancing column.

Air support. USAF B-52s bomb reserve troops and rear elements of the NVA column.

→ direction of walking barrage

The worst place in the world

'Khe Sanh was a very bad place then, but the airstrip there was the worst place in the world.... There was nothing random about the shelling there, and no one wanted anything to do with it. If the wind was right, you could hear the NVA .50-calibres starting far up the valley whenever a plane made its approach to the strip, and the first incoming artillery would precede the landings by seconds. If you were waiting there to be taken out, there was nothing you could do but curl up in the trench and try to make yourself small, and if you were coming in on the plane, there was nothing you could do, nothing at all.

'While a planeload of passengers tensed and sweated and made the run for the trench over and over in their heads, waiting for the cargo hatch to drop, ten to fifty Marines and correspondents huddled down in the trench, worked their lips futilely to ease the dryness, and then, at the exact same instant, they would all race, collide, stampede, exchanging places. If the barrage was a particularly heavy one, the faces would all distort in the most simple kind of panic, the eyes going wider than the eyes of horses caught in a fire.... Men would still be struggling on or off as the aircraft turned slowly to begin the taxi before the most accelerated take-off the machine had it in it to make. If you were on board, that first movement was an ecstasy.... There was no feeling in the world as good as being airborne out of Khe Sanh.'

Journalist Michael Herr in his book Dispatches.

Below: A direct mortar hit.

Enemy resistance faded on 7 April and next morning, at 0800, the relief of Khe Sanh was made official with the arrival of Campbell's 3rd Brigade command group at the base. That afternoon the South Vietnamese three-battalion airborne task force landed near Khe Sanh village and began sweeping west along Route 9 towards Laos.

On 9 April no enemy shells fell on Khe Sanh for the first time in 45 days and US forces moved on into the now deserted Lang Vei Special Forces camp. Route 9 was declared open on 11 April. Marine engineers had mended 14km (9 miles) of road, replaced nine bridges, and bulldozed 17 bypasses. On 12 April Colonel Lownds was relieved of command of his regiment by Colonel Bruce Meyers and went home to receive a Navy Cross from President Johnson.

The enemy still held Hill 881N, however, from where they had fired 5000 122mm and 140mm rockets at the base during the siege. The two Marine companies holding the companion Hill 881S had suffered nearly 50 per cent casualties, but during the first week of April the remainder of the 3rd Battalion, 26th Marines, joined the two beleaguered units and on Easter morning, 14 April, they jumped off in an attack against the still-forbidding Hill 881N, estimated to be held by a battalion of North Vietnamese. By 1430 hours, the Marines had taken the hill. Those North Vietnamese who had not fled were all either dead or captured. This was the last action of the battle. Next morning, at 0800 hours on 15 April, Pegasus was officially ended.

A blizzard of bombs

The North Vietnamese had employed between 15,000 and 20,000 troops in the siege, but the techniques that had succeeded at Dien Bien Phu failed them at Khe Sanh. They had done what they could to cut the aerial supply line, occasionally risking infantry action, but had got back a blizzard of bombs and shells for every shell or rocket they threw at the Marines.

As with almost every prolonged battle, getting at complete and accurate casualty figures is difficult. From 19 January until 31 March, the Marines at Khe Sanh had lost 199 men killed and 830 wounded or evacuated. Operation Pegasus cost a further 92 Marines and soldiers killed and 629 wounded seriously enough to require evacuation. South Vietnamese losses in Pegasus were listed as 34 killed and 184 wounded. About 1000 North Vietnamese were counted as dead by the Marines during the defence of Khe Sanh and another 1000 were counted after Operation Pegasus. Westmoreland's staff put the total North Vietnamese losses at between 10,000 and 15,000.

General Westmoreland believed Khe Sanh to be a 'classic example of how to defeat a numerically superior besieging force by coordinated application of firepower.' To other observers, it seemed a costly waste of resources. But the great unanswered question is how the communists regarded the operation. Did General Giap see the taking of the base as a key point in a general offensive of which Tet was the major part? Or did he merely hope to tie US forces up while Tet took place? These questions remain unanswered. In any case, Khe Sanh did not prove to be another Dien Bien Phu, either politically or militarily, nor did the Marines who were at the centre of the bull's-eye ever think it would be.

Brigadier-General Edwin H. Simmons (Ret)

Key Weapons
SOVIET FIELD ARTILLERY

Soviet military planners have always emphasised the importance of artillery and some 15 per cent of Soviet Army personnel are in artillery units. During the 1970s the Soviets placed great emphasis on the development of self-propelled guns, but towed artillery has not been neglected. It has been recognised, however, that it is no longer feasible to muster several dozen field pieces wheel-to-wheel, as was done during World War II, in order to swamp a target with fire, since such a concentration would rapidly be detected by modern sensors and attract countermeasures ranging from artillery to air and missile strikes. New tactics have evolved for the use of artillery as part of combined-arms operations, and at the same time a tendency has developed to move away from the deployment of shorter-ranging light calibre field pieces to reliance on heavier-calibre howitzers with the ability to command a greater area of the battlefield.

The backbone of Soviet artillery, from the time of the tsars until the 1960s, was the 76mm divisional gun in its various successive models. The last of these was the M1942 or ZIS-3, introduced in 1942 and produced in vast quantities during World War II and for some years thereafter. It was widely distributed throughout the Warsaw Pact armies and has been sold equally widely to Asian and African countries. By the 1980s it was only used in the Warsaw Pact as a reserve and militia weapon, and for training, but it could still be found in frontline service elsewhere. And no wonder: it is a thoroughly workmanlike and efficient piece of equipment, capable of serving perfectly adequately in any role where the calibre is suitable. The M1942's efficient design came from wartime rationalisation; its predecessor, the M1936, was efficient but heavy, and the M1942 was put together by using the M1936 barrel and marrying it to the carriage and recoil system which had been developed for a 57mm anti-tank gun. The result was a design which was 'right' from the start. Capable of firing a 6.2kg (13.7lb) high explosive (HE) shell to 13,300m (14,580yds), it was also provided with an armour-piercing (AP) shell and a hollow charge anti-tank shell, both of which were capable of dealing with most World War II tanks. As a result the M1942 was used interchangeably as a field or anti-tank gun.

In 1943-44 the Soviets developed an 85mm

weapon to supplement the 76mm design. This went into service as the 85mm divisional gun D-44, though it did not reach the hands of troops until after the war had ended. A long-barrelled weapon on a split-trail carriage, it fired a 9.6kg (21.2lb) shell to 15,650m (17,115yds) and like its predecessors it was provided with AP and hollow charge shells, giving it a useful anti-tank capability. In this latter role it was frequently fitted with a large infra-red searchlight above the shield which, in conjunction with a special sighting telescope, allowed firing in darkness against tanks to a range of about 600m (650yds).

In postwar years the Soviets expanded their airborne forces and, in order to provide them with a useful dual-purpose gun, equipped them with the 85mm D-44. The only drawback was that this needed

Previous page: A 122mm M1938 (M30) howitzer is prepared for fire by Polish troops on Warsaw Pact manoeuvres. Above: The now obsolescent 76mm M1942 field gun, mainstay of Soviet divisional artillery in the 1940s.

Below: North Vietnamese troops blast away at US positions using an 85mm D-44 field gun. Lightweight and rugged the D-44 was highly regarded by NVA field units.

Right: The SD-44, photographed from the rear to show its two-cylinder 14bhp engine mounted on the trail. Steered by one of the gun crew the drive unit is capable of a top road speed of 25km/h (15mph) and provides the SD-44 with a useful degree of cross-country mobility.

the presence of a towing vehicle, and so the ingenious Russian designers produced the first 'auxiliary propulsion' weapon to enter military service, a fashion which has since spread. The SD-44, as it was known, had a two-cylinder 14bhp petrol engine mounted on the trail so as to drive the gun wheels by a conventional prop-shaft and differential. The trail ends were supported by a single wheel which could be steered by the driver/gunner who sat on the trail ahead of the motor. On a hard road the device could reach a speed of 25km/h, and the engine could be de-clutched to allow the gun to be towed in the normal way if a tractor was available. The SD-44 stayed in service with Soviet airborne divisions until the late 1970s, at which time they were restructured as rifle divisions and their heavy support removed.

By the 1980s the D-44 was used only for training in the Soviet Army, but was still believed to be in frontline service with other members of the Warsaw Pact; it has also been widely spread throughout the Third World countries.

At a higher calibre, a 100mm field gun, the BS-3, was put into service in 1944. The barrel came from an existing naval gun and the carriage followed conventional practice, being a split trail with two dual wheels and a shield. As a field gun it fired a 15.6kg (34.4lb) shell to 21,000m (23,000yds) and with a very long barrel it could deliver a 16kg (35lb) AP shell at 1000m (1100yds) per second to pierce 185mm (7.3in) of armour at 1000m (1100yds) range, a very potent performance. It was later provided with a discarding sabot shot which had a velocity of 1415m (4641ft) per second and could pierce 200mm (7.9in) at the same range, and a hollow charge shell capable of holing 380mm (15in) of plate at any range.

Unfortunately, like most of the heavy anti-tank guns of its day, the 100mm gun was a heavy and cumbersome weapon to manhandle around the battlefield, weighing 3650kg (8050lb). It was gradually replaced in Soviet service by a specialised 85mm

Right: Leftist Muslim militia fire on Christian positions north of Beirut with a Soviet-made 122mm D-74 field gun. The D-74 can fire a 27kg (60lb) shell to a maximum range of 24,000m (26,250 yds).

Below: An Egyptian 122mm A-19 (M1931/37) field gun dug-in prior to an Israeli assault in the Sinai during the Six-Day War of 1967. Developed as a long-range counter-battery weapon during World War II, the A-19's reliability in action and its long range will ensure its continuing use in many Third World armies. Bottom: Deployed in line a battery of 122mm M1938 (M-30) howitzers awaits orders to fire.

anti-tank gun and later by a smoothbore 100mm anti-tank gun which weighed some 650kg (1430lb) less. It is still widely distributed outside the Soviet Union.

During the heyday of the 76mm field guns, the next step up was the 122mm medium artillery howitzer. The M1938 went into service in 1939 and is still present throughout the Warsaw Pact and Third World armies in vast numbers. Like the 76mm M1942 it was a sound design which can still give good service, firing a 21.8kg (48lb) shell to a range of 11,800m (12,900yds). However, its range was considered insufficient for modern warfare, and in the late 1940s it was supplemented by the 122mm gun D-74, a long-barrelled weapon capable of firing a 27kg (60lb) shell to 24,000m (26,250yds). This appeared to be satisfactory in delivering a heavier shell to a longer range, but at the same time another design bureau had developed a totally new weapon, the 130mm M-46 gun, and in comparative trials this latter proved to be even more efficient. As a result, comparatively few examples of the D-74 were made and most of them were exported, equipping among others the Egyptian, Chinese and Cuban Armies.

The M-46 was once again an existing naval gun adapted to field use, by fitting it to a two-wheeled split trail carriage. Firing a 33.4kg (73.5lb) shell to 27,000m (29,500yds), it also had an AP shell capable of piercing 230mm (9.1in) of armour at 1000m (1100yds) range, giving the weapon a very useful anti-tank performance. Its capabilities were first seen by Western agencies in Vietnam, where it was deployed from 1971 onwards. The gun rapidly acquired a reputation for phenomenal accuracy as well as destructive ability, and a remarkable quantity of US airpower was devoted to an unsuccessful effort to take the M-46 out of the war. The Egyptians used the M-46 in a counter-battery role during the 1973 Arab-Israeli

Above left: A Soviet gun crew fires a 130mm M-46 gun. Possessing a range of 27,000m (29,500 yds) the M-46 has proved highly successful in long-range artillery duels, notably in Vietnam where NVA artillery was able to outrange most US field guns with ease. Above: While Soviet armour advances in the background a battery of 122mm D-30 howitzers are prepared for action. With its wheels in the up position the D-30 has a quick 360 degree traverse, and in this picture the tow attachment can be seen below the muzzle brake.

Left: The D-30 in action – Lebanese Muslim troops pound Christian positions around Beirut from a mountain stronghold. Designed to fire both anti-tank and conventional high-explosive rounds the D-30 is a highly versatile weapon.

War with a considerable degree of success. It has been widely exported to other Asian and African armies, as well as being the standard field piece of the Warsaw Pact forces.

While the 122mm M1938 howitzer was an efficient weapon, it lacked flexibility for modern warfare, and in the early 1960s a replacement, the D-30 122mm howitzer, appeared. This was a thoroughly modern design, which was apparently based on a Skoda weapon developed for the German Army in 1943–44. Instead of the conventional split trail and two wheels, it has a platform with three outrigger legs which can be spread, and the wheels lifted from the ground, so as to allow the howitzer to be traversed and fired through the full 360 degree circle. This permits rapid employment against targets in any direction, very desirable in a war of movement. The D-30 is not towed by the trail, but by the muzzle. It fires the same 21.8kg (48lb) shell as the M1938 but to a maximum range of 15,400m (16,840yds); it also has a rocket-assisted shell which boosts the range to 21,000m (23,000yds), though with some degradation of accuracy. The howitzer has seen service in the 1973 Middle East war, and in Nigeria, Angola and Ethiopia.

The next step in traditional calibres was to 152mm, a class which had existed in Russian service since the 1870s. The current 152mm weapon in service is the D-20 gun-howitzer, mounted on the usual sort of split-trail carriage. This fires a 43.5kg (96lb) shell to a range of 17,400m (19,000yds) as standard, and is also reputed to be provided with a rocket-assisted shell which reaches to 37,000m (40,000yds) and a 0.2 kiloton nuclear shell. It is in service throughout the Warsaw Pact and in Yugoslavia, is still being manufactured in China, and has probably been supplied to various Asian and African armies.

The largest Soviet field piece is the 180mm S-23 gun, another design which began life as a naval gun

SOVIET FIELD GUNS

D-30
Crew 7
Calibre 122mm
Weight Firing 3150kg (6944.5lb)
Range 15,400m (16,840yds), rocket assisted 21,000m (22,966yds)
Ammunition HE 21.8kg (48.1lb) HEAT 14.1kg (31.1lb) and 21.6kg (47.6lb), smoke, chemical and illuminating

M-46
Crew 9
Calibre 130mm
Weight Firing 8450kg (18,629lb)
Range 27,000m (29,528yds)
Ammunition HE 33.4kg (73.5lb), AP 33.6kg (74.1lb)

S-23
Crew 15
Calibre 180mm
Weight Travelling 20,400kg (44, 974lb)
Range HE 30,500m (33,355yds), rocket assisted 44,000m (48,120yds)
Ammunition HE 84kg (185lb), AP, 0.2kt nuclear, G-572 concrete piercing

and was then grafted on to a field carriage. The carriage in this case is a large split trail design with twin wheels, the trail ends being carried on a two-wheeled limber when being towed. The gun barrel is drawn back in its recoil system and strapped to the trail while travelling, in order to reduce the vibration on the unsupported barrel. The S-23 fires an 84kg (185lb) shell to a maximum range of 30.500m (33,400yds). It is also provided with a concrete-piercing shell for attacking fortifications, a rocket-assisted shell which extends the maximum range to 44,000m (48,000yds), and a 0.2 kiloton nuclear shell. Employed by the Egyptian Army during the Yom Kippur War of 1973 the S-23 demonstrated its ability for accurate long-range fire. In Soviet service the S-23 is employed by the Heavy Artillery Brigade of the Artillery Division; it is not in general Warsaw Pact use, and outside the Soviet Union this 180mm gun can be found with the Indian, Syrian and Egyptian Armies.

Above: A Soviet 152mm D-20 gun-howitzer in its firing position, with wheels splayed outwards. Assigned at divisional level the D-30 acts in a general support capacity. Below: The largest of the Soviet Army's field guns, 180mm S-23s photographed here in Red Square, 1968.

Hitting the cities

The communist Tet offensive in Vietnam

In July 1967 senior diplomats from around the world were recalled by Hanoi to attend a top level conference headed by Ho Chi Minh and Vo Nguyen Giap which was to consider how to break the military stalemate in Vietnam. After much discussion, it was decided that an all-out military offensive should be launched in 1968 in the South using the combined forces of the North Vietnamese Army (NVA) and the Viet Cong. The declared aims were to promote a popular uprising among the people of South Vietnam, to cause the collapse of the South Vietnamese armed forces and to destroy the political and military position of the United States in Vietnam.

This crucial decision arose in 1967 because by this time the North Vietnamese had examined the situation and come to two conclusions which were to have major repercussions on the outcome of the war. In the first place, the communists appeared to be making little or no progress in their war against the South Vietnamese government and its US supporters. Secondly, while the Americans, with their sophisticated military armoury and massive logistic support, seemed capable of holding them at bay indefinitely in the field, at home US public opinion was becoming increasingly restless, with ever more strident demands for the US government to reassess its commitment to South Vietnam.

A subsidiary, but nonetheless important, element in their thinking concerned the Viet Cong, the military arm of the National Liberation Front located throughout the Republic of South Vietnam. Although close ties existed between the NVA and the Viet Cong, the apparent lack of NVA military successes was leading to growing Viet Cong dissatisfaction with Hanoi's policies. It thus became both politically desirable and militarily necessary for North Vietnam to retain the favour of the Viet Cong by launching an all-out offensive into the South. Whether Hanoi also considered the possibility that heavy Viet Cong combat losses might eliminate a potential rival for power in South Vietnam once victory had been achieved is not known.

The planned assault against the South was to be as widespread as possible with the NVA attacking into the northern provinces and the Viet Cong launching an offensive against virtually every city and town throughout South Vietnam from Saigon to the smallest district administrative centre. It was hoped that such an all-embracing operation would severely reduce the morale of the South Vietnamese government both at national and local level and allow the underground network to win the support of the vast majority of the South Vietnamese people. Power in local government would then be established and, ultimately, expanded to take control in Saigon itself. A successful operation would undoubtedly result in repercussions throughout the United States.

Having analysed the factors likely to affect a major operation, the next decision to be taken was when to launch the attack. The South Vietnamese would be least prepared at the time of the Tet national holiday, with many soldiers away on leave, and it was decided that an operation would be launched at this time in late January 1968 – to be known as the Tet offensive. At

Above: With cigarette burning and M60 machine gun at the ready, an ARVN soldier and his number two gunner move on to the offensive against Viet Cong units.

Left: General Harold Johnson Chief of Staff, US Army, meets Royal Thai Army officers during a tour of Vietnam which was aimed at establishing the effectiveness of the US military machine in Vietnam. Even before the Tet offensive serious questions were being raised about US strategy in Vietnam.

The Tet offensive 1968

Quang Tri
Khe Sanh
Hue
Phu Bai
Phu Loc
Da Nang
Hoi An
THAILAND
LAOS
Tam Ky
Chu Lai
Quang Ngai
Dak To
Kontum
Bong Son
Pleiku
An Khe
Qui Nhon
Hau Bon
Tuy Hoa
CAMBODIA
Mekong
Central Highlands
Ban Me Thuot
Ninh Hoa
Nha Trang
Da Lat
Loc Ninh
SOUTH VIETNAM
Tay Ninh
Phu Cuong
Gia Dinh
Bien Hoa
Moc Hoa
Long Binh
Phan Thiet
Chau Phu
Saigon
Sa Dec
My Tho
Phouc Le
SOUTH CHINA SEA
Vinh Long Truc Giang
Rach Gia
Phu Vinh
Can Tho
Khanh Hung
Quan Long

● towns and military installations attacked by the NVA and Viet Cong
Demilitarised Zone

this time also, the weather might well be unsuitable for American close-support operations from the air.

Planning for the Tet offensive was quickly advanced and a great deal of consideration given to deceiving the American and South Vietnamese forces as to the main objectives and scale of the assault. It was agreed that the best way to avoid alerting the enemy's suspicions would be to continue to mount operations of what might be termed a familiar nature. The decision was taken to mount two separate sets of diversionary operations. A series of minor border skirmishes was initiated in December 1967 just south of the demilitarized zone (DMZ) and at Song Be, Loc Ninh and Dak To, places remote from major garrisons in South Vietnam. They were designed to draw important troops away from the towns and cities – the major targets of the coming offensive operation.

In mid-January 1968 two NVA divisions, with a third in reserve, were deployed against the heavily defended US firebase at Khe Sanh. The attack on Khe Sanh began on 21 January and was to be sustained throughout the next 11 weeks. For the Americans, Khe Sanh became a political and military battle that they could not afford to lose. Consequently, increasing amounts of artillery and air support were used in order to maintain the besieged garrison.

In order further to conceal the build-up of men and supplies, the North Vietnamese wished their own people and soldiers to be seen enjoying the Tet holiday themselves. To accomplish this, directives were issued that the holiday should start earlier than usual, on the eve of 29 January. Careful arrangements were made to ensure that all units would be on full alert, with all men returning from leave in order to start the offensive, on the night of 30 January, just when the South would be in the midst of its own celebrations. The Viet Cong used the holiday to infiltrate into the towns and cities of South Vietnam under the guise of holidaymakers, smuggling their weapons in with them.

The North Vietnamese also attempted to ensure internal secrecy for their Tet offensive by not informing subordinate commanders and men of their intentions until the last possible moment. But despite the extreme care taken to conceal the coming offensive, on the night of 30 January a brief warning was inadvertently given to the South when a number of premature attacks were launched on towns in the Central Highlands, and some central coastal provinces, 24 hours earlier than was planned. Westmoreland was well aware that a major offensive was in the offing; on 15 January he had told his staff that there was 'a sixty/forty chance' of the communists launching an attack on or around Tet.

Nonetheless, the general assault, involving a total of some 84,000 men made up of both Viet Cong and NVA forces, began the following night. Mortar and rocket attacks were launched against targets in no less than five major cities, 36 provincial capitals, 64 district capitals and 50 villages. Fierce fighting followed these bombardments as both NVA and Viet Cong units struggled to establish themselves in the towns. Two of the main targets were Saigon and Hue. In Saigon, a number of prime targets were chosen. A small group, 15 Viet Cong guerrillas, attacked the US embassy and succeeded in setting off an explosive charge which blew an opening through the main wall. There followed a desperate firefight, in which five US military personnel died, lasting some six hours before all the Viet Cong in the raid were accounted for and control of the embassy was restored to the Americans. Elsewhere in Saigon, there were five similar attacks by small sapper groups – including one by Viet Cong in Army of the Republic of Vietnam (ARVN) uniforms against the presidential palace, though this was easily repulsed. Other attacks against the Tan Son Nhut airport and the ARVN Joint General Staff HQ were similarly defeated.

During the days that followed, five US battalions, together with ARVN forces, fought to clear Saigon of some 4000 communists who had seized areas of the city. Fierce house-to-house fighting, accompanied at times by US rocket and strafing attacks from the air, finally restored control of the city by 5 February. Throughout South Vietnam the pattern was repeated, with government and US troops retaking town after town in bloody fighting against an enemy prepared to resist to the death. In some cases, especially in the Delta region, airstrikes were called in which devastated urban areas. It was of the Delta town of Ben Tre that a US officer made the famous comment: 'We had to destroy it to save it.' Inevitably, non-combatant casualties were heavy, and the fighting left an estimated half a million refugees.

Clearing out the communists

Most cities and towns were virtually clear of communist units by the end of the first week's fighting, but in Hue the resistance was tougher. Eventually it took an ARVN division and three US Marine battalions 25 days to clear the city. Just over a month after the fighting in Hue ended, at the beginning of April, the siege of Khe Sanh was broken. Although the communists launched two smaller-scale offensives in the course of the summer, it was clear that the US Army and the ARVN had weathered the main storm.

As we have seen, the declared aims of the communists in launching the Tet offensive were: to bring the South to such a state of turmoil that the government would collapse; to cause the South Vietnamese Army to disintegrate; and finally, to undermine America's political will to continue the war. In the first two of these aims they had clearly failed. Despite widespread attacks throughout South Vietnam and momentary success, particularly in Saigon and Hue, they never looked like succeeding in their first objective. The brutal methods of the communists in Hue and elsewhere did little to earn them sympathy and their failure to enlist mass support was a major defeat.

Nor did the South Vietnamese Army collapse. Despite severe casualties during Tet (quoted by some sources as being as high as 11,000) the ARVN proved effective during the fighting. Far from disintegrating during the following months it built up its strength. This was, of course, in large part due to the US policy of Vietnamization and the introduction of general mobilisation by the South Vietnamese government. Nevertheless, volunteer enlistments into the ARVN rose sharply throughout the remainder of 1968.

Indeed, the military situation just after the offensive must have appeared somewhat alarming to

Below: A Viet Cong nurse and nine men are escorted by ARVN Rangers from the building where they surrendered in Cholon, the Chinese quarter of Saigon. Bottom: American military police inspect the bodies of Viet Cong guerrillas killed during the attack against the US embassy in Saigon.

Hanoi. In the first place, the casualties inflicted on the NVA and the Viet Cong were enormously heavy. Of the total of perhaps 84,000 men committed to the operation, reliable estimates suggest there were over 30,000 killed in the first two weeks of the battle. No army could stand such losses and certainly the communists could not have sustained the impetus of the attack longer than they did.

The great majority of the casualties were among the Viet Cong units, and it is clear that after Tet the Viet Cong were so weakened militarily that they were never again able to function effectively. For Hanoi, their destruction was perhaps less of a disaster than might have been thought. The political leadership of the southern communists was often at odds with Hanoi and its impotence after Tet eliminated the possibility of a rival for future power in the South.

The relief of Khe Sanh after some 11 weeks of siege must also have given the North Vietnamese matter for reflection. It had become clear as the fighting continued that the tactics employed by General Giap against the French at Dien Bien Phu were not likely to prove successful while the Americans remained in Vietnam in support of the South.

If Tet can be seen, then, as a military setback for the communists, it was still only a 'victory' in strictly localised terms for the US forces. And this is where the third declared objective – to weaken American resolve – becomes important. Naturally, Tet had a great impact on US public opinion, in that the sight of Viet Cong squads fighting it out in the grounds of the American embassy in Saigon was poor publicity for the US Army; but the view that the government lost its nerve mainly because of pressure from the media is a myth.

Already in the autumn of 1967, highly placed members of the government were voicing serious doubts about the war. Secretary of Defense McNamara had been one of the staunchest advocates of escalating the war, yet now he wrote to President Johnson that: 'There is ... a very real question whether ... it will be possible to maintain our efforts in Vietnam for the time necessary to accomplish our objectives there.' By November he had made clear his intention to resign. Johnson, too, was sick of the war, and well before Tet had decided not to stand for re-election in 1968. McNamara and other members of the administration, Walt Rostow and Dean Rusk for example, were in favour of halting the bombing of the North and making every effort to start negotiations.

Into this existing atmosphere of unease came the events of early 1968 which, taken in sequence, were extremely worrying. First came the attack on Khe Sanh on 21 January, which was bound to remind the Washington establishment of the start of the Dien Bien Phu siege in January 1954. Then, at the very end of January in 1968, came the Tet offensive itself. Again, whatever the communist casualties, their ability to mount such an operation after three years of US combat involvement was bound to suggest that a US victory was still far distant. And on 8 February, before the echoes of Tet had died away, came the fall of Lang Vei, the Special Forces camp west of Khe Sanh, where NVA tanks went into action, overrunning the 500 defenders.

Westmoreland's request for 200,000 more troops came at the same time as Lang Vei. It is hardly surprising, in the circumstances, that this request was investigated with care by the administration, to assess

Left: President Lyndon Johnson deep in thought at the White house in early 1968. The ability of the communists to launch an offensive on the scale of Tet after three years of US involvement convinced Johnson that an American victory was still far distant.

Below: ARVN troops take up positions and await a Viet Cong attack in the Saigon cemetery in January 1968. The 4000 communist guerrillas were eventually cleared from the city by 5 February.

what future prospects were. Clark Clifford, a well-known 'hawk', who was to take up the post of Secretary of Defense, was given the job of forming a 'Task Force' to look into the issues involved. This 11-man committee was, in the main, composed of men whose commitment to the war could not be questioned: members included General Maxwell Taylor, Richard Helms (of the CIA) and William Bundy.

Clifford completely changed his views on the war as a result of this enquiry. He was shaken when the Joint Chiefs of Staff proved unable to give him straight answers on the war. A report prepared by the CIA argued persuasively (especially in the light of recent events) that Hanoi could withstand the strategy of attrition that seemed the army's only approach. The interim report of the Task Force, on 4 March, tried to compromise on whether the troop reinforcements should be sent to Westmoreland, but the scenario it described was bleak: 'There can be no assurance that this very substantial additional deployment would leave us a year from today in any more favourable military position. All that can be said is that additional troops would enable us to kill more of the enemy and provide more security if the enemy does not offset

them.' This could only be taken as an indictment of US Army methods in Vietnam – especially the implication of the final clause that the NVA could, if it so wished, nullify the effect of the increases.

On 10 March news of Westmoreland's request for more troops reached the press and created an uproar. But the essential change in the administration's attitude was already well under way. Sober, calculating, experienced politicians and military experts had lost faith in the ability of the US Army to win the war.

So although the communists had suffered heavy losses and their previous ability to sustain a small-scale insurgency had been weakened as a result of the losses suffered by the Viet Cong, the US administration too had realised that old methods would not do. Both sides had to look for new ways. Within six months of Tet, Johnson had ordered a halt to bombing of the North, talks had begun between the US and North Vietnam, General Westmoreland had been replaced by General Abrams as US commander in Vietnam, and the shift of responsibility for the war from the US Army to the ARVN had begun. The results of Tet had not been decisive, however. Both sides had been forced to think again, and a new phase of the war began. **Major F.A. Godfrey**

Hue

Battle for the imperial city

By late-January 1968 two regiments of North Vietnamese Army (NVA) regular troops had infiltrated into the ancient imperial capital of Hue to join local Viet Cong units already present in the city. On 31 January 1968, as part of the communist Tet offensive, these forces initiated a closely coordinated rocket, mortar and ground assault, and quickly seized most of the city in an iron grip.

At the closest American combat base, Phu Bai, 12km (8 miles) to the south, there had been sporadic rocket and mortar attacks during the night and many reports of disruptions along Route 1, the spinal column of I Corps Tactical Zone. An understrength force, Task Force X-Ray, was based at Phu Bai under the command of Brigadier-General Foster Lahue, who had been both a Marine Raider in World War II and a battalion commander in Korea. At full strength the force was to comprise two Marine regiments, the 1st and the 5th. On 31 January, however, Lahue had only the two regimental headquarters and three understrength battalions under his command. With a force of less than 4000 Marines, Lahue was tasked to keep Route 1 open from Hai Van Pass to Hue, defend Phu Bai, and screen the western approaches to Hue. He was not assigned to the defence of Hue itself.

For centuries Hue had been the imperial capital of Annam. Halfway between Da Nang and the demilitarized zone (DMZ), with a population of 100,000 and an unknown number of refugees it was South Vietnam's third largest city. Two thirds of the population lived within the walls of the Old City, or Citadel, as the French had called it. Rectangular in shape, the Citadel was enclosed by two massive walls, extending 3km (2 miles) on the longest sides, with multi-channel moats outside them, except for the southeast

wall which bordered the Song Huong or Perfume River. The sea was 10km (6 miles) away and the river was not suited to ocean-going shipping. South of the river and linked to the Citadel by the Nguyen Hoang bridge was the unfortified New City.

Throughout the war, Hue had been regarded as something of a neutral zone. Even the Viet Cong treated it with respect and it had been remarkably free from active hostilities. There was a considerable US civilian presence but no US military garrison. Indeed, for most US military personnel Hue was out of bounds. Few Marines or soldiers, other than members of the advisory effort, had ever been in the city.

The Military Assistance Command, Vietnam (MACV) compound that housed the US advisers to the Army of the Republic of Vietnam (ARVN) 1st Division was located in the New City south of the river. The headquarters of the 1st ARVN Division occupied a fortified bastion in the northeastern corner of the Citadel, some distance from their American advisers. Brigadier-General Ngo Quang Truong, commanding the 1st ARVN Division, had the reputation of being one of South Vietnam's best generals and his 1st Division too was regarded as one of the ARVN's best. Truong's 12 battalions, however, were strung along Route 1, from Hue to the northern border, and were employed in pacification and area defence missions. His closest battalion and the headquarters of his 3rd Regiment were 8km (5 miles) to the north. At his headquarters compound he had only his divisional staff and his elite division reaction company, the Hoc Bao or 'Black Panthers'. On 30 January, as the Tet ceasefire broke down, Truong had brought his meagre headquarters force to 100 per cent alert in preparation for possible enemy attacks.

Above: Crouched in a ditch, a US Marine sprays enemy positions with automatic fire in order to cover his comrades who are dragging a wounded Marine out of sight for on-the-spot medical aid. After receiving first aid most US casualties requiring further treatment were evacuated from the battlefield by helicopter.

The communist attack on the city began with a rocket and mortar barrage at 0340 hours on 31 January. Two battalions of infantry from the 6th NVA Regiment together with the 12th Sapper Battalion, pushed towards Truong's headquarters from the southwest. The Black Panthers briefly stopped the 800th NVA Battalion at the Hue airstrip, then fell back to the headquarters compound which the divisional staff were defending against the 802nd NVA Battalion. By dawn the gold-starred red-and-blue flag of the Viet Cong flew over the Imperial Palace and the 6th NVA Regiment held most of the Citadel except the 1st ARVN Division headquarters compound. The 806th NVA Battalion had taken up defensive positions to block any attempt at reinforcing Truong from the north.

South of the river, elements of the 4th NVA Regiment twice assaulted the MACV compound but were beaten off, though two Viet Cong battalions succeeded in taking other government buildings in the New City. The 810th NVA Battalion was deployed to block reinforcements from the south.

The road to Hue

At Phu Bai, Brigadier-General Lahue knew very little about the situation in Hue but had received reports of damage to Route 1 and its bridges, and of 'some problems' at the MACV compound. At 0830 hours he despatched A Company 1st Battalion, 1st Marines, in trucks on a road reconnaissance. Halfway to Hue, A Company came under heavy smallarms and automatic weapons fire, probably from elements of the 810th NVA Battalion. At 1030 hours, Lahue sent out the command group of 1st Battalion, 1st Marines, under Lieutenant Marcus Gravel, with G Company, 2nd Battalion, 5th Marines, to pick up A Company and continue on to Hue. En route, Gravel was providentially joined by a 3rd Marine Division tank platoon and some engineers. The column managed to cross the bridge over the Phu Cam Canal and reached the MACV compound at about 1445 hours. The senior US Army adviser present in the compound,

Colonel George Adkisson, gave Gravel what information he had, Gravel was then ordered to cross the Nguyen Hoang bridge and push on to reinforce Truong's headquarters.

At the bridge, Gravel was joined by some ARVN tanks. These and the Marine tanks gave him some fire support but neither the South Vietnamese nor the American tanks would follow him into the Citadel. He got across the bridge but found that he was running into more than he could handle. Gravel fell back, taking out his casualties on some commandeered Vietnamese trucks, and by 2000 hours was back in the MACV compound.

The situation in the New City was not quite as catastrophic as at first surmised. There were still isolated pockets of resistance holding out against the communists – largely Regional Force and Popular Force units. Most importantly, the Landing Craft Utility (LCU) ramp on the river and the radio relay station were still in friendly hands. On the following day, 1 February, Gravel was ordered to attack towards the provincial headquarters building and prison. His attack was launched at 0700 hours but quickly encountered heavy resistance.

North of the river, Truong had ordered his 3rd Regiment, reinforced with two airborne battalions

Below: A north Vietnamese soldier crouches below a wall at an outpost on the outskirts of Hue. Bottom: An M60 machine gunner and his number two relax against a bullet-pocked wall while maintaining a close watch for possible enemy attacks.

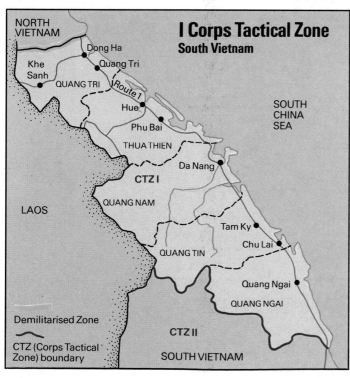

I Corps Tactical Zone
South Vietnam

NORTH VIETNAM
Dong Ha
Khe Sanh
Quang Tri
QUANG TRI
Route 1
Hue
Phu Bai
THUA THIEN
SOUTH CHINA SEA
Da Nang
CTZ I
QUANG NAM
LAOS
Tam Ky
Chu Lai
QUANG TIN
Quang Ngai
QUANG NGAI
CTZ II
SOUTH VIETNAM

Demilitarised Zone
CTZ (Corps Tactical Zone) boundary

and an armoured cavalry troop, to fight its way into the city. They reached his headquarters late on 31 January and on the morning of 1 February Truong began a counter-attack on the southern diagonal axis. With Truong's force fully occupied in the Citadel, Lieutenant-General Huong Xuan Lam, commanding general of I ARVN Corps, asked the Americans to assume complete responsibility for clearing Hue south of the Perfume River.

The northeast monsoon was at its height, bringing in rain and fog from the China Sea. On 2 February the weather turned particularly bad. That was the day that the US 1st Air Cavalry Division came into the battle. The 2nd Battalion, 12th Cavalry was tasked to seal off the city from the west and north and eventually the whole 3rd Brigade, under command of Colonel Hubert Campbell, would be used for that purpose.

At the MACV compound, Gravel had been joined by both F and H Companies, 5th Marines, and on 3 February the regimental commander of the 1st Marines, Colonel Stanley Hughes, arrived. A former enlisted man, with both a Navy Cross and Silver Star for World War II service, Hughes brought with him Lieutenant-Colonel Ernest Cheatham, commanding officer, 2nd Battalion, 5th Marines. Cheatham's three rifle companies – G, F and H – were returned to his control. On the following day, 4 February, B Company, 1st Marines, arrived. Hughes took charge of the battle south of the river with two battalions: Gravel's from his own regiment with two companies, and Cheatham's from the 5th Marines with three companies. All restrictions on the use of supporting weapons were lifted.

The Marine counter-attack began on 4 February.

Above: US Marines take cover behind an M48 tank. Although tanks were useful for supporting infantry assaults, most of the fierce fighting that took place in Hue was short range, house-to-house infantry combat.

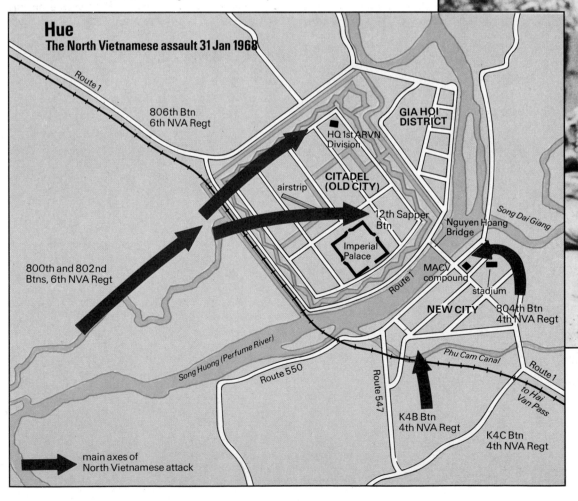

Hue
The North Vietnamese assault 31 Jan 1968

Route 1

806th Btn
6th NVA Regt

GIA HOI DISTRICT

HQ 1st ARVN Division

CITADEL (OLD CITY)

airstrip

12th Sapper Btn

Song Dai Giang

Nguyen Hoang Bridge

Imperial Palace

MACV compound

stadium

Route 1

800th and 802nd Btns, 6th NVA Regt

NEW CITY

804th Btn 4th NVA Regt

Song Huong (Perfume River)

Route 550

Phu Cam Canal

Route 1

Route 547

to Hai Van Pass

K4B Btn 4th NVA Regt

K4C Btn 4th NVA Regt

main axes of North Vietnamese attack

Above: A US Marine uses his head, but doesn't show it, as he raises and fires his M16 rifle over the top of a wall during street fighting in Hue. Right: A Marine officer, armed with a Colt M1911A1 .45in pistol, ducks down behind the tailgate of a truck to avoid sniper fire.

Left: While an M60 machine gunner keeps enemy heads down with a few bursts of automatic fire, a radio operator calls for support for his unit which has been pinned down by Viet Cong sniper fire.

Cheatham had his right flank on the river; Gravel's force was further south. The communists had converted the large government buildings they held into strong points of resistance with snipers in the upper stories, machine guns in the ground floors, mortars in hidden positions, and a web of spider holes manned by individual troops whose best weapons were the AK-47 automatic rifle, and rocket launchers. Conversely, the Marines were armed with M16 rifles, which many thought not as good as the Soviet-designed AK-47. They also had M79 40mm grenade launchers and M60 machine guns. Grenades and CS gas were used to flush the communists out of their holes. For battering their way through walls, the Marines had the 90mm guns of the M48 A3 tanks or,

even better, their 106mm recoilless rifles, some mounted in batteries of six on thin-skinned, tracked vehicles called 'Ontos'.

On the previous night, 3 February, the communists had blown up the bridge over the Phu Cam Canal, forcing the Americans to bring in supplies by helicopter or up the river by landing craft under escort of US Navy patrol craft until the bridgehead could be captured and the bridge replaced. For the Marines the battle assumed a rhythm: they would attack each morning at 0700 hours, fight all day, hope to be fed a hot meal, and would hold on to their gains at night. By 6 February they had retaken the province headquarters, the prison and the hospital. By 9 February they had crushed all organised resistance south of the river.

The battle in the Citadel

Truong's counter-attack, which had begun on 1 February, had bogged down and it was decided to give it new impetus with two battalions of Vietnamese Marines and a battalion of US Marines. The 1st Battalion, 5th Marines, which had been operating in the troublesome Phu Loc area, just north of Hai Van Pass, deployed into the Citadel by helicopter and landing craft on 12 February under the command of Major Robert Thompson. The US Marines went in on the left of the ARVN line and the Vietnamese Marines on the right. Much of the ensuing battle consisted of slow, gruelling house-to-house fighting as the density of building was much greater in the Citadel than south of the river.

Outside the Citadel's walls, to the west, Colonel Campbell's Air Cavalry Brigade had been increased to four battalions. Initially they had deployed facing outwards in order to hold off the reinforcement of the North Vietnamese in Hue by the 24th, 29th and 99th NVA Regiments, but as the operation progressed they were ordered to attack to the east, thus completing the squeeze on NVA forces in the city. Brigadier-General Oscar Davis, assistant division commander of the 1st Air Cavalry, was sent into the Citadel to join Truong and assess what forces were needed to finish the battle. Truong told him that by the time the 1st Air

Cavalry reached the walls of Hue, the battle would be over.

Entering the final phase of the operation, Campbell's brigade began an eastward attack on 21 February. They were joined, south of the river, by the 3rd Battalion, 327th Infantry, 101st Airborne Division, and on the night of 23/24 February, Truong made a surprise attack with his 2nd Battalion, 3rd Regiment, toward the Imperial Palace along the great wall itself. By dawn the red and yellow flag of the Republic of South Vietnam flew where the Viet Cong red, blue and gold flag had flown so tauntingly and the 'Black Panther' Company moved into the Imperial Palace to complete mopping up.

Within the city, the ARVN had lost 357 killed, 1830 wounded and 42 missing, claiming enemy losses of 2642 dead and 33 prisoners. The US Marines had suffered 142 killed, 857 wounded and evacuated (with 228 slightly wounded), and claimed 1959 enemy killed and 12 prisoners.

The battle for Hue had been the most violent close-range battle of the war. The commanding generals agreed that it could have been much shorter if the use of supporting arms had not been inhibited by adverse weather conditions, lack of sufficient local intelligence and the policy of sparing the city as much material damage as possible. As it was, the Marines expended 18,091 artillery rounds – high explosive, smoke, white phosphorus, illumination and CS gas. They found the 8in howitzer, with its great accuracy, the most effective of their big guns. Three cruisers and five destroyers lying offshore fired 5191 rounds of 5in, 6in, and 8in ammunition, earning the particular admiration of the US Army. Close air support was severely limited by the weather, but Marine aircraft flew 113 sorties and delivered 131,941kg (290,877lbs) of ordnance. The most effective use of close support airpower was on 22 February, when 115kg (250lb) 'snake eye' bombs and 228kg (500lb) napalm canisters were used with devastating effect at the southern corner of the Citadel in support of the 1st Battalion, 5th Marines, taking the wall as a prelude to Truong's final attack.

Additional platoons of tanks had arrived by LCU from Da Nang on 11 and 17 February and only one Marine tank was lost to enemy fire. The Ontos, with its six 106mm recoilless rifles, had proved invaluable, being able to go where tanks could not; no Ontos were lost to enemy fire. The Marines had been dubious of the newly-issued M16 rifle but, by the end of the operation, were praising it.

The 1st Marine Bridge Company had put a floating bridge across the Phu Cam Canal on 12 February and after that 104 'Rough Rider' convoys made the round trip between Phu Bai and Hue. Five LCUs further supported the operation, though losses were quite

Below: US Marines take a quiet break from the fighting as they push relentlessly forward during the final phases of the battle for Hue.

heavy; one loaded with ammunition blew up and two loaded with petrol, oil and lubricants caught fire and sank. The initial landing zone (LZ) for the resupply helicopters was at the LCU ramp but on 18 February it was moved to the stadium, which was easily visible from the air and well protected. Inside the Citadel, however, the LZ at the hospital was the only site available and it was far less secure for incoming craft. One helicopter was shot down and many received multiple hits. The Marine helicopters flew 823 sorties, lifted 1672 troops, and delivered 473,606kg (1,044,112lb) of cargo. There were also 270 medevac missions taking out 977 casualties.

The civilian populace was essentially passive, neither helping nor hindering the Americans. Inevitably, many thousand civilians were casualties of shelling, bombing and other combat operations. Refugees were numerous but presented no large problem. The price imposed upon the non-combatants by the North Vietnamese and Viet Cong was not fully known until after the fighting was over. Communist death squads had systematically eliminated South Vietnamese government leaders and employees. The bodies of some 2800 South Vietnamese were discovered in mass graves, and it was subsequently established that at least 3000 more were dead or missing.

Brigadier-General Edwin H. Simmons (Ret)

Out of Hue

At the height of the fighting for Hue, landing craft became a major form of transport in and out. Here, a journalist describes leaving Hue under fire:

'The mortar men were lousy shots. Two shells fell in the river, kicking up small geysers of water. A third one hit a packing crate, well away from the landing craft and the waiting passengers....

'When the last crate was hauled from the craft, the passengers rushed aboard. The women, children and the stretcher cases were taken below the main deck. The others, including wounded Marines who could still walk, squatted on the deck in the rain.

'It was a strange cargo. There were two priests, who had been held captive by the Viet Cong; the bodies of six Marines in green plastic bags; and a group of teachers who had found themselves trapped for nine days in Hue while artillery and mortars boomed around them....

'"If you've got weapons, you ought to get them ready," one crewman told the passengers. "It will be a miracle if we don't have to use them."

'There was no miracle. Ten minutes out of Hue, Viet Cong troops ran along the riverbank firing rifles and rockets at the lumbering landing craft. The wounded Marines rushed to the ship's railing, firing steadily....

'Bright red tracer bullets zipped over the cabin of the landing craft, a rocket shell struck a river patrol boat that had come along for protection....

'A half-an-hour later, when the shooting had subsided, one of the passengers reached under his coat, pulled out a bottle of Ambassador Scotch and passed it around to the Marines. They emptied it in four minutes. He passed around another bottle....'

New York Times, *11 February 1968*

America divided

The war at home 1965-68

In the 1964 presidential election, Lyndon Johnson was the peace candidate. His opponent, Republican Senator Barry Goldwater, projected a 'hawkish' image that the American public found disturbing. Spreading reassurance in speeches that emphasised there would be 'no wider war', Johnson won a landslide victory. But within three months of his first full term in office beginning, President Johnson had initiated the regular bombing of North Vietnam and the commitment of US ground combat forces, acting under the umbrella of the Gulf of Tonkin Resolution voted in August 1964. Despite this apparent *volte face* so soon after the election, Johnson's action enjoyed the almost unanimous support of Congress and the backing of a large majority of the American people.

But a significant minority took a different view. As soon as the president's intention to increase rather than limit US involvement in the war became apparent in the spring of 1965, anti-war groups began to organise in opposition. The focus for dissent was America's universities. During the early 1960s students – both black and white – had become deeply involved in the civil rights movement and its struggle against racial inequality in the Deep South. While many civil rights activists declined to take a stand on the war, refusing to be distracted from the pursuit of racial equality, student groups like the Students for a Democratic Society (SDS) and the mainly black Student Non-Violent Coordinating Committee (SNCC) switched some of their moral concern to the war. They were joined by pacifists, members of traditional left-wing groups and a significant number of prominent liberal intellectuals.

Through the spring of 1965 a series of 'teach-ins' was staged at universities – lengthy and well-attended sessions of speeches and discussions addressed by notable personalities who were against the war, such as baby expert and one-time Johnson supporter Dr

Benjamin Spock and novelist Norman Mailer. A solid body of student and academic opposition to the war was quickly established which soon began seeking other ways to express dissent. Students were exempted from the draft under the deferment system which ensured that the bulk of draftees would be drawn from the most underprivileged areas of society, but it was an offence to destroy or return a draft card. In August 1965 the first draft card was publicly burnt by an anti-war activist.

But support for the war remained, in political terms, overwhelming. The administration argument that it was defending a small country against communist aggression commanded popular support, and as the US death toll began to mount few politicians cared to question publicly the cause for which the soldiers were dying. Doubts about the wisdom of the war were expressed, however, by a few senators, including the influential Senator William Fulbright,

Above: A protestor offers a symbol of peace to a military policeman during an anti-war rally held by students outside the White House in October 1967.

Against the war

The American government's justifications for US involvement in Vietnam was based on the need to defend the 'Free World' against communist expansion. The anti-war movement rejected the interpretation of the conflict as an act of aggression by the North against the South; they held that the war was an uprising by a peasant population against an unpopular government and against foreign domination.

This fundamental hostility to American policy was intensified and given a weighty moral charge by concern over the *methods* of the US and South Vietnamese forces: the use of napalm and defoliant, the disregard for human life and the destruction of villages, and the support given to a regime one of whose senior police officers was happy to shoot a prisoner in the head for TV cameras.

Finally, beneath all this was a fear that the USA was abandoning its heritage; that the American commitment to liberty and human progress was being eroded by its Vietnam involvement; that the USA, in effect, was losing its soul.

and their criticisms considerably damaged the government case, at least in the eyes of the political elite. The media also became a source of discontent. Journalists sent to cover the fighting increasingly found themselves torn between a doubt and a certainty – doubt over the rightness or wrongness of US involvement and what should be done about it, certainty that the war was monstrously cruel and inhuman whatever its motives. The use of napalm – widely regarded as contrary to the Geneva Convention – the destruction of villages and the bombing of North Vietnam were vividly brought home to the American public through the media.

High on public consciousness

At the same time, the anti-war movement was becoming identified with a set of disturbances that seemed to threaten a general breakdown in American society. In early 1967 the hippy movement which had grown up on the west coast burst into public consciousness. The taking of drugs such as marijuana and LSD by young people, although never as widespread as believed, was sufficiently common to create a moral panic in middle America. Anti-authoritarianism and withdrawal from conventional society was linked to a deliberately naive anti-war posture – 'Make Love Not War' – which denied the validity of rational argument over strategy or global politics.

Hippy 'flower power' was a white youth revolt; in the black ghettos violence erupted. President Johnson had satisfied the demands of the civil rights movement with his Voting Rights bill in 1965 but his further programme to counter poverty, which would have greatly benefitted the impoverished blacks of the northern cities, was largely curtailed because of the

expense of the war. In July 1967 the black ghettos of Newark and Detroit were the scene of intense rioting and arson that could only be controlled by bringing in the army. Although in no way an anti-war protest, the riots helped convince many American politicians that the country was too fragile to support the divisions and expense of Vietnam.

It was in 1967 also that the anti-war movement first took to the streets in mass demonstrations. In April several hundred thousand protesters marched through New York. In October the Pentagon was besieged by demonstrators who were only removed after scenes of violence and numerous arrests – those arrested included such luminaries as Dr Spock, linguist Naom Chomsky and veteran pacifist David Dellinger. The effect of such disorder on the 'silent majority' in America was to confirm backing for the war, but the politicians at the top were losing their nerve.

By the autumn of 1967, Johnson could see the war wrecking his administration. His programme of social reform was coming to naught under pressure of the war; the economy was strained, and for the first time extra taxation was needed to finance the war effort; wherever the president went, in America or the outside world, taunting demonstrators dogged his footsteps; even his Nato allies were urging military withdrawal. The peace movement's perception of the war was penetrating the administration: Defense Secretary Robert McNamara had become disillusioned, writing to the president in mid-1967 that 'the picture of the world's greatest superpower killing or seriously injuring 1000 non-combatants a week, while trying to pound a tiny backward nation into submission on an issue whose merits are hotly disputed, is not a pretty one.' Worst of all, Johnson's own Democratic Party was now deeply divided.

Below: A student hurls back a tear gas grenade at a National Guard during peace protests at Kent State University in 1970. Four students were shot dead in an episode that shocked the nation.

The peace movement was determined that some anti-war candidate should be present in the 1968 presidential election. Unable to field a contender themselves, they persuaded Senator Eugene McCarthy, an anti-war Democrat, to run against Johnson for nomination as Democratic candidate. The dramatic effect of the Tet offensive on American opinion seemed to give McCarthy some real chance. Neither the president nor the 'silent majority' believed any longer in military victory in Vietnam. Johnson withdrew from the presidential race, replaced by Hubert Humphrey, and Robert Kennedy joined in, splitting the peace vote but lashing the administration with his rhetoric (for example, quoting Tacitus, 'they made a desert and they called it peace'). Kennedy might well have won the Democratic nomination, but his assassination in June (three months after that of another anti-war figure, Martin Luther King) left the anti-war nomination campaign weak and divided. All the movement could achieve was a demonstration at the Democratic convention in Chicago in August which provoked an exceptionally brutal police response and ensured Humphrey an easier victory over McCarthy. These deep divisions in the Democratic Party guaranteed the Republican candidate Richard Nixon a safe passage to power on a platform of 'de-Americanisation of the war'.

Under President Nixon the scale and intensity of anti-war activities was if anything to increase, but their effectiveness declined. The peace movement could influence the Democratic Party, ensuring in the long run a president, Jimmy Carter, committed to putting morality first in foreign policy, but Nixon could base himself securely on his constituency – the 'silent majority' – for whom his policy of 'bringing the boys home' was enough.

Most of the peace movement leaders came to believe in retrospect that their activities had no effect on the course of the war. Senator McCarthy has said that 'the war would have ended just when it did even if there had been no protest . . . .' Certainly, large areas of American society – including those represented by the labour unions and rural Americans – remained fixedly hostile to anti-war ideas. Some have claimed that the movement prolonged the war by encouraging Hanoi to fight on, and there is evidence that the North Vietnamese did take it into account. But the truth – an embarrassing truth for the US Army – would seem to be that the war was decided, like most other wars before it, on the battlefield. The US needed a victory it could not achieve. Neither the support of the silent majority nor the hostility of the vocal minority could outweigh that simple fact. **Graham Brewer**

Below: A South Vietnamese woman demonstrates in favour of continued US aid to South Vietnam. The prospect of US withdrawal and life under the harsh communist regime that Hanoi would impose was anathema to those with dependants in the Republic.

At home, US public opinion was dramatically affected by the Tet offensive and more people than ever before took to the streets (right, a peace march in San Francisco) to protest against the war. Even ex-GIs (inset right) formed a peace movement – the Veterans against the War. This reflected the deep-seated divisions within all sectors of US society.

THE 25-POUNDER GUN-HOWITZER

During the 1914–18 War the divisional artillery of the British Army was composed of two different types of weapon, the 18-pounder field gun and the 4.5in howitzer. Both these weapons had been designed in the aftermath of the Boer War, and by 1918 their designs had been taken to the limit. In the mid-1920s work began on replacements and one of the main requirements was that the new weapon had to be capable of rapid and large changes of direction so as to be able to engage moving tanks. Replacement of the existing gun and howitzer was imperative since the 18-pounder high-explosive shell was badly designed and too small to be very effective, while the 4.5in howitzer had limited range and traverse and was quite unsuited to shooting at moving targets.

Designs based on salvaging existing equipment soon proved useless and the Ordnance Committee was asked to investigate totally new designs which would provide a range of 13,700m (15,000yds). At the same time the weight was limited to 1525kg (3360lb) since this was considered to be the maximum which could be drawn by a six-horse team on active service. Calculations soon showed, however, that a gun capable of firing to the desired range would exceed the specified weight, so the proposal was changed and eventually, in late 1926, a firm specification was drawn up, for a 105mm howitzer firing a 15.9kg (35lb) shell at 1600 feet per second to a range of 10,970m (12,000yds). By this time the weight restriction had also been eliminated by the decision that in future motor vehicles would be used to tow field artillery. One of the ideas which appeared in this specification was that of having a firing platform, a circular steel plate which could be dropped to the ground, the gun-wheels run on to it, and the gun then swung around the smooth perimeter of the platform so making the weapon capable of rapid and large changes of direction.

Accordingly, in 1931, the Vickers 105mm howitzer appeared and was tested on Salisbury Plain, but a decision on its acceptance was deferred until another new project, a 3.3in field gun, capable of anti-tank fire and ranging to 10,970m (12,000yds) could be tested as well. By this time, however, financial considerations made it highly unlikely that two new weapons would be approved, particularly since the whole programme had begun on the assumption that a single equipment could replace two. Back in 1928 the first suggestions of a 'combination weapon' or 'gun-howitzer' had been made, and after much discussion a firm proposal was put forward in 1933 for a 3.7in gun-howitzer firing an 11.3kg (25lb) shell. In September 1934 construction of a pilot model of the 25-pounder was ordered.

Unfortunately, the question of finance still hung over the project, and so it was decided to economise by using as much existing equipment as possible. By reducing the calibre to 3.45in it was still possible to fire an 11.3kg (25lb) shell but the barrel could now be designed so that it would fit into the jacket and use the breech mechanism of existing 18-pounder guns, thus saving the cost of a carriage. But at the same time, the design of a purpose-built modern carriage went ahead.

The 18-pounder conversion was officially approved as the Ordnance 3.45in Mark 1 on 26 August 1936, but in February 1938 the nomenclature was changed to Ordnance 25-pounder Mark 1. To almost all the army, however, it was known as the 18/25-pounder. Just over 1000 were made and they armed the Royal Artillery field regiments in time for the outbreak of war in 1939. The 18/25-pounder saw action with the British Expeditionary Force in France in 1940, but its performance was marred by lack of numbers, poor communications and endless enemy air attacks. Most of the Royal Artillery's inventory had to be left behind at Dunkirk and from then on the remaining 18/25-pounder conversions were maintained for training purposes and for coastal-defence service.

Above: The Ordnance 3.45in Mark I , or 18/25-pounder as it was generally known, utilised a slightly modified version of the pre-World War I 18-pounder carriage, while also retaining the basic recoil and breech mechanisms. The standard box-trail version of the carriage shown above was the 4P, while a split-trail model, the 5P, became available later. Officially approved in 1936, the 18/25-pounder saw action in Norway and France in 1940, but many were lost during the retreat from Dunkirk when most of the Royal Artillery's inventory was left behind on the beaches. By the end of May 1940, some 700 of the original 1000 conversions had been lost.

Previous page: A 25-pounder Mark 2 is put through its paces by a Royal Artillery crew on a training exercise on Salisbury Plain. With the loss of the 18/25-pounders in 1940, the Mark 2, with its new carriage and circular firing platform, became the backbone of the field artillery of the British and Commonwealth armies.

The design of the all-new carriage led to some interesting technical proposals, but eventually the choice was made of a split-trail two-wheeled carriage; two designs were constructed, one by Vickers and one by Woolwich Arsenal, but neither was liked by the artillerymen who were going to have to use them. They were too heavy and cumbersome, awkward to move and difficult to operate. A fresh design was requested, but instead the box-trail carriage of the Vickers 105mm howitzer was resurrected and a barrel mounted on it for test. At a comparative trial at the School of Artillery early in 1938 the box-trail model was judged superior to either of the split-trail types, and the decision was taken to go into production.

The new howitzer, the 25-pounder Mark 2, had a new vertical sliding block breech mechanism and was approved in December 1937. The new carriage, however, did not receive approval until late 1939 and from then on very few changes in the design were made until the gun was retired from British Army active service in 1967 and replaced by the 105mm Italian OTO-Melara Model 56 pack howitzer. The only significant change to the basic gun was the adoption of a muzzle brake in 1942 to allow the firing of armour-piercing ammunition with an extra-powerful charge to maximise muzzle velocity, but this was only adopted in areas where major armour was likely to be met. The 87.6mm calibre 25-pounder weighs some 1800kg (3970lb) and is served in action by a detachment of six men, although this number can be reduced once firing has begun. It has a maximum range of 12,250m (13,400yds) and depression/elevation of minus four to plus 40 degrees is provided. Crew protection against smallarms fire is provided by a large flat shield of bullet-proof steel. A wide range of ammunition can be fired by the 25-pounder including high-explosive, armour-piercing, squash-head, smoke, flares and incendiary rounds.

The carriage, however, saw some changes to meet special demands. The Indian Army developed a version with narrower track, so that it could be towed behind a jeep through jungle, and also be loaded into a C-47 Dakota aircraft without having to remove the wheels. The Canadian Army adopted this and also added a hinge in the middle of the trail which allowed the gun to be elevated some 30 degrees above its normal maximum for high-angle fire. This became the 'Mark 3' carriage and it was used to arm airborne artillery regiments.

In 1943 the Australian Army developed the 'Short 25-pounder' specially for use in the jungles of New Guinea. This was a massive redesign; the carriage was completely new, much simpler, with small wheels and a heavy spade, the shield and firing platform being discarded. The gun itself was drasti-

Top: The 25-pounder Mark II was provided with a circular firing platform which enabled rapid changes of direction to be made in action; this was crucial to its deployment in an anti-tank role. Centre: A 17-pounder anti-tank gun mounted on a Mark 2 carriage. Above: The 'Baby', or shortened version of the 25-pounder was developed in Australia to meet the specialised requirements of jungle warfare. Right: To increase elevation, the Mark 3 was fitted with a hinged tail. Left: The breech mechanism and sighting apparatus on a 25-pounder Mark 3.

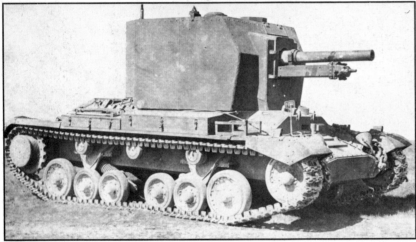

cally shortened, but a flash cone had to be fitted to prevent blast and flame damaging the recoil system when firing. It could be broken into 14 pack loads for mule transport and weighed about 430kg (950lb) less than the standard equipment. The principal drawback was that due to the short barrel it could not fire the full range of charges and was restricted to a maximum range of only 9875m (10,800yds).

Apart from the abortive Lloyd Carrier project, the first operational self-propelled version of the 25-pounder, known as the Bishop, was developed in 1941, mounting the gun in a box-like structure on a Valentine tank chassis. A hundred were built and sent to North Africa in 1942, but due to the restricted space inside the vehicle the gun could only fire to a range of 5800m (6400yds) and was not popular. The replacement for the Bishop was a far better weapon in every respect. It was based on the chassis of the Canadian 'Ram' tank (itself based on the Sherman) in which the body was built up into an armoured open-topped superstructure with the gun mounted in the forward face and capable of full elevation and 25 degrees of traverse each side of zero, thus allowing the gun to deliver its full range. Called the Sexton, this equipment was built in Canada from 1943 to 1945, over 2000 being produced. They remained in British service until the late 1950s, by which time the spares problem had become acute, and they were to remain in service with the South African, Portuguese and other armies until the 1980s.

During World War II, the 25-pounder proved an extremely robust and reliable weapon and was very highly thought of wherever it saw action with the Allied armies. Many Commonwealth forces retained it after the war, and the 25-pounder was still in use in the early 1980s. Since World War II it has seen action the world over. Most post-World War II British actions have involved the 25-pounder including Suez, Aden, Oman and Malaya and it was still in service with the British Army for training, ceremonial and experimental trials purposes in the early 1980s.

In retrospect, the only defect of the 25-pounder was the lightness of its shell; in comparison with the American and German 105mm howitzers, which were its equivalent in employment, it had better range but their 14.9kg (33lb) shells packed more destructive power. On the other hand it weighed 455kg (1000lb) less than the American weapon and 227kg (500lb) less than the German, and was better balanced and easier to operate than either of them. The circular firing platform gave it the edge in rapid changes of direction, and as an anti-tank weapon it was far superior and undoubtedly saved the Eighth Army from disaster many times in the desert in 1941–42. Simple to maintain and operate, there can be no doubt that, on balance, it was the best field gun of its generation.

Left: The Saluting Battery of the 1st Battalion, Sierra Leone Regiment practises its gun drill with a pair of 25-pounders in 1959. Although phased out of active service with the British Army in the 1960s, the 25-pounder continued to equip many foreign armed forces throughout the 1970s and into the 1980s.

Opposite page: The Lloyd carrier (top) was the first of several designs for a self-propelled version of the 25-pounder. Its immediate successor, the Bishop (centre above) suffered the same lack of space and gun movement as the Lloyd carrier and it was not until the open-topped Sherman-chassied version, the Sexton (centre below), was introduced that the full 40-degree-plus elevation of the gun could be achieved.

Right: A 25-pounder, with the four-port Solothurn muzzle brake attached, on active service with a detachment of the Royal Canadian Artillery in Korea in October 1951.

Above: A row of British 25-pounders on ceremonial duty on the Thames Embankment in London. Above right: A 25-pounder on tow behind a No 27 limber. The limber stowed 32 rounds of ammunition, on 16 trays, and a selection of stores and spare parts. It could also be used to transport the circular firing platform.

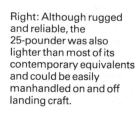

Right: Although rugged and reliable, the 25-pounder was also lighter than most of its contemporary equivalents and could be easily manhandled on and off landing craft.

Below right: The sighting apparatus of the 25-pounder. To the extreme top of the picture is the black dial-sight which mounts the gun layer's eyepiece and measures the horizontal angle of direction. Below the dial-sight is a circular brass disc with a wing nut which provides the setting to compensate for shell drift. Shell drift is caused by the spin of the shell due to the rifling of the barrel and so the vertical axis of the dial-sight has to be altered to allow for this. The conical range-setting hand wheel is situated directly beneath it. To its left is the range cone with its charge slider and range-scale reader fitted below. The charge slider is set to the particular charge being fired and is also used to compensate for changes in muzzle velocity caused by wear to the barrel. When the range cone is set, the complete sighting mechanism comes to a tilt and the barrel is then elevated until the sight becomes level. At the bottom are the elevation hand wheel (right) and the traverse hand wheel.

25-pounder gun-howitzer

Crew 6
Weight 1800kg (3968lb)
Dimensions (Travelling) Length 7.92m (25ft 9in); width 2.12m (6ft 10½in); height 1.65m (5ft 4¼in)

Calibre 87.6mm
Maximum muzzle velocity 518mps (1700fps)
Maximum range 12,250m (13,396yds)
Rate of fire 5rpm

Above left: The breech mechanism in the closed position. The firing handle is situated on the left side of the breech, directly to the right of the conical range-setting hand wheel. Above right: The breech in the open position. The handle on the right opens and closes the breech while the brass device at the bottom of the vertical-sliding block is the automatic cocking mechanism.

Below left: Some of the ammunition and charge types available to the 25-pounder. Back row, left to right: cartridge case, armour-piercing shot, cartridge case, high-explosive shell, smoke shell. Front row: Charge 1 (red bag), Charge 2 (red plus white bag) and Charge 3 (red, white and blue bags combined). Below right: The muzzle brake which was adopted in 1942 to accommodate an anti-armour supercharge.

Prague '68

The Soviet invasion of Czechoslovakia

The 'Prague Spring' of 1968 in Czechoslovakia was, on the face of it, one of the least likely events of modern history – a movement for democracy and liberalisation initiated from within the ruling Communist Party and led by a pro-Soviet communist who became a hero for his own people and for the capitalist West. And the suppression of the movement contained many surprising elements too, for the Soviet leadership seems to have been genuinely split over its response to events in Czechoslovakia.

Although the brutal repression of the Hungarian uprising of 1956 by the Soviet Army had left no doubt that the Soviet Union would refuse to tolerate change beyond a certain point in its East European satellites, pressures for reform continued to emerge within the communist system as its leaders struggled to cope with their economic and political problems. Czechoslovakia was the most industrially developed state in the Eastern bloc, but it lagged behind in the 'de-Stalinisation' of its political system. Since 1957 the mediocre Antonín Novotný had combined the posts of first secretary of the Communist Party of Czechoslovakia and president of the republic. Through his appointees in the bureaucracy, the police and the army, Novotný kept a tight grip on the country and blocked any efforts from within the Party to reform the system.

There were three main groups within the Communist Party discontented with Novotný's rule. One consisted of those Slovaks who felt Novotný's centralist policies discriminated against their part of the country in favour of the Czechs. Another was the 'intellectuals', who were oppressed by the heavy-handed censorship and climate of conformism which stifled all forms of expression and creativity in a country with a long-established tradition of active cultural and intellectual life. Finally, and most important, there were the 'economists' who argued for change as a matter of economic necessity. As a relatively advanced country, Czechoslovakia could expect to enjoy a higher standard of living than its Eastern bloc neighbours and to maintain a level of sustained, balanced economic growth, but the economy was suffering badly from the combined influence of the Soviet Union itself and Soviet-style central bureaucratic planning. Since the end of World War II the Soviet Union had systematically 'milked' its more economically advanced satellites, and Czechoslovakia was in effect subsidising the Soviet economy while being forced to develop its own industry in an unbalanced manner to meet the Soviet need for heavy manufactured goods. The economy was also suffering from the hopeless inefficiency which plagued all the centrally-planned economies of the Eastern bloc, where the heavy hand of bureaucracy prevented managers taking necessary decisions and proved inflexible in response to changing circumstances. By the mid-1960s the Czechoslovak economy was in a mess that could no longer be ignored.

Throughout the 1960s, Novotný made small concessions on all these fronts, but his response was woefully inadequate. In October 1967, the frustration felt by other top Party members broke into open opposition at a Central Committee meeting. The Central Committee now contained a considerable number of members who recognised the need for change; at the same time, if any changes were to be made they must not appear as a radicalisation of the

Above: A street scene in Prague after the Soviet invasion of August 1968. Czechoslovakia offered no armed resistance to the overwhelming numbers of troops and armour poured in by the Warsaw Pact invaders, but crowds of civilians took to the streets to express their frustration and outrage at the Soviet action. Here, a student runs off after emptying a can of kerosene onto a street fire, while a Soviet T55 tank stands immobilised.

country. The major spokesman for the malcontents was Alexander Dubček; he was first secretary of the Slovak Communist Party and an 'economist' and therefore combined two of the major strands of discontent, but he was, at the same time, a resolutely pro-Soviet communist, with nothing suspicious in his past that could worry hard-liners.

Novotný appealed to the Soviet leaders to defend him against his enemies in the Party, but the Soviets showed little interest. Novotný clung on tenaciously to power, planning to use the army to arrest the reformers, but his position was clearly weakening. The decisive blow fell on 5 January 1968 when Dubček was elected by the Party leaders as first secretary. Dubček had been a lifelong member of the Communist Party, and knew the methods of control in eastern European states very well, yet he did not take typical steps to establish his power base within the Party in Czechoslovakia – he did not move to replace Novotný's appointees by his own, for example, nor even conspire to remove Novotný from the post of president which he still retained; instead Dubček encouraged a popular mood of reform and revival in the country which grew to such a pitch that, on 22 March, Novotný was forced to accept defeat and resign. He was replaced by General Jan Svoboda, who had been a victim of Stalin's displeasure in 1950, and in April a new government was formed with Oldřich Černík, a Dubček supporter, as prime minister, and Professor Ota Šik in charge of revitalising the economy.

On 10 April the government produced an 'action programme' designed to create 'socialism with a human face'. Its proposals included the abolition of censorship – which had already virtually collapsed – the release of political prisoners and reparation for those who had suffered injustice, a federal system to satisfy Slovak aspirations, and decentralisation of the economy, freeing managers from bureaucratic controls and shifting the emphasis away from heavy industry. The revival of democracy and political debate within the Communist Party was to be accompanied by permission for other political organisations to operate freely. Dubček believed that a revitalised Party could win the hearts and minds of the masses without the need for censorship or repression.

That spring of 1968 saw a remarkable efflorescence of political debate, artistic activity and social reawakening in Czechoslovakia, centred on the capital, Prague. Despite the breakneck speed and scope of developments in the Czechoslovak media, in workplaces and in the universities, Dubček refused to try to call a halt, maintaining his faith that the movement he had unleashed would neither undermine the 'gains of socialism' nor harm relations with the Soviet Union. The new government repeatedly affirmed its adherence to the Warsaw Pact. The Soviet leaders in Moscow were not reassured, however. Czechoslovakia was considered vital to Russia's defences (in effect, a liberalised Czechoslovakia would be an enormous salient piercing the Warsaw Pact), and could on no account be allowed to slip away from the Eastern bloc. The example of an alternative form of socialist system was not welcome, and might have a disturbing effect on neighbouring states like Poland or Hungary. There was also the economic question: the Soviet Union wanted to keep the financial and industrial tribute from Czechoslovakia that the new policies would almost inevitably withhold. But there is good reason to suppose that the Soviet leaders were divided on their response. As early as April or May, contingency planning for a military intervention must have been carried out, yet clearly some of the leadership opposed military action, either believing

Above: Antonin Novotný, whose narrow and bureaucratic rule was incapable of winning popular support or solving economic problems.

Above: Alexander Dubček, the unlikely hero, an unassuming communist who led the reform programme and won the respect of his people.

Dubček's assurances that he could keep the situation under control and maintain Czechoslovakia's loyalty to the Soviet Union, or believing that pressure stopping short of invasion could bring about a change of policy.

At first the Soviet Union limited itself to strongly-worded criticisms of Dubček's policies, but at the end of May and again towards the end of June the Czechoslovak government was forced to agree to the holding of large-scale military manoeuvres over much of its territory. The Soviet Army streamed into the country and set up huge military camps (notably at Milovice, near Prague) to which the Czechoslovak military had no access but which had regular connection by air with the Soviet Union. This gave the Soviets an excellent opportunity to prepare the way for a future invasion, but for the moment they held back.

From 29 July to 1 August, a dramatic meeting was held between the Czechoslovak leadership and practically the whole of the Soviet politburo at the little frontier town of Čierna nad Tisou. Hard words were exchanged but an agreement appeared to be reached. Dubček accepted the reintroduction of a measure of press censorship and agreed to clamp down on political organisations outside the communist-dominated National Front. Two days later, on 3 August, Leonid Brezhnev, Dubček and the leaders of the other four hardline Warsaw Pact countries (East Germany, Poland, Hungary and Bulgaria) met at Bratislava and signed a joint statement on the need to consolidate the international communist movement. After the meeting, Brezhnev and Dubček appeared hand-in-hand and kissed each other on both cheeks.

The storm breaks

All was, it seemed, sweetness and light; the crisis was over, the statesmen and newsmen dispersed in the belief that the next event of importance would be the congress of the Czechoslovak Communist Party in September, at which the Dubček reforms would be endorsed. The Czechoslovak leadership had never believed the Soviet Union would use force to stop their democratic reforms, since their fidelity to communism and to the Soviet Union was unquestionable. Even Nato intelligence experts watching the situation did not think a Soviet invasion was imminent, despite evidence of Soviet troop movements.

What decided the Soviets to invade is unknown. In one view, the smiles of agreement at the start of August were mere play-acting, designed to put the Czechoslovaks off their guard. Others believe that the arguments in the Soviet politburo were finally won by the hardliners after visits to Prague by two other unorthodox communist leaders at the start of August – Tito of Yugoslavia and Nicolae Ceausescu of Romania. It is even possible that the Romanian leader, who had refused to take part in any of the threatening moves against Czechoslovakia over the previous months, suggested to Dubček an alliance of Yugoslavia, Romania and Czechoslovakia to counter Russian influence. Five days after Ceausescu's visit, the Soviet invasion began.

At 2300 hours on the night of 20 August 1968, military units of the Soviet Union, Poland, East Germany, Hungary and Bulgaria crossed the frontier into Czechoslovakia – without any previous warning whatsoever – and moved at great speed to occupy the whole country. The first wave consisted of 70,000

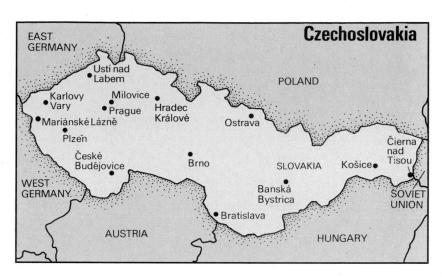

Soviet troops based in eastern Germany, another 100,000 from the Soviet Union itself, plus units from East Germany (20,000), Poland (40,000), Hungary (10,000) and Bulgaria (5000). The Russians are believed to have thrown altogether nearly 500,000 men into the operation – twice as many as were used to suppress the Hungarian uprising. In less than 24 hours the Soviet Army, under the command of General Pavlovsky, was effectively in control of the whole country.

The main thrust of the invading force came from the north. The First Soviet Guards armoured corps, consisting of four Soviet divisions and one motorised East German division, drove south from Karlovy Vary (Karlsbad) through Mariánské Lázně (Marienbad) to Plzeň (Pilsen) and České Budějovice (Budweis) near the Austrian border thus sealing the western frontier of Czechoslovakia.

Another force, consisting of five Soviet divisions, including an airborne division, and an East German armoured division, advanced on Prague from the northwest and northeast and occupied the city. Four Polish divisions were given the task of occupying the central part of the country, while five Soviet divisions entered Slovakia from the east and moved swiftly to occupy the principal towns. Four other Soviet divisions, plus two Hungarian divisions, crossed from Hungary into Slovakia in the south and occupied Bratislava, the capital. At the same time 20 squadrons of the Soviet Air Force based in East Germany

Below: Leaders from the Warsaw Pact countries (including Brezhnev, far right) confront the Czechoslovak administration (left) at Bratislava on 3 August 1968. The meeting ended in a joint declaration, hugs and smiles; but within three weeks Warsaw Pact forces would be streaming into Czechoslovakia and the main Czech leaders would be virtual prisoners in Moscow.

occupied all Czechoslovakia's airfields.

From the political point of view by far the most important operation carried out by the Russian invading force was the seizure of Prague's Ruzyně airport, which in turn made possible the arrest of the leaders of the Czechoslovak government and Party. Even before Soviet troops crossed the Czechoslovak border on the night of 20 August a huge specially-equipped Soviet Antonov transport plane landed at Ruzyně, taxied to the end of the main runway and remained there without any explanation and without disgorging any passengers or freight. The moment the invasion began, however, Russian paratroopers poured out of the plane and quickly seized the airport buildings, while the plane itself began to function as a radio beacon and flight control for a continuous stream of incoming planes bearing invasion forces. More than 250 aircraft were counted arriving on the morning of 21 August alone.

The Antonov also brought in a task force of special troops who rushed into the centre of Prague and stormed the offices of the Communist Party where the Czechoslovak leaders were meeting. Dubček, Černík and Smrkovský, the head of the National Assembly, were seized and bundled off to Moscow. With these

Taken by surprise

When Warsaw Pact troops crossed the frontiers of Czechoslovakia on the night of 20 August 1968, I was sleeping peacefully in a small hotel high up in the Tatra mountains, having spent the day walking and climbing with my wife and son. I had already spent many weeks in Prague following events as the correspondent of the London *Daily Telegraph*. But, with the conclusion of the Warsaw Pact meeting in Bratislava on 3 August, tension had eased and I had decided to seize the opportunity to take a few days off in Slovakia.

I had a shock, therefore, when I switched on my short-wave radio to catch the 7am news bulletin from the BBC in London – the one sure source of reliable news. To my amazement I learnt that the Warsaw Pact troops were already well inside Czechoslovak territory, occupying its cities and towns. Involuntarily I looked out of the window, but saw nothing but the same trees and mountains. It took us only a few minutes to gather ourselves together, pack our bags and scramble down the mountainside to where our car was parked. I decided to make for Bratislava and the frontier near Vienna. Neither I nor my wife, born in Czechoslovakia, wanted to be caught in a country occupied by the Russians.

There was no mistaking the fact that complete occupation and control of Czechoslovakia was what the Russians were about. No half-measures,

no 'summer manoeuvres' this time. This was for real. As we sped along the almost deserted roads we suddenly discovered that we were in danger of being overtaken by some Soviet troop transporters. I had to push my little Austin 1100 to the limit in an effort to keep ahead of them.

In Banská Bystrica I stopped to talk to the friendly editor of the local newspaper, only to find a tank stationed right outside his office with its gun barrel pointing up the stairs. Near Zvolen the air was full of Russian helicopters delivering troops who were about to seize the town. When at last we drove into Bratislava we found the Soviet Army already in occupation and all the main streets lined with tanks, while others were still trundling through the city. The population eyed them sadly and helplessly. Some tried to talk with the Russian soldiers, but with little success. Most of the Russians looked exhausted, thick with dust, showing they had been many hours on the road. They appeared not to have the slightest idea where they were or why.

We parked among the tanks and debated what to do next. In the end we set off for Vienna. It was no use remaining in Bratislava, cut off from London. I needed to write my story and get it back to Fleet Street, and I doubted whether the Russians would help me. From Vienna I was able to send a first-hand account of the Soviet Army in action back to my office in London. **David Floyd**

The Soviet invasion was met with days of street protest. Top left: Students demonstrate their continuing support for Dubček. Above: Soviet troops, mounted in a BTR-152 APC, look bemused by the angry crowds that surge round their vehicle. The invading forces were visibly astonished by the reaction of the population. Left: A vehicle burns fiercely as the street protests in Prague gather momentum. In the background, students have climbed onto a Soviet T55 tank. Below: A soldier clears debris from a tank with a sledgehammer.

leaders arrested and silenced, the Russians expected to be able to set up a new 'revolutionary' government to replace them and give an air of legitimacy to the invasion. But although Soviet propaganda claimed they had entered Czechoslovakia at the request of its own citizens, they could find no one of any standing to cooperate with them. President Svoboda proved uncooperative and was also flown to Moscow, where he refused to negotiate until united with the others. Consequently, the Russians found themselves compelled to negotiate with Dubček and his colleagues.

Meanwhile, in Czechoslovakia the Soviet position was uncomfortable. The well-prepared invasion had gone extremely smoothly. The Czechoslovak leaders regarded military resistance as futile and the armed forces were confined to barracks. They could do no more than watch the Warsaw Pact forces stream past them. The leadership also did their best to discourage popular armed resistance. But the invading forces encountered a barrage of hostility: crowds jeered at the tanks, shouted slogans, posted protests on the walls. Underground radio and television stations managed to keep operating, at times almost taking over the function of a temporary administration, issuing instructions and coordinating opposition. The Communist Party even succeeded in holding its 14th Congress in secret in a Prague factory and elected a new reformist leadership. But resistance was unorganised and the odds against it were overwhelming.

Under the yoke

On 27 August, negotiating under extreme duress, the Czechoslovak leadership agreed to a humiliating 'protocol' which in effect abandoned all the aims of the reform movement under a veneer of compromise. The leaders returned to Prague and took up their posts again, but Dubček was a broken man. He could not accept his betrayal by the Soviet Union which he had admired and respected all his life. In appearance, some of the aims of the reform movement were fulfilled – a federal system was introduced, for example, to meet Slovak demands – but in fact the spirit of liberalisation and democratisation that had been the flower of the 'Prague Spring' was crushed. In October a Soviet-Czechoslovak Treaty legalised the temporary stationing of Soviet troops in the country; 15 years later the troops were still there. The Czechoslovak contribution to Soviet economic development was restored. Rapidly, the frost of censorship and repression settled once more on Czechoslovakia.

In April 1969 Dubček, already powerless, was replaced by the complaisant Gustáv Husák. It was in fact at the insistence of Marshal Grechko, then Soviet minister of defence, that Dubček was finally removed. The Soviet Army wanted to be quite sure that its command of the heartland of Europe would not be disturbed again.

The brutal suppression of the 'Prague Spring' did not have a lasting effect on East-West relations. But it did lead to the formulation of the 'Brezhnev Doctrine', declaring that countries with Soviet-style political systems under Russian influence enjoyed only limited sovereignty, since their governments had no right to move away from socialism – as defined by the Kremlin – or to endanger the collective security of the 'socialist' states. This clear warning discouraged further attempts at reform in the Eastern bloc, until the people of Poland embarked on another attempt ten years later. **David Floyd**

Going West

Defectors from the Soviet bloc

One evening in the autumn of 1969 I was about to sit down to dinner with some guests in my home in London when I was called to the telephone. The caller, a man, spoke in Russian from a public call-box in the city, said he wanted to speak to me urgently and asked how to reach me. His name was Anatoli Kuznetsov, a well-known Soviet author. I did not ask him any questions; he was far too agitated and appeared to be in some danger. I simply spelt out my address for him as clearly as possible and told him to stop the first taxi and come to my house.

Half an hour later he arrived and in a few minutes had explained that he was on an officially sanctioned visit to Britain, accompanied by an official who was responsible for returning him to Russia. But he did not wish to return, and had succeeded in giving his watchdog the slip. All he wanted to do was to disappear and to remain out of the limelight for a few days, so as to give his mother and former wife in Russia time to adjust to his departure. I told Kuznetsov his troubles were over: he could stay with me as long as he liked. I would not reveal his whereabouts to anyone.

Kuznetsov thus became a 'defector' from the Soviet Union. He was not the first nor by any means the last Soviet citizen to 'choose freedom' in the West. Ever since the founding of the Soviet state in 1917 and the erection of practically impassable barriers between Russia and the outside world there has been a steady stream of 'defectors' – people who for one reason or another can no longer tolerate life under the Soviet version of socialism. Few of the defectors have been ordinary citizens, mainly because the average Soviet citizen has very little chance of travelling to the West legally. Illegal crossing of the Soviet frontier, with its thousands of miles of barbed-wire fences, landmines, watch-towers and armed frontier guards, is far too dangerous an enterprise which very few have accomplished.

Most defectors are people who have succeeded in leaving Russia legally, as Soviet diplomats or officials of some kind, or as members of organised tours. Even for them defecting is not an easy task. No Soviet citizen is allowed to go abroad unless he or she has first-class credentials, a clean political record and preferably long membership of the Communist Party.

Every would-be traveller has to go through a long process of 'vetting' before an exit visa is issued. Even if he passes all the tests, he is still unlikely to be allowed to leave Russia if he does not have a hostage for his return – a wife or child – to leave behind. And, when the traveller is abroad, he or she will be carefully shepherded by one or more members of the secret police included in the group. It is not easy to explain the lengths to which the Soviet authorities go to prevent their citizens leaving the country.

Anatoli Kuznetsov was one of the few genuine 'ideological' defectors: he had honestly found life under the Soviet system, especially the censorship of everything he wrote, impossible to bear any longer. He really wanted to live in freedom and was delighted when he achieved it, though it was not easy for him, a writer with only Russian as a language, to make his

way. Other defectors of the postwar period, like the ballerina Natalia Makarova, the male dancers Nureyev and Baryshnikov, the musicians Rostropovich, Yuri Shostakovich and many others, also sought greater artistic freedom but were less concerned with intellectual or political freedom. In any case, since ballet and music are an international language, they had no difficulty in earning their living.

All defectors from the Soviet Union have one thing in common, however: they cannot go back to their country. To have left Russia without permission is a serious crime, tantamount to treason in the eyes of the Kremlin, and a returning defector would almost certainly land in prison. What is more, the defector knows that if he has left his family behind in Russia, they will never be allowed to join him. The Soviet government does not reward defectors.

Writers and dancers who defect are welcomed in the West and granted asylum because they appear to demonstrate the superiority of democracy over totalitarianism. But the really valuable defectors are those members of the Soviet or East European intelligence services who 'cross over', often bringing with them dossiers of information as their credentials. Some of them have accounted for the most important exposures of communist espionage in the West. Such defectors are always assured of a warm welcome by Western intelligence agencies and are usually well taken care of. In some cases, after they have been 'de-briefed', they are provided with a new identity and are started in a new life, safe from pursuit by the Soviet KGB, which does not like to see defecting agents going unpunished.

Defections from the Soviet or East European intelligence services are seldom on 'ideological' grounds. They are more often the result of some personal conflict within the intelligence organisation, disappointment, jealousy, entanglement with the opposite sex or sheer greed. Soviet agents operating in the Western world tend to be cynical professionals who have long ceased to believe in Soviet propaganda

Czech defector General Jan Šejna (bottom left) brought the West valuable secrets; Makarova and Nureyev (below) and musician Rostropovich (bottom) brought artistic skills.

and the official ideology, but who are well aware of the higher standard of living the West offers.

Hundreds of Russian and East European agents defected to the West in the 1960s and 1970s, many of them with disastrous consequences for the Soviet spy network. One of the most valuable was Anatoli Golitsyn, who was an officer in the Polish intelligence service (the UB) but was actually an agent for the KGB within that organisation. He first offered his services to the West in a letter he managed to smuggle out to the US embassy in Switzerland in March 1959. Although intelligence men are usually very wary of such offers, since they may be a 'plant' by the other side, Golitsyn proved his sincerity and his worth in the series of letters which he sent until the end of 1960, when he slipped into West Berlin and the safety of the CIA.

It was information from Golitsyn that led to the exposure in 1961 of George Blake, the Soviet agent working in the British SIS, and it was Golitsyn's information that enabled British counter-intelligence to identify Harry Houghton as a Soviet agent in the Portsmouth shipyard and so to trap the 'illegal' Soviet agent Gordon Lonsdale and the Krogers. Golitsyn is said to have provided Western intelligence agencies with more than a hundred leads to communist agents operating in the West.

Desire and defection

No less sensational in its effect was the defection in London in 1971 of Oleg Lyalin, who worked in the Soviet trade delegation in Britain but was primarily a KGB agent. Lyalin's motive was romance: he was in love with his Russian secretary and decided to elope with her, abandoning both the KGB and his family in Russia. His work had put him in a position to know exactly who among the employees of the Soviet embassy and trade delegation in London were using their jobs as cover for their real business of spying. Lyalin's revelations prompted the British government, exasperated by the brazen way the Russians had expanded their diplomatic staff to accommodate spies, to expel 105 Soviet 'diplomats' from Britain. It was a serious blow to the operations of the Soviet intelligence services in Britain.

The Soviet occupation of Czechoslovakia in the summer of 1968 was followed by a number of important defections from the Czechoslovak intelligence services. General Jan Šejna was a deputy minister of defence in the Czechoslovak government and principal liaison officer with the rest of the Warsaw Pact forces. He was also said to have been a trusted adviser on military affairs to Antonín Novotný, leader of the Czechoslovak Communist Party until he was replaced by Alexander Dubček. Šejna was able to get away to the US where his knowledge of the state of the Warsaw Pact armies was of enormous value. He claimed to have knowledge of Soviet plans for overrunning western Europe, about which he later wrote in some detail.

Another Czech who got away at the end of 1968 was Josef Frolík, a major in Czechoslovak intelligence who had served for some years in his country's embassy in London. He made some sensational revelations about contacts between communist agents and certain prominent figures in British public life. A colleague of his, Major Ladislav Bittman, who defected at the same time, later made public some 'disinformation' operations in which he had been involved.

The flow of defectors continued throughout the 1970s, and always in the same direction: from East to West. There were no significant defections at all from West to East, and the unhappy postwar years that had seen Burgess, Maclean and Philby disappear behind the Iron Curtain were long past. In view of the vast scale of their intelligence operations in the West and the ever-present temptations offered by the West's high standard of living, it seemed that the Soviet authorities had no choice but to accept the fact that some of their agents would 'choose freedom'.

They were, however, always ready to resort to the most extreme measures to prevent a defector from getting away and into the hands of a Western agency. A dramatic example of the lengths to which they were prepared to go was provided by the case of Vladimir Tkachenko, a Russian scientist whom the Soviet authorities suspected of planning to defect in 1967. They kidnapped him in broad daylight on a London street and injected him with a fatal drug for which the British doctors had no antidote. Following a sensational move to prevent the departure of an airliner with Tkachenko aboard, the British government was finally forced to hand him over to the Soviets and let him leave for Russia. He was never heard of again.

David Floyd

Above: Anatoli Kuznetsov, the well-known Soviet author, could no longer tolerate life under the Soviet version of communism and defected to Britain in 1969.

Right: Gaunt and dazed, Vladimir Tkachenko, a Soviet scientist, is led towards an Aeroflot plane after his dramatic street-capture in London by Russian security officials who feared he was about to defect. He shows clearly the effects of a deadly drug with which he had been forcibly injected by his captors. British doctors knew of no antidote to the drug and were forced to let Tkachenko be flown back to the Soviet Union.

The Presidium of the Supreme Soviet of the USSR decrees: the formation of the Committee for State Security under the Soviet of Ministers of the USSR.' With these words the Komitet Gosudarstvennoi Bezopasnosti (Committee for State Security – KGB) came into being on 13 March 1954. The idea of a secret police force in the Soviet Union was not new; but at the same time it would be a mistake to assume that its role and position in Russian and Soviet society has gone unaltered since 'the Third Department' was established by decree under Tsar Nicholas I in July 1826. While a major justification for such a force was, and remains, the Russians' inherent distrust of foreigners, the secret police has undergone a number of changes during its history; some, admittedly, merely cosmetic, involving little more than a change of title, but others more fundamental.

The biggest change followed the October Revolution of 1917 which brought the Bolshevik Party to power. Unlike the Red Army, which recruited many disaffected officers and men from the old Imperial Army, the first political police force of the new era, the Cheka, did not staff its ranks with former officials of the Tsar's Okhrana; rather, it relied on those who had become acquainted with the Okhrana's methods from the other side, having been imprisoned or exiled fighting for the revolutionary cause. Felix Dzerzhinsky, the head of the Cheka, was just such a man. At first

his police force was designed to be an investigatory body, rather than an instrument of repression. The Bolsheviks had not thought of political terror as a good way of attempting to seize power; but within months of achieving power they had come to realise that it was an excellent way of hanging on to it. Thus by the time the Cheka was reorganised as the GPU in February 1922, arrest, imprisonment and execution not only of avowed enemies of the state, but also of those who might conceivably become enemies in the future, was an established principle.

By the time the title USSR was adopted for the new state in November 1923 (and with it the GPU became the United State Political Administration – OGPU) the extremes of police terror used by the Cheka during the Civil War had largely disappeared, albeit temporarily. The OGPU period (November 1923–July 1934) was marked by the introduction on an ever growing scale of labour camps run by GULAG, the Main Administration of Camps, and, from 1928, by the use of the political police to impose collectivisation of agriculture on the peasantry. This period also saw the death of Lenin in January 1924 and the rise to power of Stalin; and the death of Dzerzhinsky in July 1926 and of his successor Menzhinsky in May 1934. When the secret police was reorganised into the NKVD in July 1934, it was under Genrikh Yagoda's leadership.

It was as the NKVD that the Soviet secret police reached new extremes of terror. As well as being responsible for the deaths of millions of ordinary Soviet citizens, there were specific purges on the orders of Stalin against Party members, army officers, and even the NKVD itself. This last claimed as a victim not only the NKVD's head from 1934 to September 1936, Yagoda, but also his successor Nikolai Yezhov, who was replaced by Lavrenti Beria in December 1938. Within a matter of months, Beria was given the opportunity to demonstrate how efficient the NKVD machine of terror had become. In 1939–40, the Soviet Union acquired vast areas of land in Finland, the Baltic States and Poland, and thus millions of new citizens who had to be taught respect for the Soviet system. Thousands were deported to

The Soviet secret army

Left: Two KGB agents are photographed from the window of an apartment they are supposed to be discreetly observing – clearly their guise as lovers was not convincing. It has been estimated that there are as many as 500,000 KGB personnel within the Soviet Union, a large number of whom are actively engaged in surveillance of the local population.

camps in Siberia, where their slave labour was to be a valuable asset to the Soviet war economy.

Between February and July 1941 the NKVD was divided into two separate commissariats: the NKVD, responsible for internal affairs, and the NKGB, which specialised in political police matters. Temporarily suspended after the outbreak of war, in April 1943 the NKGB re-emerged, and the division continued until the death of Stalin in March 1953. In 1946 people's commissariats were renamed ministries, and thus these two became the MVD and the MGB. An exact delineation of functions in this period is not possible, although it seems that Beria was still largely in charge of the actions of both ministries. One important area where MVD/MGB influence was extended was in the eastern European countries now under Soviet domination.

The KGB and the Party

On the death of Stalin, Beria's position as head of the security services made him potentially the most powerful man in the Soviet Union, but he lost the power struggle which followed. Within four months Beria had been arrested on the orders of Stalin's successors, and he was executed in December 1953. Thus, when the KGB came into being in March 1954, it was a somewhat different body to its predecessors. Nevertheless, although it was limited in its powers, and although the MVD continued to exist, it was not subordinated to any ministry, and its chairman was an *ex officio* member of the council of ministers. However, its history since 1954 shows that the Party leadership remains determined that it will not rise to the heights of power achieved by Beria, and that it will be kept subordinate to the Party. None of its first three chairmen – Serov, Shelepin, or Semichastny – was made a member of the Presidium/Politburo, and even though Yuri Andropov was elected to candidate membership after his appointment as KGB chairman in 1967, and full membership six years later, it must be remembered that Andropov's rise to prominence was as a member of the party, not as a policeman. Furthermore, it is highly likely that one reason for Andropov moving from the KGB to the post of a secretary to the Party Central Committee in May 1982 was so that this potential successor to Brezhnev as Party General Secretary could distance himself sufficiently from the secret police before taking over.

The image that the modern KGB tries to present of itself is one of a noble guardian of the Revolution. Under Andropov's leadership the total silence surrounding the Soviet secret police which characterised the earlier periods was lifted, and books have even been published in the USSR praising its work. It is compared to Dzerzhinsky's Cheka, while those bodies which existed between 1922 and 1954 are largely ignored. A major difference between the Cheka and the KGB, of course, is its size and organisation. Sixty years experience has produced a large, yet generally well-organised and efficient body. 'State Security', the *raison d'être* of this 'Committee', falls into two categories: home and abroad. Estimates put the number of KGB employees – officials, agents and informers – within the Soviet Union at 1,500,000. Abroad they are reckoned to have 250,000 operatives in Soviet embassies (the so-called 'legals'), trade and other delegations, foreigners sympathetic to, or blackmailed into supporting, the Soviet system, and 'illegals', Soviet-born

spies who have been trained at home and equipped with false identities, under cover of which they run espionage cells. The intelligence systems of the other Warsaw Pact countries also feed all information back into the files of the KGB.

Three of the four chief directorates of the KGB are concerned with domestic affairs. There is the Border Guards Chief Directorate, whose role is self-explanatory. The Second Chief Directorate is responsible for internal security generally, involving both Soviet citizens and foreigners in the USSR. Observation of Soviet citizens is made easier by the system of internal passports and personal work books issued to everyone and shown on demand to anyone in authority, and by the need to register with the local police if you are in any place for more than 24 hours. Six of the 12 departments of the Second Chief Directorate are tasked with observing foreigners in the USSR, and if possible compromising or otherwise recruiting them to work for the KGB. This involves personnel from foreign embassies, journalists,

The secret police have been an arm of the Soviet state, under a variety of titles, since the earliest days of its existence. Founded by Dzerzhinsky (shown top, fourth from the left, at Lenin's funeral), the secret police have been headed by such men as Beria, (centre left) Andropov (centre right), and Chebrikov (centre middle) who took over in December 1982. The hub of KGB activities is Lubyanka (above), the infamous prison in central Moscow where an extensive range of interrogation methods is practised.

Above: Soviet border guards, on duty near the frontier with China, question a worker. The Border Guards Chief Directorate is a branch of the KGB.

Below: Top-ranking officer of the West German Federal Counter-Intelligence Agency Heinz Felfe was arrested for spying for the Soviet Union. Below centre: Geoffrey Prime, who was arrested in November 1982 for supplying the Soviet Union with British secrets over a period of 13 years. Below right: Soviet diplomat, Yuri Pavlenko and his family prepare to fly out after being expelled by the Italian authorities for spying in March 1967.

students or even foreign tourists. One of the most common ploys for snaring diplomats is sexual entrapment, which often involves luring the foreigner to a specially prepared flat where hidden cameras and tape-recorders can capture a potentially embarrassing record of the diplomat's misdemeanours. In some cases drugs are used too, resulting in photographic 'evidence' of a homosexual liaison. One victim of both heterosexual and homosexual blackmail was a clerk at the Indian embassy in Moscow in the late 1950s. After his initial seduction by an attractive girl working for the KGB, she arranged a 'foursome': pictures were produced of the clerk in bed with another man; he agreed to supply the KGB with Indian Foreign Office secrets.

Department number seven of the Second Chief Directorate had its greatest challenge in 1980, when the 22nd Olympic Games were held in Moscow. For this it worked jointly with the Fifth Chief Directorate, which was created in 1969 with the specific task of dealing with dissenters of any kind. One of the principal tasks of the Fifth Chief Directorate in the months leading up to the event was to remove from

Moscow any potential troublemakers. The most prominent of these, Andrei Sakharov, was sent into internal exile to the city of Gorky in January 1980; foreigners are not allowed to visit Gorky. Department number seven had the job of training the 10,500 interpreters and translators, patrolling tourist routes, and manning the listening devices installed in new hotels, as well as keeping a close watch on foreigners who had contact with Soviet citizens. Above all, it was vital to ensure that no demonstration or act of violence took place, and that no reports on anything other than the Games themselves were sent out of Moscow by foreign reporters. On all these counts, the KGB was able to congratulate itself when the Games were over.

Constant surveillance within the Soviet Union provides the KGB with the routine and often unpleasant bulk of its work to protect the country's security. However, because threats to security may come from outside too, a vital part is played by KGB operations abroad. This is often thought of as the 'glamorous world' of the spy. There is indeed an element of glamour: a KGB agent working in a Soviet embassy or trade legation abroad has already achieved something most of his fellow countrymen will never attain – he has travelled abroad. Also, he probably lives more comfortably than he would back home. But this aside, the operations directed by the First Chief Directorate of the KGB are more sordid than glamorous. Basically these operations cover two areas: the protection of Soviet officials abroad; and the penetration of foreign security and intelligence services. It is the espionage role which is pursued most vigorously. One of the best ways to penetrate foreign security is to find a foreign national working for his country's security service who can be persuaded to spy for the KGB. For some, like Philby, Burgess and Maclean, there is an ideological commitment to communism which leads them to believe that the espionage work they carry out is right, and in accordance with their principles. For others pressure can be brought to bear by sexual or financial blackmail.

It is believed that foreigners working abroad such as Nato servicemen stationed in West Germany are

particularly susceptible to this approach. In 1952 the KGB recruited a US Army sergeant called Johnson, who was serving in Berlin. Up until April 1963 Johnson provided the KGB with vital Nato defence documents. Also serving in Berlin was Geoffrey Prime, when he was picked out by the KGB in 1968. Working later at the Cheltenham communications centre, he supplied the Soviets with top secret information for 13 years; he had already ceased his spying activities when he was arrested in November 1982. One form of pressure which is particularly effective in West Germany is 'family blackmail': threatening to harm relatives of West Germans who live in East Germany, unless the West German supplies the KGB with information. Other West Germans have been forced to cooperate because they fear exposure of their past, if, for example, they were in the Nazi Party or the SS. Although numerous cases of such spies in Western security services have come to light, it must be assumed that many more have not.

In 1826, Tsar Nicholas I included among the roles of his secret police force: 'Information relating to the number of varying sects and dissenting movements existing in the state; questions relating to the exile, disposal and accommodation of suspicious and harmful persons; all edicts and regulations concerning foreigners residing in Russia, entering and leaving the confines of the state.' Almost 160 years later, the KGB is concerning itself with those same problems. A major difference, however, is in the role of the service abroad. In the period after the 1917 Revolution, when it was feared that foreign powers might be planning an attack on the new Soviet state, espionage was essential to determine whether or not these intentions posed a genuine threat. With much of this information now provided by satellite, the primary aim of Soviet espionage today is to obtain technological secrets, to reduce the time and money the Soviet Union must spend in an area where she realises she still lags behind the West. Nevertheless, although the USSR does not want another war, planning for just such an eventuality is seen as vital in Moscow, and, should it ever happen, the KGB's worldwide network of agents could prove devastatingly effective in carrying out their sabotage operations. **Anthony Canon**

Right: A newspaper report on the death of Bulgarian emigré writer Georgi Markov, murdered on a London street in September 1978 by an agent of the Bulgarian secret police. As in the case of Stefan Bandera, the method employed was fiendishly sophisticated: a tiny capsule filled with slow-acting poison was concealed in the tip of an umbrella and stabbed in the back of Markov's leg by an apparently innocent passer-by.

Agent of death

Above: Bogdan Stashynsky.

Ever since the revolution of 1917 the Soviet secret police have resorted to assassination as a means of silencing Russian emigrés who were causing them trouble in the West. The best known example of this is the murder of Leon Trotsky in 1940. After World War II one of the most notable Moscow-directed assassinations was that of Stefan Bandera, leader of the Ukrainian nationalists-in-exile.

The man sent to kill Bandera in Munich was Bogdan Stashynsky, a professional killer employed by the KGB. The weapon used by Stashynsky was a metal tube, seven inches long, that was capable of dispensing prussic acid, a poison that looked like water, which escaped from the tube as a vapour. If fired at a person's face from a distance of about 18 inches, the poison would cause the person to drop dead immediately on inhaling the vapour. Since the vapour leaves no traces it is impossible to determine the real cause of death.

One day in 1959 Stashynsky went to Bandera's flat in Kreittmayer Street in Munich and discharged the poison into Bandera's face. The Ukrainian leader died within minutes. After disappearing to East Germany Stashynsky later defected to the West, where he eventually stood trial and received a relatively mild sentence in return for cooperation with Western security agencies.

Ready for action

Warsaw Pact Manoeuvres

Training is an essential task in all armed forces. Large-scale exercises provide an opportunity to harden troops for the rigours of combat and to test equipment and operating procedures. Exercises demonstrate to potential opponents the capabilities of a state's armed forces and so may help to deter the war they are training for. When alliances organise exercises they are also likely to have the aim of demonstrating the political unity of the alliance. Warsaw Pact exercises naturally have all these objectives but, more unusually, they have been used to put pressure on a Pact member whose loyalty to the Soviet Union has been in doubt. More than this, Pact exercises have been used to prepare for military intervention in member states to ensure the discipline of the alliance.

The Warsaw Pact was founded in 1955 but at first the Soviet Union paid little attention to its potential military value. A change in the Soviet attitude was signalled in 1961 by the first of a series of major exercises. Two reasons for this activity have been identified. Firstly the Soviet ground forces were under pressure from the Soviet leader, Nikita Khrushchev. He believed that the Strategic Rocket Forces had become the most important part of the Soviet armoury and wanted to reduce the size and budget of the ground forces. Major international exercises were not only a public relations ploy, but helped to improve the standards of the Soviet allies to compensate for Khrushchev's cuts. The other explanation offered is that the Soviet bloc was under considerable internal

pressure. The quarrel between China and Russia was serious in itself but it was being exploited by Russia's other allies to secure greater freedom to manoeuvre. Albania abandoned the military structure of the Pact from 1961 and Romania was showing signs of independence. Both countries were developing doctrines of total national defence, in effect preparing for guerrilla warfare against any invader – including by implication the Soviet Union. The new series of exercises prepared the Pact armies for offensive action, generally accompanied by nuclear weapons. Whether or not the Soviets were actually planning such a war, it was certainly convenient for them that their allies should be ill-prepared to defend their national territories against invasion.

It is worth noting that Romania has not permitted exercises on her territory since 1963, nor has she sent more than small delegations to exercises elsewhere.

The first major exercise, Buria, was held in October 1961 and ranged over training areas in East Germany, Poland, Czechoslovakia and the western USSR. It was organised by the Pact's new commander-in-chief, General Alexei Grechko, who was known in the Soviet Army as a hard and realistic trainer of men. Between 1961 and 1979 at least 71 major Warsaw Pact exercises were noted by Western analysts and no doubt there were many other smaller-scale and command post exercises which were not widely publicised. Since the Helsinki Agreements of 1975, which included clauses on the size of exercises, prior notification and the attendance of observers, the scale of the exercises and the publicity given to them has been somewhat reduced. However, a description of one of the largest exercises of recent years, Exercise Shield of 1982, will give the flavour of these events.

The Shield exercises are held regularly and members of the Pact take turns to act as host. In 1972 the exercise was held in Czechoslovakia, in 1976 in Poland and in 1979 in Hungary. In 1982 Bulgaria was the setting and 60,000-80,000 troops were involved.

It was stressed that the exercise was intended to strengthen the defensive capabilities of the alliance, but it is interesting to note that the exercise 'enemy' (the Southerners) were usually defending and 'friendly forces' (the Northerners) usually on the offensive. The exercise began with a night approach march on 27–28 September. Next morning, under cover of live artillery barrages and air attacks, gaps were made in the Southerners' defences and ground troops passed through. Driven from their positions the Southerners tried to establish a new line holding a mountain pass, but were driven out on 29 September by specially trained mountain troops. The main activity on the final day, 30 September, was a large-scale landing on the Black Sea coast which was watched by political and military notables including Todor Zhivkov, the Bulgarian leader, Marshal Ustinov, Soviet Minister

Right: Soviet T62s move through snowbound forest during military exercises in eastern Europe. Despite the proliferation of nuclear missiles in the Soviet armoury, the tank still has a leading role in the Russians' concept of modern warfare.

Far left: Aircrews scramble towards their Kamov KA-25 helicopters aboard the Soviet vessel *Minsk* during a practice manoeuvre. Below: Pilots discuss combat procedures as they prepare to embark upon a military exercise in their MiG-21s.

of Defence, Marshal Kulikov, Commander-in-Chief of the Warsaw Pact and his Chief of Staff General Gribkov.

On 1 October the allied forces paraded in Burgas, the nearest city. Medals were presented to officers who had distinguished themselves and speeches made. For many, no doubt, the highlight of the whole exercise was the dinner held that evening, culminating in more speeches. Bulgaria is the most loyal (or sycophantic) of Russia's allies so it was not surprising that the Bulgarian minister of defence described the then Soviet leader, Leonid Brezhnev, as the 'outstanding peacemaker of our epoch' and that Todor Zhivkov stressed Bulgaria's 'supreme patriotic and international duty to consolidate fraternal friendship and all-round cooperation with the Soviet country, with the party of Lenin, with the Soviet people, with its army.'

Putting on a spectacle

The military value of such training is hard to determine. These inter-allied jamborees tend to involve a series of heavily-rehearsed demonstrations for the benefit of the VIP spectators. They follow a set pattern from year to year and it is very doubtful whether they help to develop the qualities of initiative and creative leadership which Soviet military authors have recently been demanding from commanders at all levels.

In these exercises it often seems that more attention is given to political work than military training. Before an exercise begins a 'joint operational group' is formed by the political directorates of the armies involved. The group prepares a programme of fraternal meetings for the troops involved and visits to local sites of interest. If these include some memorial to the Soviet Army's role as 'liberator' of eastern Europe, then so much the better. The group also controls the media coverage of the exercise and arranges newspapers and broadcasts in the languages of the participants. Thus the world, particularly in eastern Europe, will be presented with a picture of united and efficient armed forces.

However, Warsaw Pact exercises do sometimes have a more direct operational relevance. It has already been noted that the Soviet Union has employed exercises to enforce Pact discipline. In 1972, for example, Romanian foreign policy was very favourable to China and the Romanians even applauded the growing links between China and the United States. This was hardly consistent with Soviet attitudes and to remind Romania that there were limits to Russian patience Exercise Opal was arranged in neighbouring Hungary.

The clearest example of the intimidation process occurred during the Czech crisis of 1968. Soviet political pressure on the Dubček regime was backed by military demonstrations in the form of hastily-organised 'exercises'. The first, at the end of May, included the landing of Soviet airborne troops at Prague airport. The second, Exercise Sumava, ran from 20 to 30 June. Sumava was in effect a rehearsal of the Warsaw Pact invasion which took place two months later and it was reported that the Soviet contingents did not withdraw completely at the end of the exercise. Other exercises, generally Soviet-controlled, but with Warsaw Pact participation, covered the deployment of the main invasion forces along the Czech border and the establishment of the signals and logistic framework which supported the invasion.

In 1981 the Warsaw Pact exercise Soyuz-81 played a vital part in preparing for the declaration of martial law in Poland. The exercise was held in Poland between March and May and included Soviet, East German and Czech forces. Like other exercises held since the start of the Solidarity trade union movement in Poland it emphasised the threat of intervention, but during the exercise communications were established sufficient for an army of 300,000 men. This communications network was not dismantled at the end of the exercise but remained dormant until required to control the Polish Army's takeover in December.

It is clear that the Soviet Union gains a great deal from the Warsaw Pact's exercises. Planning the exercise programme gives the Soviet officers in the Pact's Joint High Command a means of controlling training standards in all the Pact countries. The exercises do have a military value and also provide a major source of favourable propaganda. Pact exercises help to ensure that the Soviet Union's allies are poorly-prepared to defend their territory against interventions like that of 1968. If such an intervention should be necessary as a last resort, the Soviets can prepare their own and allied forces for the task under the cover of Warsaw Pact exercises. **Michael Orr**

Below: SA-4 Ganef missiles, on tracked transporters, are moved into position during a firing exercise. The missiles weigh 2500kg (5500lbs), have a maximum speed of Mach 2.5 and a range of 70km (45 miles).

The F-100 Super Sabre was the first combat aircraft capable of exceeding the speed of sound in level flight. Conceived by North American Aviation between 1947 and 1949 as a private-venture design, it was officially adopted by the United States Air Force (USAF) in 1951, when the appearance of the MiG-15 over Korea demonstrated the necessity for an air-superiority fighter with substantially improved performance over the F-86 Sabre. So urgent was this requirement that the USAF decided to order quantity production of the F-100 before the prototype made its first flight on 25 May 1953. Consequently, when prototype testing revealed a number of major deficiencies in the F-100's design, it was too late to apply corrective measures to the early F-100A production aircraft, the first of which began flight testing in October 1953. The real problems lay in instability and control under certain flight conditions, coupled with poor visibility from the pilot's cockpit. Nevertheless, despite these shortcomings, the USAF considered the F-100A superior to any other fighter in its inventory and its supersonic performance had been conclusively demonstrated.

The eventual solution to the F-100's stability and control problems was the introduction of larger-area wings and vertical tail surfaces on the F-100D, but as an interim measure the F-100As were fitted with stability-augmentation devices. The Super Sabre entered service with Tactical Air Command's 479th Fighter Day Wing (FDW) at George air force base (AFB), California, in September 1954. The initial production version was a clear-weather air-superiority fighter, armed with four 20mm Pontiac M39 cannon, with 200 rounds of ammunition per weapon. As increasing numbers of supersonic MiG-19s were by then reaching Soviet fighter regiments, the USAF decided to accelerate production of the F-100. The following month, however, the USAF was forced to ground all its F-100As after six major accidents, one of which resulted in the death of North American's test pilot George Welch. The resulting

delay while corrective modifications were made set the F-100 programme back by some six months, and the 479th FDW did not achieve its initial operational capability until September 1955.

In the spring of 1955, Super Sabre production switched from the F-100A (203 of which had been delivered) to the F-100C which was fitted with integral wing fuel tanks, in addition to the fuselage tanks, and could carry up to 2268kg (5000lb) of ordnance when operating in its secondary fighter-bomber role. Its high speed at low level made the F-100C particularly suited to a tactical nuclear strike role employing the low altitude bombing system (LABS) technique. This method involved the aircraft making a high-speed bombing run at low level and pulling up short of

Previous page: An F-100C Super Sabre drops twin napalm canisters over a target in Vietnam. Below: A flight of four F-100C Super Sabres reveal the distinctive 45-degree sweepback of their wings. Bottom: The first in the Super Sabre series, the F-100A, which suffered from extensive teething troubles caused by in-flight instability. The Super Sabre's high landing speed made an air brake parachute essential.

its target into a climb, during which its nuclear weapon was released towards the target at a point determined by a weapons-release computer. After dropping its bomb, the fighter bomber could then dive away so as to be well clear of the target area when the weapon detonated. The F-100C's greater internal fuel load, which could be augmented by underwing drop tanks and in-flight refuelling by means of the probe and drogue system, made it a more useful and versatile tactical fighter than the F-100A and over 150 of the 476 built were deployed to USAF bases in West Germany, the Netherlands and Morocco. The F-100C, however, retained the F-100A's pernicious tendency to yaw at high speeds and then go into an uncontrollable roll. This fault was alleviated by the

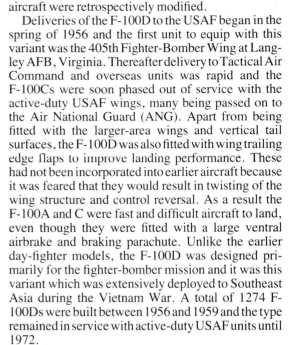

Bottom: An F-100D in the markings of a pilotless target drone. Although by the end of the 1960s the F-100 had been superseded as a front-line aircraft, it continued to be deployed in other, less exacting roles.

fitting of a hydraulically-activated yaw damper to later production F-100Cs and earlier models of the aircraft were retrospectively modified.

Deliveries of the F-100D to the USAF began in the spring of 1956 and the first unit to equip with this variant was the 405th Fighter-Bomber Wing at Langley AFB, Virginia. Thereafter delivery to Tactical Air Command and overseas units was rapid and the F-100Cs were soon phased out of service with the active-duty USAF wings, many being passed on to the Air National Guard (ANG). Apart from being fitted with the larger-area wings and vertical tail surfaces, the F-100D was also fitted with wing trailing edge flaps to improve landing performance. These had not been incorporated into earlier aircraft because it was feared that they would result in twisting of the wing structure and control reversal. As a result the F-100A and C were fast and difficult aircraft to land, even though they were fitted with a large ventral airbrake and braking parachute. Unlike the earlier day-fighter models, the F-100D was designed primarily for the fighter-bomber mission and it was this variant which was extensively deployed to Southeast Asia during the Vietnam War. A total of 1274 F-100Ds were built between 1956 and 1959 and the type remained in service with active-duty USAF units until 1972.

In 1957, a two-seat version of the F-100D appeared as the F-100F combat-proficiency trainer. The two-seater retained a measure of combat capability, although the warload was reduced from the F-100D's 3193kg (7040lb) to 2268kg (5000lb) and two of the 20mm cannon were deleted. F-100Fs were attached to all USAF wings operating the Super Sabre and 339 examples of this version were built. In August 1959 two F-100Fs became the first jet fighter aircraft ever to fly over the North Pole. Seven F-100Fs were modified as Wild Weasel Is to operate against North Vietnamese SA-2 Guideline surface-to-air missiles. They were fitted with a range of radar homing and warning receivers which operated on the various wavebands

Right: An F-100D streaks across the sky, returning from a ground-attack mission in South Vietnam. Below: With afterburners on, two F-100Ds take-off from a US airbase. The Super Sabre excelled as a ground-attack machine and was responsible for more close-support sorties over Vietnam than any other aircraft.

used by North Vietnamese early-warning and missile-control radars. These systems enabled the F-100F's electronic-warfare officer to detect any SA-2 site which was preparing to engage USAF strike-bomber forces and to direct an attack against it, either by his own aircraft or by accompanying fighter-bombers. The Wild Weasel Is first deployed to Korat airbase in Thailand at the end of 1965 and were assigned to the 388th Tactical Fighter Wing which was operating Republic F-105D Thunderchiefs against targets in North Vietnam. Operational experience, however, showed that the F-100Fs were too slow and vulnerable for these operations and they were replaced by specially-modified F-105Fs in 1966.

The first F-100Ds to operate over Southeast Asia were detachments from the Thirteenth Air Force in the Philippines, which were deployed to Thailand in May 1962 to carry out air attacks over Laos. Three years later, following the Gulf of Tonkin incident, F-100s were further deployed to South Vietnam for close air support missions and also took part in the Rolling Thunder bombing campaign against the North. Yet it was as a close air support aircraft that the F-100 made its greatest contribution to the war. During the late 1960s four tactical fighter wings (12 squadrons) operated in this role, and three further squadrons, recalled to active duty from the ANG, were briefly assigned to combat service. During 1969 F-100s carried out 52,699 close air support sorties over South Vietnam, by far the greatest number by any single aircraft type. F-4 Phantoms took second place with only 19,185 sorties flown. This high level of combat activity, however, resulted in a correspondingly high rate of loss, with some 50 F-100s being shot down in a single year. The stringent demands of

Above: A Super Sabre stands on the runway, displaying the distinctive oval air-intake of this type as well as the refuelling probe positioned on the underside of the starboard wing. Above right: A Super Sabre on display, here in natural metal finish instead of the more usual green and brown camouflage scheme.

close air support in South Vietnam meant that the F-100Ds were retained in frontline service for longer than had been originally anticipated and the re-equipment of ANG units with this type was consequently delayed. Nonetheless, by the early 1970s the US policy of Vietnamization had led to a considerable reduction in the USAF's war effort, and as F-4 Phantoms and A-7D Corsair IIs were becoming available for ground-attack missions, the F-100Ds were phased out. In 1971 the USAF had 364 operational F-100Ds on strength, but by the middle of the following year the number had dwindled to a mere dozen, while the ANGs inventory had risen to 335 fighters of this type.

Until such specialised aircraft as the AC-47C Dragonship became available in sufficient numbers, F-100s were also required to fly night-attack missions over South Vietnam. These so-called Night Owl sorties made considerable demands on the pilot's skill and stamina, as the only available means of target

illumination were air-dropped magnesium flares. These flares provided a harsh light which made accurate perception of distance very difficult during the run-in to the target. The pilot then had to make the transition from flying by sight to instrument flight, with the ever-present risk of vertigo totally disorientating him. F-100Fs were also used as high-speed forward-air-control aircraft over North Vietnam, locating and marking targets with smoke rockets for attack by the F-105 fighter-bombers. Most F-100s operating in Southeast Asia were modified with Combat Skyspot ground-directed radar bombing equipment, which allowed them to lead formations of F-105s on blind bombing missions over the North when adverse weather conditions obscured the targets.

Following their retirement from active-duty service with the USAF, the F-100D/F Super Sabres continued to equip ANG units until 1979. Since then a number of them have been converted to QF-100

pilotless target drones. Super Sabres have also served with the air forces of Denmark, France, Taiwan (Nationalist China) and Turkey. The Chinese Nationalist Air Force received 118 F-100As under the US Military Assistance Program and four of these were fitted with reconnaissance equipment as RF-100As. Super Sabres were operated in Taiwan from 1959 until the early 1980s primarily in the interceptor role. France's Armée de l'Air flew the F-100D and F-100F from 1958 until 1978, 12 of the 100 aircraft delivered being two-seaters, while Denmark was supplied with 48 F-100Ds and 10 F-100Fs in 1959, forming three fighter-bomber squadrons on the type. The Danish Super Sabres, however, suffered a high attrition rate, as they did amongst all the air forces which flew the type, forcing the Danes eventually to disband one squadron in 1971. The remaining two units, reinforced by 14 two-seater Super Sabres supplied by the United States in 1974, served on until they re-equipped with the F-16 in 1982. By 1983 the only remaining operator of the F-100D/F was the Turkish Air Force with three Super Sabre squadrons on strength.

F-100D Super Sabre

Type Single-seat fighter-bomber
Dimensions Span 11.8m (38ft 9in); length 14.36m (47ft 1in); height 4.95m (16ft 3in)
Weight Empty 9524kg (21,000lb); maximum take-off 15,814kg (34,832lb)
Powerplant One 7687kg (16,950lb) thrust Pratt & Whitney J57-P-21A afterburning turbojet

Performance Maximum speed at 11,000m (36,000ft) Mach 1.3 or 1390km/h (864mph)
Range Combat radius clean 885km (550 miles)
Ceiling 15,250m (50,000ft)

Armament Four 20mm M39 cannon with 200 rounds of ammunition per gun; up to 3193kg (7040lb) of ordnance including Sidewinder AAMs, Bullpup ASMs, bombs, napalm tanks, 2.75in rockets, one tactical nuclear weapon

Despite the fact that the Super Sabre was a 'difficult' aircraft to fly, North American received a considerable number of export orders from overseas nations. Top: The two-seat F-100F trainer in the distinctive markings of the Turkish Air Force. Centre: Complete with low-visibility markings, an F-100F of the Danish Air Force. In the early 1980s the ageing F-100s were replaced by the considerably more advanced F-16s which now equip several air forces in Europe. Above: A Super Sabre depicted in the national colours of the United States of America. Left: A rear view of an F-100D of the French Air Force.

Trading places

Vietnamization and pacification 1968-72

The Tet offensive of early 1968 was a pivotal event in the war in Vietnam. It precipitated the American public's disenchantment with President Lyndon Johnson's war policy and brought changes in America's role in the conflict. In the aftermath of that major communist offensive, the separate but interrelated programmes of Vietnamization and pacification assumed a crucial place in the war strategy of the United States and its South Vietnamese ally.

Vietnamization involved the three-part process of reducing the American role by turning over US bases and installations to the Army of the Republic of Vietnam (ARVN), improving their weaponry and training, and ceding to them the combat responsibilities borne previously by the withdrawing American units. A natural complement to Vietnamization, pacification sought to make the Vietnamese capable of providing for their own internal security with their own police and territorial forces. To this end, a campaign was launched to destroy the communists' political organisation in the villages, accompanied by a programme of land reform and economic development, designed ultimately to rally the peasants to the Saigon government. In contrast to other aspects of the war, pacification never had to be turned over to the South Vietnamese – that is, Vietnamized – it was always chiefly their responsibility even at the height of the US military involvement. The Americans were involved in pacification primarily as bankers and advisers.

Although President Richard M. Nixon received public credit for Vietnamization, the policy's beginnings can be traced to the previous administration. It had always been official US policy that South Vietnam was being helped to defend itself, and that eventually the South Vietnamese would have to take responsibility for their own defence, but in the early years of US troop involvement the ARVN was in practice ignored. General William C. Westmoreland, the head of the Military Assistance Command, Vietnam (MACV), concentrated on the effort to defeat the communists with US forces. The ARVN did not command respect, being ill-led, ill-equipped and plagued by corruption and desertions. But by the summer of 1967, faced with mounting costs and escalating public criticism, President Johnson was inclined to resist General Westmoreland's requests for more US troops. Instead, it was hoped to improve the ARVN's performance through upgraded training and equipment, so that they could assume much of the burden of the fighting. This would also satisfy the demand to reduce US combat casualties. General Westmoreland's deputy, General Creighton W. Abrams, was put in charge of revitalising the ARVN.

At around the same time, in May 1967, it was decided to unify the military and civilian branches of the American management of the pacification effort in one organisation – Civil Operations and Revolutionary Development Support (CORDS). CORDS was an integral part of the US military command, but

Above: Members of the 38th Ranger Battalion ARVN, armed with newly-received M16 rifles, lay down a cover of protective fire into a Viet Cong position during fierce street-fighting in the Cholon sector of Saigon. The ARVN's surprisingly good performance during the 1968 Tet offensive raised hopes that they could become a match for the North Vietnamese.

it was headed by a civilian – initially Robert Komer, later William Colby – and included personnel from such organisations as the CIA and the Agency for International Development (AID) alongside the military. With enthusiastic backing from the US ambassador, Ellsworth Bunker, the CORDS team set out to build up intelligence, attack the Viet Cong political presence, strengthen the South Vietnamese pacification forces, and channel development resources into pacified villages.

Neither pacification nor Vietnamization had progressed far before the Tet offensive, but the aftermath of Tet provided new incentives and new opportunities for both programmes. In March 1968 the US took the definitive decision that American troop levels would not rise further, and urgent planning for upgrading the ARVN began. Production of the M16 rifle was accelerated so that the ARVN could be issued with the new weapon to replace their World War II-vintage M1s. Helicopters, armour and artillery were supplied to the Vietnamese in ever-increasing numbers. In June 1968 General Abrams, already engaged in the Vietnamization programme, took over from General Westmoreland as head of MACV.

At the same time, the South Vietnamese government of President Nguyen Van Thieu for once took a useful initiative. In June 1968 it passed a general mobilisation law which made some form of military service an obligation for all able-bodied males between the ages of 16 and 50. Also, for the first time, the government agreed to the arming of the peasantry with the establishment of the People's Self Defense Force, a militia with some weapons and training to protect their home villages. In the course of 1968 the number of ARVN personnel – both regular and Regional and Popular Forces – rose from 643,000 to 820,000.

When President Nixon took office at the start of 1969, the US commitment to Vietnamization became even clearer. Nixon's administration pursued a policy

Right: General Creighton Abrams (right) was involved from the outset in Vietnamization, which gathered pace after he took over as US commander in Vietnam. Below: South Vietnamese in an American M113 APC move up to resist the North Vietnamese offensive in the spring of 1972.

of gradually reducing the US combat role while enlarging and modernising South Vietnamese forces and simultaneously negotiating a settlement with the communists. US troop withdrawals began in June 1969 and training programmes to improve South Vietnam's air, ground and naval units were accelerated. Delivery of new weapons was also speeded up: by April 1969 all ARVN regular forces had the M16 rifle, and by February 1970 most Regional and Popular Forces units had also received the new weapon.

Below: South Vietnamese troops assault a Viet Cong position near Tan Son Nhut airbase using M60 machine guns and hand grenades. With the M16 rifle and the M60 in their hands, the ARVN were well equipped. But a question-mark remained over morale.

ARVN force levels 1964-71

	1964	1967	1969	1971
Regular	250,000	343,000	493,000	516,000
Regional	96,000	151,000	190,000	284,000
Popular	168,000	149,000	214,000	248,000
Total	514,000	643,000	897,000	1,048,000

The pacification effort also made great strides from 1968 to 1970. In the weeks immediately following the 1968 Tet offensive security in the countryside fell – that is, fewer villages were under the government's control – but it soon became clear to the US leadership that the heavy Viet Cong losses in Tet had left the communists in no position to counter the advance of pacification teams into previously contested villages. In November 1968 CORDS initiated an Accelerated Pacification Campaign to exploit this weakness. The campaign goal was the raising of 1000 contested hamlets to 'relatively secure' status within three months. The goal was largely achieved, although normally it would have been unusual to improve security in that many hamlets in the course of an entire year. US statistics showed visible progress in the number of refugees resettled and the number of enemy defectors – US advisers had persuaded the South Vietnamese to treat people coming over from the enemy side reasonably, instead of imprisoning or shooting them.

Under the CORDS Phoenix programme aimed at Viet Cong political operatives and cadres, around 15,000 communists were reportedly arrested or killed both in 1968 and 1969. To fill the political and military vacuum left by the set-backs to the Viet Cong, a positive effort was made to introduce South Vietnamese cadres and Regional and Popular Forces into the villages. By 1970 most villages had elected councils after a drive to introduce local democracy, and in March of that year a sweeping land reform bill was passed, known as the Land-to-the-Tiller Law.

The pressure of pacification

With Vietnamization and the success of pacification came increasing burdens on South Vietnam's armed forces. As the secure areas became more extensive, and as pacification cadres moved into previously contested and enemy-controlled areas, the responsibilities of the ARVN and the territorial forces to protect settlements likewise expanded. The withdrawal of US combat units also left the ARVN to assume increasingly the combat and support role for the so-called main force war against the North Vietnamese Army. This in turn put greater pressure on the police and Regional and Popular Forces: if the ARVN had to carry on the fight against the enemy's main force units, it could not at the same time devote as much energy to providing a shield for the territorial forces. The Regional and Popular Forces would have to provide local security without the accustomed amount of support from the ARVN regular units.

Fortunately for the ARVN, their assumption of responsibility for the ground fighting through 1970 and 1971 coincided with a lull in communist military activity. On paper, with a strength of over one million men, almost evenly divided between regular and territorial units, and the latest US equipment, the ARVN should have been able to guarantee the South's security, especially since by 1971 it was estimated that less than five per cent of the South Vietnamese population was under communist control. But the Americans knew that the ARVN's mettle had not yet been seriously tested, and there were reasons to doubt its will to fight. The desertion rate from the ARVN was astonishingly high – there were over 126,000 desertions in 1970, and regular combat units were losing about one-third of their strength in this way each year.

The Phoenix programme

Above: A captured Viet Cong is led away.

The Phoenix programme grew out of American attempts to find a more effective way of fighting the Viet Cong than the use of overwhelming firepower in combat. It was only one element of the general 'pacification' effort that had begun to get under way in late 1967, under the energetic direction of Robert Komer. In Komer's words: 'We realistically concluded that no one of these plans – relatively inefficient and wasteful in a chaotic, corrupt Vietnamese wartime context – could itself be decisive. But together they could hope to have a major cumulative effect.'

In 1967 the CIA tried to improve intelligence from sources in villages by bringing all agencies responsible for such work within one organisation; by July 1968 the South Vietnamese government had formally assumed responsibility for this, and called it *Phuong Hoang* (Phoenix). In theory, the CIA advisers were phased out in January 1969. The programme itself came to an end in 1972, after the final American withdrawal of combat troops.

Phoenix offices were set up at district and provincial levels. The American involvement was always present; in 1971 there were 600 military and 50 civilian advisers on the staff. Information was collected from all possible sources on individuals and families, and then collated. Using this information, the South Vietnamese government would arrest suspect individuals, who could be held in detention at the decision of a Provincial Security Committee (a process known as *an tri*) or tried immediately by a military court.

This straightforward administrative procedure (whereby Americans helped collect information to be used by the Vietnamese authorities) was only part of the picture, however. Phoenix rapidly became known as a programme of counter-terror. The number of deaths during arrests of suspects (some 24,800 between January 1968 and February 1972) and the frequency of the involvement of Special Forces-trained Provincial Reconnaissance Units, that registered a high percentage of kills in their activities, led many observers to suspect that this was a CIA-run programme of selectively slaughtering any possible Viet Cong cadres in the villages of Vietnam; while many of those actively involved in the Phoenix, such as Barton Osborne who was in charge of operations around Da Nang in late 1968, have described how torture was routine and indiscriminate killing common.

To some of those who have defended the activities of the Phoenix programme, the fact that the Viet Cong carried out similar terrorist activities as a matter of course justified the use of counter-terror; and it is certainly the case that various US directives and many individual Americans did their best to limit torture and murder. Phoenix began to assume the proportions of an unchecked 'hit' list, however, and there were allegations that President Thieu was using it to remove political opponents who were in no sense communists. The intelligence gathered by Phoenix was often suspect, and the innocent quite clearly suffered with the guilty when a Provincial Security Committee had to make a decision based on a dossier containing some hearsay evidence.

Probably about 40,000 suspects were arrested during the Phoenix programme; it had helped weaken Viet Cong cadres, but had made little headway in winning the 'hearts and minds' of the peasantry.

Vietnam 1968-72

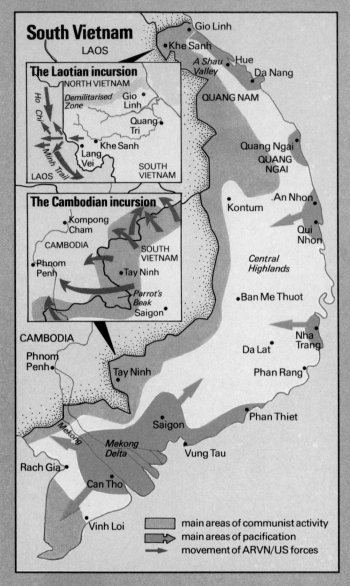

South Vietnam

The Laotian incursion

The Cambodian incursion

main areas of communist activity
main areas of pacification
movement of ARVN/US forces

US military commitment South Vietnam 1968-71 (as of 31 Dec)

	1968	1969	1970	1971
Military personnel	536,100	475,200	334,600	156,800
Deaths in action	14,592	9414	4221	1380
Wounded in action	92,820	70,216	30,643	8936

The year of 1968 was a watershed in the Vietnam conflict. After the carnage in South Vietnam's cities in the February Tet offensive and the prolonged bloodletting at Khe Sanh through to April, the Vietnamese communists knew they could not achieve military victory against the US Army, but American politicians were equally aware that the US public would not allow them to keep the army in Vietnam indefinitely.

When Richard M. Nixon took over the office of president in January 1969, he inherited peace talks, officially opened in Paris that same month, and a twin policy of Vietnamization and pacification in South Vietnam. Under the influence of General Creighton W. Abrams, who had replaced General Westmoreland as US military commander in Vietnam in June 1968, the Army of the Republic of Vietnam (ARVN) was increased to over a million men by 1971 and progressively re-equipped with the latest in military hardware. At the same time, pacification – treated as a sideshow under Westmoreland – proceeded apace. Taking advantage of the weakening of the Viet Cong by their losses in the Tet offensive, a series of coordinated measures – land reform, village elections, and the Phoenix programme to eliminate Viet Cong cadres – established a degree of government control over much of rural South Vietnam.

As Vietnamization proceeded, Nixon gradually fulfilled his elec-

tion promise 'to bring the boys home'. The first troop withdrawals were announced in June 1969. By early 1972 the number of US personnel in Vietnam had fallen to a quarter of the 1968 level.

Changes of policy were not always immediately translated into new combat methods, however. General Abrams wished to move away from the war of attrition (the 'body count') and stop the use of excessive firepower in densely populated areas, but armed sweeps in Quang Ngai Province and in the Delta (Operation Speedy Express) in the first half of 1969 and by the Marines in Quang Nam Province later in that year continued the old tactics, causing appalling civilian casualties. In May 1969 a major attack launched against communist main force units in the A Shau Valley resulted in heavy US losses which caused an uproar in America; after A Shau, the US Army ceased actively to seek to engage large enemy units.

Nor were the communists keen for battle. They had launched three relatively small offensives since Tet – in May and August 1968 and in February 1969 – but they were clearly weakened by their losses. From the end of 1969, perhaps coincidentally after the death of Ho Chi Minh in September, the communists reduced their combat operations. During 1970 and 1971 the level of fighting in South Vietnam fell sharply.

President Nixon's policy on the war combined a willingness to negotiate – as well as the official meetings in Paris, secret talks between Nixon's foreign policy adviser Henry Kissinger and North Vietnam's Le Duc Tho began in August 1969 – and a firm commitment to bring US troops home with a readiness, if necessary, to widen the scope of the war to bring pressure to bear on the communists. As early as March 1969 he ordered the secret bombing of communist sanctuaries in Cambodia and in April 1970 ARVN and US troops invaded that hapless country. American opinion was outraged by this widening of the war, and Congress repealed the Gulf of Tonkin Resolution which had given the president a free hand to conduct the war as he saw fit. In anti-war protests in May 1970, four students were shot by National Guardsmen at Kent State University, Ohio. But despite the protests, the widening of the war continued, and in February 1971 ARVN forces backed by US airpower invaded Laos in a failed attempt to cut the Ho Chi Minh Trail.

The style of the Laos incursion was a sign of the future: the ARVN using American methods and equipment was to be left to defend South Vietnam under the umbrella of US air power. In March 1972 the acid test came, as heavily-armed North Vietnamese regular forces poured into the South. In the event, the ARVN held on.

The period from 1968 to March 1972 saw the transition from a Northern-backed insurgency resisted by US troops to a conventional war between the regular armies of North and South Vietnam. It would be three years before this final phase of the conflict was decided.

Leadership of the armed forces was perhaps the most critical issue confronting South Vietnam. The military had long been politicised. High rank and advancement depended more on political loyalty than military expertise, leadership abilities or performance. Much to the dismay of an American adviser who might have persuaded the government to remove an incompetent military officer (or political official) from a position of authority, that person would often reappear in another unit or province in the space of a few months. Without a solid corps of trained and capable NCOs and officers, South Vietnam's forces were likely to have difficulty meeting the military threat of the North Vietnamese Army whose leadership attained a higher level of professional competence and performance.

There was also little likelihood of South Vietnam becoming self-sustaining. The ARVN had been taught to fight American-style, with an expensive combination of mobility and firepower – indeed, they were known to outdo the Americans in their readiness to call in airstrikes and artillery fire as a substitute for infantry action. They depended on the American umbilical cord for all kinds of supplies to support this style of warfare, from spare parts to ammunition and heavy equipment. The South Vietnamese economy could supply military uniforms; almost everything else came from outside. The ARVN was also crucially dependent on US close air support. ARVN units preferred to have a US adviser out in the field with them, because it meant the Americans would come to their assistance if they were in trouble. But Vietnamization meant ultimately the departure of American advisers, and the day would come when US airpower would disappear too.

The solidity of the pacification successes was equally open to doubt. More of South Vietnam's villages were under government control than at any previous time, but were the improvements lasting? The land reform programme and village democracy were soon to be compromised by the Saigon regime's ineradicable hostility and distrust for the peasants, and events would show that if active opposition in rural areas had ceased, positive support for President Thieu's government was far from being won.

Vietnamization and pacification successfully played their part in covering the withdrawal of US troops without an admission of defeat or dishonour. But the only guarantee for the long-term existence of South Vietnam as an independent state remained the commitment of the US government to continue the supply of air cover, arms and money. Saigon's future still lay in the hands of Washington. **Richard A. Hunt**

Talking peace

Above: The Paris peace talks.

The inability of either side to win the war in Vietnam led logically to the opening of peace negotiations, from which each side, equally logically, sought to seize a decisive advantage.

Preliminary discussions were held in Vientiane and Paris from April 1968; official negotiations opened in Paris in January 1969. The talks were four-sided: they involved the North and South Vietnamese communists, the United States and the government of South Vietnam. There were two major stumbling blocks: the Americans demanded the withdrawal of all North Vietnamese forces from the South as a precondition for the withdrawal of US troops, while the Vietnamese communists demanded the resignation of President Thieu and his replacement by a coalition government, including communists, in Saigon. It was a dialogue of the deaf. The talks soon settled down into a stultifying ritual of propaganda statements, denunciations, proposals and counter-proposals and even secret talks begun in August 1969 between President Nixon's adviser Henry Kissinger and the head of the North Vietnamese team, Le Duc Tho, failed to produce any results.

Above right: Within the perimeter fence of strategic hamlets like this one at Kien Hoa the inhabitants would be defended against guerrilla intimidation.
Bottom right: From 1968 onwards the South Vietnamese government agreed to arm the peasants, forming Self-Defense Force militia units like the one being inspected here. Despite these efforts, however, the peasants remained cool towards the government.

Saigon at war

Sarah Coombe was in Saigon, where her father was military attaché in the British embassy, from 1968–70. She worked for Newsweek *magazine for six months in 1970 as a stringer, and was the youngest member of the Saigon press corps. Her press pass enabled her to travel extensively in South Vietnam.*

"Night beauty observed from a balcony tucked under the eaves of an elegant residential house in Saigon in 1970: terracotta rooftops, discreet court-yards and dusky palm trees, all encircled by a fire-works display of phosphorus flares clumsily flicker-ing over the outer perimeters of the city and dotted lines of red tracer crackling upwards, perhaps from some Viet Cong outpost. In the precious hour before dawn one could appreciate the former style of the 'Paris of the East' – the straight, tree-lined boulevards leading into spacious parks, empty and peaceful before the lifting of the curfew.

The harsh light of day, however, revealed Saigon as a stinking, overcrowded city. It teemed with dis-placed persons and homeless refugees, living along-side thousands of government officials and military personnel all feeling very vulnerable since the Tet offensive 18 months before. Daybreak did have some compensations, however; it brought some respite from the vague terrors of darkness. The sound of bombs from US airstrikes in the country near Saigon that rattled the window panes night and day was not so alarming during daylight when it competed with the roar of tanks on Phan Than Ghan heading for Route 1, or the unceasing clatter of helicopters.

By 7.30am the morning rush-hour was in full swing. The hot cloying winds that never cleared the air would irritate even the Vietnamese schoolgirls, impeccably dressed in the Vietnamese kimono, the white *ao dai*, as they wove their way through the packed streets, neatly perched on their Hondas like young blackheaded gulls picking their way through a garbage dump. Their waist-length shining black hair streamed behind them, as they competed with emaci-ated siklo-drivers, wolf-whistling American service-men and trucks piled to overflowing with baskets laden with Mekong Delta produce heading for mar-ket. An early morning rocket or car bomb would merely add to the confusion, an inconvenience rather than cause for alarm, too commonplace for concern. This was a city whose inhabitants had survived 25 years of war, and who were now coping with the temporary, tawdry vitality created by the American involvement, a vitality nurtured by dollars and desperation.

The large enclosed houses of the residential area, populated by foreigners and the wealthy, remained relatively unsullied, though the American properties tended to be trussed up in chickenwire and sandbags. Refugees would, however, sometimes squat outside the walled edifices, on the tree-lined pavements. They would appear without warning and ingeniously construct temporary homes of makeshift materials; printed aluminium sheets stolen from the local Coca-Cola canning factories were very popular and warded off the worst of the monsoon rains. The most helpless

Saigon was a city of extremes: the physical grace of Vietnamese girls (above) contrasted with the squalor of the war; there were thousands of refugees (top right) who lived in the streets, while at the same time there was a booming economy, exemplified by the ubiquitous Honda (above right), which was a consequence of US dollars being pumped into circulation. The fine residences of foreign officials (far right) contrasted with the rambling riverside shantytowns (right).

of all, the abandoned bastard babies, were housed in over-crowded orphanages run by various missionary groups, exhausted by a losing battle against numbers and the misappropriation of charity funds. Despite this, the foreign adoption agencies had great difficulty in getting the necessary clearance from the Vietnamese authorities, and babies would often die before their emigration papers came through. It was a sickening business. The pretty young orphan girls soon found a home in the bars downtown, and they could be seen in ill-fitting clothes, with immaculately painted faces, impassively accosting GIs on their three-day rest and recreation – 'You number one, you drink tea with me!'

Entertainment could be found for all at every level. The Cirque Sportif, still patronised by the considerable French community, attracted foreigners and the wealthy. Exquisitely-dressed Vietnamese women, wives of high-ranking officers and politicians, or mistresses of influential American residents decorated the pool side. Many of them were running highly successful businesses in scrap-metal, antiques or prostitutes. They invested their wealth in diamonds and gold. In the *Newsweek* office where I worked, the Vietnamese secretary, the wife of a colonel in the ARVN, would amuse the journalists by showing off a latest sparkling purchase, her insurance for when the inevitable day of reckoning came along.

Cholon, the Chinese district, was not so readily frequented, though it was reasonably safe during the day. Situated around a swamp it was a rambling shantytown, a confusion of ill-lit streets, offering sanctuary to the Viet Cong and any military personnel who decided to go AWOL. Here, as in many other parts of the city, the black market proliferated, and the pavements would be piled high with goods from the American PX stores – everything from tape recorders to Rolex watches.

Journeys for Europeans outside the city were strictly controlled by the national embassies, though of course the press were a law unto themselves and their MACV passes enabled them to use military transport of all kinds within South Vietnam. The British embassy insisted that any journey was registered in case of mishap or 'diplomatic' incident.

When on the road outside the city, it was usual to carry arms, and an occasional lunchtime invitation to the French plantation at Swan Lok would involve a convoy of two or three civilian cars, with hand grenades in the glove compartment and an M16 or two

Above right: The city had swollen outwards from its elegant French centre to makeshift litter-strewn suburbs where soldiers on leave provided an ever-present reminder of war. Right: At Qui Nhon orphanage young victims of the conflict exhibit a stubborn cheerfulness in the face of misfortune. The same United States that had sent the bombers and the heavily-armed troops which had left the children crippled or parentless also furnished the Coca-Cola and Miami-style shorts with which they were cheered and comforted.

handy in case of ambush. Helicopters and C-130s were normal transport for longer journeys, and it was from the air that the effects of the B-52 bombing and defoliation programme became only too evident. Rich plantations of rubber and banana trees had been reduced to a brown wasteland interspersed with shining pools of water in the clusters of bomb craters. Much of the country between Saigon and the coastal resort of Vung Tao was like this, though there were still areas of paddy that flourished around the villages.

US ambassador Ellsworth Bunker maintained a luxurious yacht outside the town of Vung Tao, and would fly his weekend guests down by helicopter from the roof top of the American embassy, with accompanying gunships to assure a safe arrival. A relaxing lunch fanned by cool breezes, away from the unremitting tensions of Saigon, was only occasionally disturbed by US helicopter assaults on the volcanic outcrops – steep-sided hills riddled with caves where the Viet Cong took refuge – that overlooked the coast.

Cruises on ambassador Bunker's yacht may have revealed the paradoxes of this war but for me a visit to Qui Nhon did far more than merely stir the intellect. The Save the Children Fund maintained a hospital on the coast there, in an insecure mountainous region, surrounded by a free-fire zone, and the town was constantly under attack. A major battle had taken place the day I arrived, and there was a severe shortage of blood. A visit to the hospital as blood donor and make-shift nurse was a salutory experience. I found beds overflowing into the corridors and courtyards, filled with horribly wounded victims – the chaos compounded by accompanying relatives who squatted alongside makeshift bedding with bundles of food, praying for the wounded. I remember being physically sick, feeling horribly ineffectual and very shocked, and yet glad that I had for once escaped the cocoon of Saigon, and the 'armchair' war.

It was while I was at Qui Nhon that I heard first-hand from GIs about maintaining 'body count' levels at any cost. They sat on the beach, outside a hospital set up by the Save the Children Fund, on a warm evening, and talked to me of a recent massacre of small children in the free-fire zone as casually as if returning from a hunting party in the Rocky Mountains. Here, at Qui Nhon, the war was no longer a fireworks display outside a beautiful colonial city; it was a chilling combination of maimed limbs and murdered children – and for me, as a 17-year-old, a difficult mixture to stomach. 99

POW

US prisoners in Vietnam

During the 12 years of US involvement in the Vietnam War about 800 Americans, including 100 civilians, fell into enemy captivity, the majority of them being air force and naval aviators shot down over North Vietnam and Laos. But this relatively small number of individuals played an inordinately significant and visible role in the conduct and final political settlement of the war. The US manifested enormous concern over the fate of its nationals held by the communists, while for its part the government of North Vietnam saw the prisoners as one of its most potent bargaining counters.

The prisoners who had been shot down over North Vietnam were placed in a variety of camps throughout the North, and their basic physical conditions, although harsh, were generally survivable. Those captured in the South by Viet Cong field units, however, found that they were in a very difficult physical situation. Food was scarce, disease was hardly treated and the troops who had captured the Americans manifested very little concern for their charges. For the Pathet Lao and the communists in Cambodia, too, the Americans they held were burdens, who consumed food and time, and sending them to North Vietnam might incur further problems in breaking cover or sending soldiers away to escort the Americans northwards. Although in the North the prisoners were seen as a valuable source of propaganda, and were exploited accordingly, this admittedly unpleasant process at least saved some of the prisoners from the brutal maltreatment that occurred in the South.

From 1965 on, when pilots were first shot down, the attitude of the North Vietnamese, the Viet Cong and the Pathet Lao was that captured Americans were not prisoners of war (POWs) but criminals, holding no rights under the Geneva Conventions and subject to the laws of their captor, arguing that no formal state of war existed. The North Vietnamese described the prisoners as 'capitalist hired guns' or 'imperialist air pirates', and forced them to appear in propaganda films, to face press conferences, and to parade in public.

In 1966 the Hanoi government advertised its apparent intention to hold war crimes trials. In this effort they were supported by the Bertrand Russell War Crimes Tribunal, then trying to gather evidence of genocide and locate a nation willing to act as host for an actual tribunal predisposed to find the US guilty. The threats drew powerful reaction throughout the US from all parts of the political spectrum, and President Johnson despatched private messages through several sources warning President Ho Chi Minh that any such trials would bring on grave consequences. The

Right: A wounded US aviator is transported in a cart, under armed guard, to a POW camp, while an East German cameraman (far right) prepares for some propaganda filming.

powerful American public reaction gave Hanoi further indication of the value of the prisoners it held.

Treatment of prisoners was in theory 'lenient and humane', but torture was justified as punishment for violation of regulations, and it was any relief from this torture that was counted as lenient and humane treatment. Punishment itself, the interrogators explained, was never the wish of the captor. Rather, the prisoner brought it upon himself by an 'incorrigible,' 'recalcitrant,' 'unprogressive,' or 'reactionary' attitude.

The US prisoners developed a resistance organisation, devised resistance policies, and struggled to avoid exploitation. The most vital element of their resistance programme was communication. Denied the right to converse at most camps until late 1970, the prisoners developed a covert system of communication based upon a 25-letter alphabet set in a 5×5 matrix omitting the letter K:

	1	2	3	4	5
1	A	B	C	D	E
2	F	G	H	I	J
3	L	M	N	O	P
4	Q	R	S	T	U
5	V	W	X	Y	Z

Once they memorised the matrix, prisoners communicated by tapping, blinking, flashing fingers, coughing, scraping food plates, snapping clothing,

Below: A US pilot, captured after his plane was shot down, is paraded through the streets of Hanoi. The communists made great political play with the POWs.

scratching – and other, more exotic methods. Prisoners organised cellblocks so that men in interior rooms could communicate while those at the ends kept lookout. The noon siesta period and the early evening after mealtime were good times for communication in many camps. One effective method was the 'cup telephone'. A prisoner in one cell, covering his head with a blanket to muffle sound, held the bottom of his cup to the wall and spoke into the cup's open end while a prisoner in the adjacent cell held his cup the same way and pressed one ear into its opening.

To make the resistance function, the Hanoi prisoners established a chain of command based upon rank on day of capture – a practice they never abandoned. The captors tried to shatter the prisoners' organisation by punishing them for communication, by isolating senior officers and tough resisters, and by transferring captives from prison to prison. This last tactic actually served to unite the various camps and spread the policies and influence of the leaders.

The rope trick

As the captors grew to suspect the existence of this clandestine communication, they increased their use of torture. The worst torture in North Vietnam was one called 'the rope trick' or simply 'the ropes'. The victim's arms were tied together behind him at the elbows and wrists; then he was forced to sit, legs flat out before him, while torturers raised his arms, forcing his head down between his thighs. Another rope was used to secure his ankles, then wrists and ankles were joined by a fourth rope. Pulling on this last rope could dislocate shoulders, cause fearful leg and groin pains, threaten suffocation, and destroy bowel control. Certain interrogators favoured it over more obvious methods because it left few visible signs. Men so tortured were presented to press conferences and visitors to Hanoi because, apart from prison pallor and gauntness, they did not appear severely maltreated. In addition, standard prison punishment procedures such as solitary confinement were common, while the denial of food, medicine and clothing was commonplace.

For its part, the Johnson administration created two committees to work confidentially on the POW problem – the Department of State Committee on Prisoner of War Matters in April 1966 and the Department of Defense Prisoner of War Policy Committee in July 1967. The first, reflecting a desire to treat the prisoner question as a humanitarian matter separate from the war itself, departed from the tradition in the US government that each armed force looked after its own POW and Missing-in-Action (MIA) members, following service regulations written to support portions of the Missing Persons Act and other legal guidelines. The second, by studying the POW-MIA issues as matters of policy involved in waging the war, as well as by coordinating practices of all the armed forces and serving as liaison between the services and the Department of State, similarly departed from tradition. Both committees, by their existence and actions, revealed US sensitivity to the subject; and naturally the repatriation of prisoners and accounting for those missing in action became major items of negotiation at the Paris peace talks of 1968–72.

In spite of US attempts to effect an exchange of prisoners, the Hanoi government denied sending any troops outside its borders, therefore denying the

A case history

In 1968 Colonel Norris Overly was one of only nine US POWs who had been released by the North Vietnamese. Under pressure from peace groups, he revealed his story.

On 11 September 1967, Colonel Overly was engaged in a bombing raid against a convoy of enemy trucks 100km (60 miles) north of the demilitarized zone. Effective ground fire knocked out his controls and he ejected safely, landing in a rice paddy. Despite an overnight attempt to evade the enemy, he was captured by some 200 civilians the following morning. He was then wired to a 50-gallon oil drum, placed in a truck and driven slowly northwards to Hanoi. A cut on his back, suffered during his ejection from his craft, became infected and the journey stopped while he was treated – Overly was tied face down on a board with his legs in stocks and his arms held by wet ropes. He remained in this position for 29 days. After seven weeks he finally reached Hanoi.

Interrogation followed shortly. Twice Overly was smashed in the face with a rifle butt for crossing his legs, blood and broken teeth falling from his nose and mouth. But worse was to follow. The incarceration in a cell 245cm by 335cm (8 by 11 feet) for months on end with no company was punctuated only by meals – and those consisted of little more than limp gruel and stale bread. As time wore on conditions seemed to improve. Overly was allowed to listen, twice daily to political broadcasts and local civilians came to see him, sometimes to jeer and sometimes out of curiosity. Indeed, as Overly recalled, one young Vietnamese was so impressed by the colonel's ability to read Latin, that he returned several times with a catechism that he carried in his pocket.

Eventually, Overly was released. Despite having spent only five months in captivity, he had lost 20kg (45lbs).

existence of North Vietnamese in enemy captivity; while covert arrangements, under the code-name 'Buttercup', to exchange Viet Cong and US prisoners within South Vietnam itself – an effort plagued by the accidental deaths of messengers and the Saigon government's uncooperative attitude – accomplished little. The Viet Cong had begun a limited programme of releasing prisoners in 1962, eventually freeing about 70, including 30 news correspondents, civilian workers, missionaries and students. The Viet Cong typically announced releases to coincide with major anti-war demonstrations in the US. An American sponsored programme of model POW camps managed by South Vietnamese and open to international inspection began in 1967 but inspired no reciprocation.

In 1968 and 1969, three groups of three prisoners each were released by Hanoi, and the individuals involved were fully exploited for propaganda purposes by the communists. This caused deep bitterness among the other prisoners, who felt most of the men had compromised their honour, ignored the policies of senior officers, and violated the protocol of the Geneva Conventions which calls for repatriation of ill and injured first. But the released men carried out valuable information, including the names of more than 300 previously unidentified prisoners, and gave aid and comfort to the POWs' families as well as practical advice to survival training programmes.

In 1969 the Nixon administration ended its predecessor's five-year-old policy of confidentiality about the POWs. In what was called the 'Go-Public' programme, the government launched a wide range of protests against Hanoi's treatment of prisoners, releasing damning photographs and films, sponsoring a series of public appearances and speaking tours by released prisoners, and encouraging active, vocal, international appeals by several private groups of relatives of POWs.

An end to isolation

In 1970, still fearing that American prisoners in remote camps in North Vietnam could be suffering harsh treatment, the US launched a commando raid upon a camp at Son Tay, a few miles west of Hanoi. Although the prisoners had been moved from the camp before the raid, the commando attack itself demonstrated American ability and will to venture into the enemy's stronghold, and it helped persuade Hanoi to gather all the prisoners into large compounds within the city. Coincident with the death of Ho Chi Minh in October 1969 and the 'Go-Public' effort in Washington, treatment had begun to improve in the North Vietnamese prisons. The congregating of all prisoners into three compounds further improved conditions. No longer were individuals isolated in solitary confinement, for example.

Following visits by President Nixon to communist China and the Soviet Union in 1972, and Hanoi's unsuccessful spring invasion of South Vietnam, North Vietnamese and American representatives at the Paris talks reached an agreement on repatriation. Even as they negotiated while mounting a large offensive, the North Vietnamese transferred more than 200 POWs from Hanoi to a location near the Chinese border, holding them in reserve against various contingencies.

On 27 January 1973 the peace accords were signed, and 600 prisoners were repatriated in February and March. In the group were 591 Americans, 26 of them

civilians, two Thai sergeants and one South Vietnamese Air Force captain, and two civilians each from Canada, West Germany and the Philippines. Officially, three men were released by the People's Republic of China, nine by the Pathet Lao, and the others by North Vietnam and the Viet Cong's Provisional Revolutionary Government. In South Vietnam, the Republic of Vietnam released more than 25,000 communist prisoners and the Viet Cong freed 5000 South Vietnamese.

More than 70 Americans are known for certain to have died in captivity, but the real total may have been as high as 300. More than 30 Americans successfully escaped from captivity, chiefly in South Vietnam, most of them during the first few days of captivity before incarceration in a prisoner compound. One army officer escaped in 1968 after a five-year captivity in the South Vietnamese Delta. An equal number attempted to escape but were recaptured, half of them

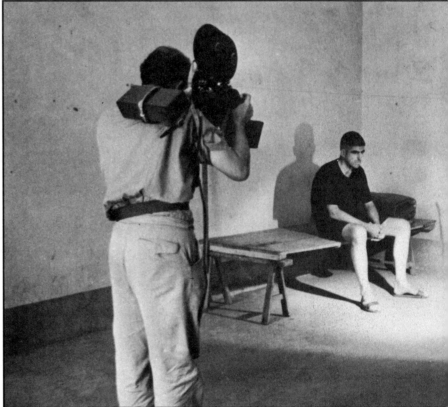

Left: The haunted face of a POW reveals vividly the mental strain of interrogation and imprisonment. Below: An East German film crew make a propaganda documentary on the US POWs. Titled 'Pilots in Pyjamas', it was widely shown, but gave no impression of the extensive maltreatment to which the Americans were being subjected. Bottom: Dejected POWs are paraded through the centre of Hanoi. The North Vietnamese people felt intense hostility towards the pilots who had been bombing their country.

dying as a result. It has been established that, during wars involving Western nations in this century, fewer than two per cent of all prisoners attempted escape. The rate for American POWs in Indochina 1961–1973 approached five times that percentage. No one successfully escaped from North Vietnam, although one air force officer evaded recapture for two weeks and nearly reached an American outpost at the demilitarized zone separating North and South Vietnam. Two young flyers – an air force pilot and a navy navigator – broke out from a Hanoi prison and swam 24km (15 miles) down the Red River toward the Tonkin Gulf before recapture. An army officer escaped from a jungle camp 48km (30 miles) from Hanoi, reached that city and was but a few blocks from sanctuary at the French or Canadian embassies when a policeman arrested him. A dozen other known attempts resulted in recapture.

In 1976 a review of the Armed Forces Code of

Conduct determined that it had served well as an ethical standard for prisoners of war. The Department of Defense made no change in the Code save for a slight rewording in one article to eliminate an ambiguity. Nearly all prisoners were judged to have resisted the enemy adequately and many heroically. Ten – two officers and eight enlisted men – were considered to have collaborated with the North Vietnamese. The two officers – one navy, one Marine Corps – were censured by the secretary of the navy and retired 'in the best interest of the Naval Service'. Charges against the enlisted men, who had all been imprisoned in South Vietnam at least two years before transfer to Hanoi in 1970–71, were dropped.

The American prisoners were welcomed home with great enthusiasm and relief, seen by many as both victims and heroes of the war. Their return symbolised the end of the war to most Americans. They were fêted, lionised, and decorated – three receiving the Congressional Medal of Honor for actions while in captivity. The group repatriated in 1973 was an uncommon one, averaging 32 years of age at capture and being largely officers and aviators. Any group experiencing the sort and duration of imprisonment this group underwent would be expected to suffer subsequent difficulties in health, psychological readjustment and careers. This group certainly encountered such difficulties but has met them as they met their captivity, with courage, character and intelligence. **Fred Kiley**

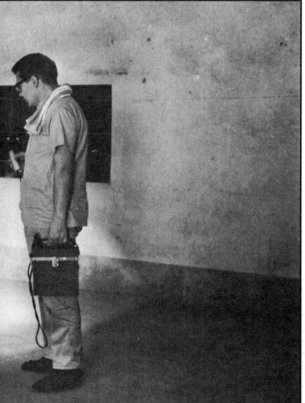

Below: An ex-POW walks down the gangway to a tumultuous welcome home after his release from captivity. Returning POWs were fêted by the American media as public heroes, but many of them found it difficult to adapt to life at home after their harrowing ordeal.

Raid on Son Tay

A daring bid to free the POWs

In early May 1970 US intelligence officers at Fort Belvoir, Virginia, identified a new North Vietnamese prisoner of war (POW) camp from aerial photographs. The camp was located in an isolated area approximately 50km (30 miles) west of Hanoi. At the same time, what appeared to be coded messages for help from the prisoners were also received.

The findings were passed to the US Joint Chiefs of Staff (JCS) and, with unusual haste, the Office of the Special Assistant for Counter-Insurgency and Special Activities (SACSA) was charged with preparing a feasibility study for a rescue attempt under the direction of Brigadier-General Donald Blackburn (head of SACSA). Throughout the following four weeks, Blackburn's 15-man research unit (in cooperation with representatives from the four services and the intelligence agencies) studied all available information and concluded that the intelligence was correct, and also that a rescue bid could be successful. The results of their research, together with a tentative plan of operation, were then placed before the new JCS chief, Admiral Thomas Moorer.

It was estimated that approximately 70 prisoners were held at the camp which was located 1.6km (1 mile) from Son Tay City. The camp itself was formed by two main features: a walled compound and an administrative area.

The walled compound, in which the prisoners were assumed to be held, was bounded by a 2m (7 feet) wall with two guard towers on the western wall of the compound and a third at the gate of the eastern wall which separated the compound from the administrative section. It was estimated that the camp itself was held by only 45 to 55 communist soldiers.

The main threat to a rescue attempt was not formed by the prison garrison but by surrounding military installations and units. The Defense Intelligence Agency and the CIA calculated that up to 12,000 communist troops were within 15 minutes drive of the camp. Further problems were posed by the fact that the North Vietnamese constantly juggled their air defence system and that, close to the Laotian border, radar installations had been deployed with no masking territory in between.

The plan for the rescue called for a night attack launched from Laos using a ground assault team of about 50 men. A six- to eight-man assault group from the team would crash-land into the actual prison compound and secure the prisoners. The guard towers would be taken out by air support while the bulk of the rescue force would land outside the compound, breach the main wall with explosives and cover the extraction of the prisoners by the original assault team. Blocking positions would be assumed while evacuation was completed. Other helicopters would also fly in with the raiders but were to wait to the rear of the attack zone at a holding zone, on call to touch

down at Son Tay when needed. Diversionary raids would be mounted by USAF and US Navy aircraft around Hanoi and Haiphong. The safe time allotted to the entire operation was 26 minutes. October or November were estimated as providing the best weather conditions.

The plan was approved by Moorer, and Blackburn immediately began to recruit his force. The assault was to be led on the ground by Colonel Arthur Simons, while overall planning command was given to the air force Brigadier-General Leroy Manor. Simons and Manor, using the facilities at the Eglin air force base in Florida, produced a complex but effective training programme and raised an assault force from scratch. The operation relied upon simplicity, speed of execution and, above all, security. Indeed, security was so great that virtually the entire staff directing the war in Southeast Asia was unaware of the operation until it had happened.

During the build-up to the raid, Simons and Manor encountered many difficulties. Even the most basic equipment requirements were often unfilled. In one particular instance, it was discovered that the US military had only six individual-weapon night sights in its entire armoury (and these were experimental), the force could, and did, purchase far more effective sporting night sights from the Armalite company for $49.00 each.

Sufficient intelligence was particularly hard to come by as the various intelligence-gathering organisations involved in Vietnam were reluctant to impart information and those photographs that were obtained by low-altitude drones and high-altitude SR-71 reconnaissance aircraft proved of little value on their own. Thus, despite extensive planning, the commanders remained uncertain of what they would actually find when they arrived.

There were also serious logistics problems to be faced. The assault helicopters would have to be accompanied and refuelled by larger fixed-wing tankers, all flying at under 30m (100 feet) at night and over extremely uneven terrain. The diversionary attacks that would take place to the east of Hanoi and occupy enemy air defences would, under current political bombing restrictions, be forced to use only simulation flares instead of ordnance.

In fact it was these political factors that affected much of the raid. As late as 24 September, Defense Secretary Melvin Laird informed Manor that a deferment on the October launch would be necessary

Above: An HH-53 helicopter of the type used by the raiding force. This helicopter has a maximum speed of almost 315km/h (196mph). Below left: Troops and equipment prepare to mount a Lockheed C-130 aircraft, as used to transport the raiders to their forward staging post.

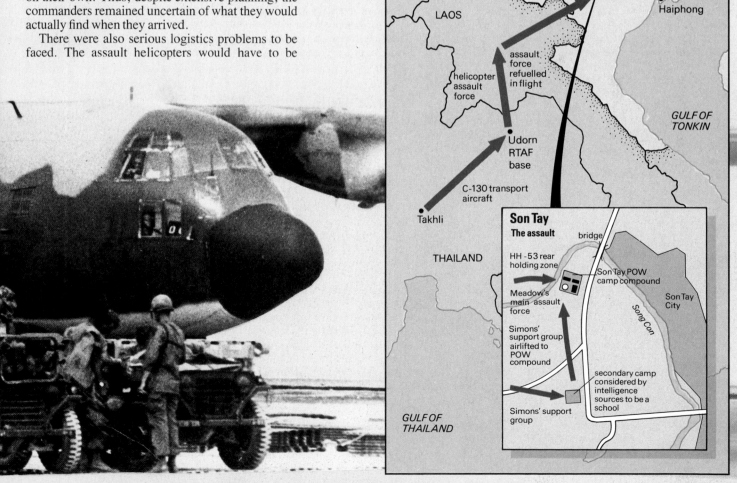

Son Tay
The approach route

CHINA

NORTH VIETNAM

LAOS

Son Tay · Hanoi

· Haiphong

assault force refuelled in flight

helicopter assault force

GULF OF TONKIN

Udorn RTAF base

C-130 transport aircraft

Takhli ·

THAILAND

GULF OF THAILAND

Son Tay
The assault

bridge

HH-53 rear holding zone

Son Tay POW camp compound

Son Tay City

Meadow's main assault force

Song Con

Simons' support group airlifted to POW compound

secondary camp considered by intelligence sources to be a school

Simons' support group

Left: A CIA model of the Son Tay prison camp and its surrounding buildings, code-named Barbara, reconstructed from aerial photographs. Despite the high level of security surrounding the operation, there were no prisoners present when the raiding force arrived to rescue them.

pending 'coordination with higher authority'. The truth of the matter was that last-minute diplomatic efforts were being made with Hanoi to secure the release of the prisoners. It seems, however, that the communists remained intransigent.

On 18 November 1970 President Nixon finally approved the plan and gave the go-ahead. By that time the force had deployed into Thailand and was awaiting orders. At 1800 hours on 20 November, the force was finally briefed on its mission. At 2230 hours the 56 men moved from their staging base at Takhli in Thailand to the Udorn Royal Thai Air Force Base. On arrival at Udorn the force disembarked from its C-130 transports and mounted helicopters. Between them the men carried 111 weapons, 15 claymore mines, 11 special demolition charges and 213 hand grenades. They also carried special rescue equipment such as chainsaws and oxyacetylene cutting torches and, between this small force, 92 radios were issued to cover the eight networks that would be used for the raid. At 2325 hours the last helicopter was signalled airborne.

Storming the cell-blocks

At shortly after 0218 hours on 21 November 1970 the assault force hit Son Tay prison camp. With loudspeakers blaring out a message to the prisoners, the small team that crash-landed into the compound streaked toward the cell-blocks. The compound wall was breached and more troops poured in from outside. But Simons' contingent, 22 men, supposed to support the attack, provided the first error of the mission – they had landed in a secondary camp 400m (440 yards) to the south. While an alternative rescue plan was adopted by the force at Son Tay prison, Simons was in fact engaged by some 500 communist troops whose presence at the secondary camp had not been revealed by intelligence data.

After inflicting casualties of almost 200 enemy dead, Simons' force was rapidly airlifted to the Son Tay camp where the demolition team immediately went into action, clearing the command building outside the front gate (where they encountered limited communist resistance) and demolishing the bridge north of the prison. Inside the prison compound, the assault teams encountered only sporadic enemy fire and quickly accounted for most of the 55 guards.

Ten minutes into the raid it was suddenly discovered that there were no prisoners in the camp. Major Richard Meadows, commanding the assault team, reacted instantly and radioed the news over the command network. Simons ordered all troops to withdraw to the landing zone for extraction as soon as his photographers had taken pictures of the empty cells. Eighteen minutes into the raid, the first of the Sikorsky HH-53 helicopters arrived at Son Tay from the rear holding zone. Major Meadows' men were mounted and evacuated. Twenty-seven minutes into the raid, Simons and the last of the combat force were airborne – having taken a couple of minutes to destroy four enemy vehicles which had been tearing up the road towards them. The operation had been precise, the withdrawal smooth; one flesh wound was the total US casualty. But there were no prisoners released and in this sense the raid had not been a success.

Quite why the prisoners had been moved from Son Tay is open to speculation. Although it may have been merely coincidence, it has been suggested that the increased diplomatic pressures to gain the release of the prisoners may well have alerted the North Vietnamese to the prospect of a US rescue operation. As it was, and despite the fact that the raid did not achieve its aim, the operation can be seen as a partial success. A raid was launched deep into enemy territory, severe casualties were inflicted on the communists and there were no US casualties. It was conceived, planned and executed from the highest political-military level and appeared to retain its security throughout the long build-up. Furthermore, it established a pattern for future rescue missions – although the attempt to free the US hostages held in Iran in 1980 was to show once more how difficult such an operation was to carry out and how high were the chances of failure.

Simon Innes

Above: Brigadier-General Donald Blackburn, head of SACSA, whose 15-man research team developed a feasibility study and an operation plan for the Son Tay raid.

THE F-18 HORNET

McDonnell Douglas's futuristic Hornet began life in 1966 as the Northrop P-530 Cobra lightweight-fighter project. Designed as an advanced-technology successor to the company's highly successful F-5 series, the Cobra was developed into the F-17 which competed unsuccessfully with the General Dynamics F-16 to fulfil a USAF requirement for a lightweight fighter issued in 1972. A 'fly-off' between the two designs took place in 1974, an event which was paralleled by the formulation of a US Navy requirement for a multi-mission aircraft to replace the A-7 and the Marine Corps' F-4.

This second programme, known as VFAX, produced paper designs from McDonnell Douglas, Grumman and Ling-Temco-Vought and considerable interest in the possibility of an aircraft derived from one or other of the USAF types. The navy's consideration of a VFAX F-16 or F-17 was prompted in part by political pressure to reduce development costs and eventually a derivative of the F-17 was chosen to fulfil the requirement.

At first sight, it may seem odd that the navy chose the unsuccessful competitor in the USAF evaluation – indeed, considerable criticism was levelled at the programme on just such grounds – but the decision was justified on the basis of the F-16's inability to carry the required electronic systems and the F-17's use of the YJ101 engine which was a close relative of the F404 turbofan specified for use in VFAX.

Considerable work was needed to turn the F-17 into a carrier aircraft and Northrop's inexperience in the field led the company into an agreement with McDonnell Douglas whereby the latter would act as prime contractor on the type, now known as the F-18. Northrop retained responsibility for the aft section of the new aircraft and took charge of the development and sale of any land-based derivatives. Initially, the consortium envisaged three distinct models, the F-18 as a Marine Corps fighter, the A-18 as an A-7 replacement and the F-18L for the air force market. The two naval models were eventually merged, hence the currently-unique service designation of F/A-18.

In order to fulfil the VFAX specification, the basic airframe was modified to incorporate a stronger fuselage and landing gear, an arrester hook, increased fuel capacity, a revised weapons system, an enlarged wing, the F404 turbofan and the Hughes AN/APG-65 radar system. The prototype F/A-18 made its first flight on 18 November 1978 and began an extensive test programme run jointly by the navy and the

manufacturers in January 1979. This evaluation, which included sea trials, used 12 aircraft and continued until the summer of 1982, by which time several fundamental changes had been made to the design. The undercarriage proved incapable of withstanding the repeated stress of deck landings and major modifications had to be made to the wings and tailplane in order to cure instability at low speeds, a long take-off run and a poor roll rate.

The mature F/A-18A emerged as a 17.07m (56ft) long, single-seat, all-weather fighter-bomber. At the heart of the type's capabilities lies the APG-65 radar. This unit was designed specifically for the Hornet and incorporates the HOTAS (hands-on-throttle-and-stick) concept, allowing the pilot to operate the radar without letting go of his two major controls. For air-to-air combat, the APG-65 offers three operational modes and can display up to eight targets at any given time. In the ground-attack role, the radar provides navigational information and has the ability to

Previous page: The underside of a US Marine Corps F/A-18, displaying a wide variety of stores including Sidewinder missiles on the wing tips, twin general purpose bombs on each wing and three large drop tanks. In between the drop tanks are two sensors: low-light TV (starboard) and infra-red (port). Above: Two Northrop YF-17 prototypes take-off from Edwards AFB in 1974 to undertake air combat trials.
Below: The YF-18 prototype lifts off from the runway. The Northrop/McDonnell Douglas collaboration led to the development of the F/A-18.

track both moving and stationary targets and to discriminate between individual targets in a closely spaced group such as a tank formation.

As a back-up to the radar, the F/A-18A can carry a forward-looking infra-red sensor pack, a laser designator for 'smart' weapons delivery and an electro-optical 'low-light' TV. Information from all these systems is displayed on a 'head-up' unit and three panel-mounted VDUs (visual display units). These displays have been designed for ease of use and can provide the pilot with systems information – fuel state, for example – as well as sensor data. Despite the obvious care which has gone into the design of the Hornet's cockpit, the overall sophistication of the aircraft has led to extended training periods before pilots are fully proficient in handling all the aircraft's capabilities.

Built-in armament comprises a single 20mm M61A-1 rotary cannon with 400 rounds of ammunition. Externally, there are nine weapons stations capable of carrying a theoretical maximum load of 7711kg (17,000lb). In the fighter role, AIM-9L and AIM-9J Sidewinder or AIM-7 Sparrow missiles are carried whilst for ground-attack sorties Mks 82, 83, 84 and 117 'iron' bombs can be carried alongside the full range of 'smart' weapons, fuel tanks and such specialised munitions as the AGM-109 Harpoon anti-shipping missile and the AGM-88 HARM anti-radiation missile.

Power is provided by two 7257kg (16,000lb) thrust

Top: The Marine version of the F/A-18. Above: A US Navy F/A-18 fires a Sparrow air-to-air missile. The Sparrow is an intermediate-range missile employing a semi-active radar system, in which the F/A-18's fire-control radar illuminates the target so that the missile homes onto the energy reflected off the target. Left: An underside view of a navy Hornet.

Left: A YF-17 takes-on fuel during one of the many trials designed to eradicate teething problems.

Right: Immediately following take-off an A-18 prototype retracts its wheels. Capable of acting as both an interceptor and a strike aircraft the F/A-18 has evolved into a highly versatile combat machine.

Right: A combination of four
Marine and navy F/A-18s
form up in line, armed with
Sparrow and Sidewinder
missiles. Below left: A
navy F/A-18, fitted with a
centre-line drop tank,
comes into land aboard the
aircraft carrier USS
Constellation.

General Electric F404-400 afterburning turbofans. These engines have proved particularly reliable in service and give the Hornet a high rate of acceleration and a maximum speed of Mach 1.8.

The first F/A-18 squadron, VFA-125, was formed in November 1980 and acts as the training unit for the type. Marine Corps squadron VMFA-314, commissioned in January 1983, became the first operational Hornet squadron with VMFA-323 and VMFA-531 converting to the F/A-18 during the course of the year. Although the introduction of the F/A-18 has been successful in service terms, politically the Hornet has become something of a hot potato. By mid-1982 Congressional disquiet about various aspects of the programme had reached the level where series production of the Hornet was put in doubt. The main areas of contention concerned the type's escalating unit cost, its relatively low maximum speed – when

compared with the F-14 – and its short range.

As originally conceived and understood by Congress, the VFAX programme was to provide the navy with a cheap 'dog-fighter' to complement the large and expensive F-14. Having established the programme, the navy proceeded to alter the specification so that VFAX became a multi-mission, all-weather fighter-bomber. Congress was convinced of the wisdom of these changes by a subtle campaign which played up the advantages of such an aircraft whilst hiding the disadvantages inherent in a system forced to compromise between a number of roles.

The politicians remained happy with the programme as long as they believed that they were getting more aeroplane for their money. When the F/A-18 finally appeared, the realisation dawned that the actual hardware was much more expensive and less capable than they had been led to believe. As the first

Below: F/A-18s on the flight deck of USS *Constellation*. Of interest is the aircraft in the right foreground with its wings still folded-up for below-deck storage. The two forward aircraft are being prepared for take-off, with blast deflectors raised.

Above: The clean lines of the F/A-18 can be seen in this photograph; also, the gun muzzle sited in between the gas vents of the aircraft nose. While lacking the performance figures of the F-14 the F-18 can deploy an impressive range of ordnance.

Below left: A navy F/A-18 climbs into the sky, armed and prepared for its role as an advanced interceptor aircraft.

F/A-18s became operational, the arguments continued and by the end of 1982 the Pentagon had come out firmly against sanctioning the purchase of the planned 1366 F/A-18s required by the navy. The current plan is to continue with the conversion of Marine Corps units with the type but limit navy use to four squadrons. These units will undertake a re-evaluation of the Hornet's potential as an attack aircraft after which a decision will be taken as to the final 'buy'.

Despite these domestic problems, the Hornet has proved to be a success in the world marketplace, with Canada, Australia and Spain placing orders for land-based versions. Canada selected the type as a replacement for its CF-101s, CF-104s and CF-5s during 1980 and has ordered a total of 138, including 24 of the two-seat TF/A-18 trainer which first flew in December 1979. Known as the CF-18, the Hornet entered Canadian service in October 1982 and deliveries were

due to continue at the rate of two a month until 1988.

The Australian contract was signed in October 1981 and called for 75 aircraft to be delivered from late 1984 onwards. Seen as a replacement for the Mirage III, Australian F/A-18s, apart from three imported aircraft, will be produced locally. The Spanish order, now apparently confirmed after several re-evaluations, is for 84 aircraft with delivery commencing in 1986. Interestingly, all land-based Hornets sold so far are based on the naval model, and the original 'land' Hornet, the F-18L, is being developed by Northrop as a simpler, cheaper aircraft for sale to Third World countries.

Apart from the single-seat F/A-18A and its two-seat trainer derivative, only one other Hornet model has appeared, this being the RF-18 reconnaissance platform. In this aircraft, the M61 cannon is to be replaced with a camera/sensor package comprising a

Above: Painted in low-visibility insignia a Canadian CF-18 is given its first public demonstration in July 1982. Canada has ordered a total of 138 Hornets. Above right: The ergonomically designed cockpit of the F/A-18 comprises two HUDs (head-up displays) and three HDDs (head-down displays) and is unique in allowing the single crewman to simultaneously deal with single-pass attacks and self-defence requirements.

Below: Maintenance crew set to work on an F/A-18 on the flight deck of a US carrier.

mix of F-924 panoramic and KS-87B forward/oblique cameras or an AAD-5 infra-red line scan unit. Ground testing of the package has been undertaken but flight trials, and indeed the aircraft itself, have been put in doubt by the current indecision over the numbers of Hornets the US Navy will eventually acquire.

There is no doubt that, within certain limitations, the F-18 Hornet is a very capable and sophisticated warplane. Well liked by its crews, the type does however illustrate the difficulty Western nations are facing in arms procurement. Whilst designers and users strive to create and obtain the best possible system for a given role, often with little regard to cost-effectiveness, the political will to fund such expensive military research and development programmes is wavering. This is especially true in America, fuelled in part by an increasing struggle for authority in such matters between the civilian and military components of government. The F/A-18 Hornet is both a product and a victim of this trend and it remains to be seen if the type is allowed to reach its full and obvious potential as a weapons system.

F/A-18A Hornet

Type Single-seat, carrier-borne, multi-role combat aircraft
Dimensions Span 12.31m (40ft 4¾in); length 17.07m (56ft); height 4.66m (15ft 3½in)
Weight Empty 9336kg (20,583lb); loaded (attack role) 21,887kg (48,253lb)
Powerplant Two 7257kg (16,000lb) General Electric F404-400 afterburning turbofans

Performance Maximum speed in clean condition Mach 1.8 or 1915km/h (1190mph)
Range Combat radius in interceptor role 741km (461 miles)
Ceiling Over 14,935m (49,000ft)

Armament One 20mm M61A-1 Vulcan rotary cannon (400 rounds) internally mounted plus nine external weapons stations capable of lifting a maximum load of 7711kg (17,000lb). In the interceptor role, AIM-9L and AIM-9J Sidewinder and AIM-7 Sparrow air-to-air missiles are carried whilst for the attack mission Mks 82, 83, 84 and 117 'iron' bombs can be carried in combination with a range of 'smart' weapons and other specialised munitions

Power to the people

Student revolt of the 1960s

The 1950s and early 1960s were a period of complacency for the advanced industrial societies of North America, Western Europe and Japan. Challenges to their dominance occurred in the Third World – in Asia, Africa or South America – but at home all was quiet, because the capitalist economies delivered the goods. Since the end of World War II the West had experienced a quite unprecedented growth in prosperity, with nearly full employment. The rise in living standards coupled with, in most cases, stable democratic institutions, undercut any revolutionary tendencies among industrial workers. Communist parties, where they existed, were discredited by their association with the Soviet Union, and their stolid leadership pursued a cautious policy.

But in 1968 this calm and complacency was shattered by a student revolt which seemed momentarily to throw the whole of modern society into question. The student population had risen rapidly through the 1960s to meet the economic demand for highly trained staff: in the United States, for example, the number of students rose from 3.6 million in 1960 to over 7 million in 1968, in France from 350,000 in 1965 to 680,000 in 1968. But why should these privileged children of affluence turn to revolt?

Partly it was a phenomenon common to a wider cross-section of the young. The conflict between the generations was a 1960s' cliché, as a 'youth culture' emerged with its own music, drugs, lifestyles and hairstyles, pitting young people against their parents

Top: French students take to the streets under a variety of banners, including the Palestinian flag. Left: Digging up cobblestones for use as missiles. Above centre: West German student leader Rudi Dutschke. Above: Daniel Cohn-Bendit.

and other authority figures. In the universities, this sense of hostility to authority and desire for change took on a political direction.

To the new generation of radicals, known as the New Left, the repressive bureaucracy of the Soviet Union offered only a mirror image of the authoritarian hierarchy in their own society, but the Marxist tradition still provided the main basis for a critique of capitalism – whether free-market capitalism in the West or state capitalism in the Eastern bloc. They lighted upon the works of thinkers like Herbert Marcuse and Wilhelm Reich who linked the concepts of social revolution with arguments for a sexual revolution based on their interpretation of Freud's theories. Marcuse's argument that modern industrial society manipulated and distorted all people's lives, offering consumer goods as a substitute for a full human existence, enabled the students to see themselves as an oppressed group in need of liberation, despite their privileged economic status. Industrial workers were no longer seen as the revolutionary class, a role which now devolved upon marginal minorities – blacks in America, the unemployed, and, of course, the students.

Capitalism unmasked

A major problem for the New Left was how to reveal the hidden repression and violence which they were convinced lay at the heart of the apparently peaceful and tolerant Western societies; and here the Third World played a vital role. In the casual brutality of many of the regimes in Latin America and above all of the Americans in the Vietnam War, the students claimed to see the true face of capitalism unmasked. Che Guevara, Ho Chi Minh and Mao Tse-tung – whose 'cultural revolution' was seen as an officially-directed youth revolt against bureaucratic hierarchy – were popular student heroes. The very violence of the guerrilla fighters was much praised and glamourised, seen less as a technique for winning wars than as a form of personal liberation. Although some students joined Trotskyist and Maoist groups where a traditional concern was shown for the details of revolutionary ideology, the majority of the New Left were more interested in direct action and immediate change.

The issues which brought these left-wing currents into contact with the main body of students were the Vietnam War and, much nearer to home, dissatisfaction with the state of university life. Throughout the West and Japan, anti-American demonstrations over Vietnam were the harbinger of student revolt. In the United States, for obvious reasons, the anti-war movement began earliest and was most important. The agitation from 1965 onwards at Berkeley, Columbia and other universities across America created many of the techniques of student action – the teach-ins, sit-ins and occupations. By 1967 mass student protests against America's war had spread to most of Western Europe and Japan.

Still there seemed no threat to established authority, even in the US where the black ghettos were in flames and Vietnam threatened a debacle. That students had posters of Che on their walls and marched in support of North Vietnam was marginal to national politics. But in Western Europe a second source of discontent developed as the anti-authoritarian, libertarian spirit of 'youth culture' and the New Left met the rigid conservatism of the universities.

In West Germany, the Sozialistischer Deutscher Studentenbund (SDS), a radical student group heavily involved in opposition to the Vietnam War, established an alternative university in West Berlin to protest against the authoritarian structure and uncritical transmission of ideas at the university proper. In April 1968, Rudi Dutschke, one of the SDS leaders, was shot and seriously wounded by a right-wing fanatic; student riots broke out in major West German cities, particularly directed against the Springer newspaper group which the students claimed encouraged violence against left-wingers.

Meanwhile, in France trouble was developing at the newly-built faculty of Nanterre, incongruously sited amid the shanty towns and slums of northern Paris. Led by the anarchistic 22 March Movement, whose most prominent member was a third-year sociology student, Daniel Cohn-Bendit, students had entered into conflict with the academic authorities. The specific grievances of French students were numerous: the highly centralised and conservative system was breaking down under the weight of

Left: A French riot-policeman discharges a canister of CS gas.
Below: Street violence in Milan, April 1968, as demonstrators assault an isolated policeman.
Bottom: Bemused residents survey the wreckage after violence between students and police in the Latin Quarter of Paris. Right: These postal workers in occupation of their depot and (inset) the Renault workers being addressed by students were among the 10 million French citizens who joined a nationwide strike. This outburst of libertarian radicalism was very worrying to all established bodies – including the French Communist Party.

numbers, but attempts to introduce selective exams were highly unpopular; teaching standards were poor and rules of conduct archaic – for example, no student was allowed into the room of a member of the opposite sex on campus at any time.

On 2 May 1968, faced with persistent disturbances, the authorities closed Nanterre faculty; the following day the students took their protest to the Sorbonne in central Paris and some arrests ensued. From that point events developed with dizzy rapidity. After a week of student demonstrations and riots, on the night of 10/11 May French riot police, the much-feared CRS, attacked student barricades in the Latin Quarter. Students threw Molotov cocktails and paving stones, but police brutality through the long night's fighting was such that the students won massive public support throughout France. On 13 May over a million people marched in protest, and the following day young workers at Sud-Aviation in Nantes occupied their factory. Within days, workers throughout the country, ignoring the communist union leaders who had denounced the student action from the outset, occupied factories and established a spontaneous general strike. Almost all schools, universities and factories of any size were occupied, and with over 10 million people on strike a demand was launched for workers' control – threatening to turn France into a revolutionary state.

For young radicals in France and beyond, these startling events seemed to herald an exciting new era in human affairs. A poster in the Sorbonne expressed the spirit of the moment: 'We are inventing a new and original world. Imagination has seized power.' The mood was completely utopian: favourite slogans demanded an end not only to advertising, private ownership and the consumer society, but also to work, the family and the state. But although they were in control of the streets of Paris, the radicals had no plans for the seizure of power – ruled out by their essential anarchism which rejected leaders and central organisation.

While the students and their allies from all walks of French life rode the wave of revolutionary optimism, discussing and planning the new society, however, other forces worked to reinstate the old order. In the last week of May, President de Gaulle moved to reassert his authority, and found his most useful allies in the French Communist Party. Fixed in their hostility to the student revolutionaries and young radical workers, the communists negotiated a pay rise and increase in union rights in return for the ending of the general strike, and on 30 May welcomed de Gaulle's call for elections to end the upheaval. The subsequent elections were a disaster for the left – including the communists – and a triumph for the Gaullists.

The events of May 1968 in France had worldwide repercussions. There were student riots and occupations in countries as diverse as Brazil, Switzerland, Italy, Mexico, Spain and Japan. The 'Prague Spring' in Czechoslovakia, already under way, was certainly encouraged by the French events. In England, student imitators of the Parisians were concentrated in Essex University and Hornsey College of Art.

But if 1968 was a year of hope for the radicals, it was also a year of disillusion. The French events dissipated in June; in August Soviet tanks rolled into Prague; in the US, there was not even an anti-war candidate for the autumn presidential election, in spite of the sufferings of student demonstrators in the Chicago 'police riot', also in August. In Italy and Germany the student agitation lasted longer, but could never obtain broad popular support. In West Germany, especially, the mass of the population remained fixedly hostile to the student radicals. In the US, student protests lasted as long as the American involvement in Vietnam, but rarely opened out into wider issues.

In the ashes of their hopes, many convinced activists recognised the need for contact with broader areas of society, either through working in factories, infiltrating traditional left-wing parties, or forming parties of their own. Others, disillusioned, withdrew into private projects. But some small groups refused to abandon the call for immediate revolutionary action and turned to terrorist violence and urban guerrilla warfare. Such organisations as the Baader-Meinhof group in West Germany, the Red Brigades in Italy, the Angry Brigade in Britain, the Weathermen in the United States and the Red Army in Japan, were the bitter aftermath of the idealistic student revolts of 1968. **R. G. Grant**

The Angry Brigade

From protest to bombing in the UK

On 5 December 1972, after an Old Bailey trial lasting 109 days, four ex-university students – John Barker, James Greenfield, Anna Mendelson and Hilary Creek – were each sentenced to 10 years imprisonment on a charge of conspiracy to cause explosions. Together with Jake Prescott, an habitual criminal sentenced to 15 years on a similar charge in November 1971, they constituted what was known as the 'Angry Brigade', a British terrorist group held responsible for 25 bomb attacks against property, chiefly in or around London, between May 1970 and August 1971.

The Angry Brigade had its origins in the wave of student unrest which swept through the Western world in the late 1960s, coming to a head in Paris in May 1968. In Britain student disaffection showed itself in protest marches – the largest of which was the anti-Vietnam War protest at Grosvenor Square on 27 October 1968 – demonstrations, sit-ins and a general disregard for accepted norms of behaviour. In the vast majority of cases this was a superficial youthful rebellion, to be abandoned with age and leaving few permanent traces, but in a small minority it created an anger and alienation which led them to dedicate their lives to opposing existing society and its rules. Barker and Greenfield at Cambridge University and Mendelson and Creek at Essex were among this minority, expressing their disaffection by 'dropping out' of academic life and drifting to London, where libertarian 'communes' seemed to offer an alternative society. By early 1970 all four were living in one of the poorer districts of North London, acting out their beliefs by helping to organise 'squats' for homeless people in empty properties and a Claimants' Union among the jobless.

Unfortunately their efforts rarely made much headway against entrenched bureaucracy, producing feelings of deep frustration which soon hardened into a belief that the only way to change society was to use violence to trigger a revolutionary upheaval. Exactly what would fill the ensuing vacuum was never adequately explained, for the Angry Brigade saw themselves as the expendable instigators of change rather than the future leaders of a new utopia. They took as their inspiration the Spanish 'First of May' group, an anarchistic anti-capitalist organisation already involved in terrorist operations, some of which – such as a sub-machine gun attack on the American embassy (20 August 1967) – had taken place in London. Contact between this group and the embryonic Angry Brigade was made sometime in early 1970, with the British dissidents agreeing to mount attacks on Spanish targets in exchange for arms and explosives. They started their campaign in May when, as part of a coordinated 'First of May' operation in four European cities, a bomb was planted on board an Iberia Airlines jet at Heathrow. The airline was hit again in August and September, but by then specifically British 'Establishment' targets – including the homes of the commissioner of the metropolitan police, and the attorney general – had also been attacked.

Above: Anna Mendelson, one of the four members of the Angry Brigade sentenced to 10 years imprisonment. Far right: Detective Chief Superintendent Roy Habershon who tracked them down.

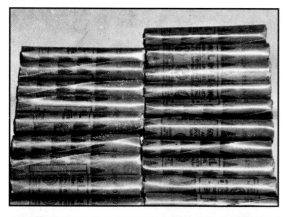

On 20 August 1971 the police closed in on the headquarters of the Angry Brigade – a flat in Amhurst Road, North London. A wide range of armaments (left, sub-machine guns, pistol and sheath knife) and explosives (far left, the rows of gelignite) was discovered there. Below left: The victim of one of the bomb attacks – the motor car of the Conservative Employment Secretary Robert Carr.

Right above: Angry Brigade communiqués expressed an intense belief in the essential injustice of British society, a point of view regarded sympathetically by many of their associates, including Catherine McLean, Angela Weir and Stuart Christie (right, left to right) who were acquitted of conspiracy to cause explosions.

These early bombs, claimed by people signing themselves 'Butch Cassidy and the Sundance Kid' or 'The Wild Bunch', did little actual damage and tended to be dismissed as the work of cranks. But the situation changed on 12 January 1971 when two explosions rocked the house of Robert Carr, secretary of state for employment, since in the prevailing atmosphere of social unrest caused by the Conservative government's Industrial Relations Bill, such attacks (as the Angry Brigade hoped) had the potential to trigger a bitter class divide. A police team, led by Detective Chief Superintendent Roy Habershon, began to track down the terrorists. The authorities were beginning to get worried.

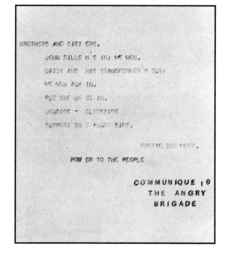

Habershon had very little to go on, but the political sentiments of the Angry Brigade, expressed through communiqués which appeared in the 'underground' press, made it obvious that the group belonged to the anarchist fringe. The police, assisted by the Special Branch, therefore concentrated upon known dissidents such as Stuart Christie, thought to have contacts with the First of May group, and Ian Purdie, an ex-student with a record of extreme political action. Suspects were watched and communes raided, although at this stage all that was uncovered was a thriving business in stolen cheque-books which, quite fortuitously, led to Greenfield and Mendelson. They promptly disappeared.

An unexpected breakthrough occurred on 20 January when Prescott, arrested on drugs charges, boasted to his cell-mates of his involvement in the Carr bombing. His known association with Purdie led to both men being charged with conspiracy, and although Purdie was to be acquitted at the subsequent trial, documents in his possession helped to narrow the field of suspects to a small group which included Barker, Greenfield, Mendelson and Creek. But they could still not be found, and the bombings continued. In May 1971, for example, the fashionable Biba boutique in Kensington High Street was hit and the police computer centre at Tintagel House attacked; on 22 June the home of William Batty, chairman of Ford UK, was bombed and on 31 July a woman – the only casualty of the campaign – was injured in an explosion outside the apartment of John Davies, secretary of state for trade and industry.

In fact Barker and his three friends were living together in a flat at 359 Amhurst Road, Stoke Newington, and it was through the continuing investigations into cheque-book theft that the police closed in. A raid on the flat on 20 August 1971, aimed at the arrest of Greenfield and Mendelson, uncovered the headquarters of the Angry Brigade, complete with 33 sticks of gelignite (recently picked up in France by Barker and Creek), weapons and a stack of incriminating documents. A further six suspects, including Christie, were arrested over the next few weeks, although in the end only the four from Amhurst Road were found guilty. No more bombings took place and the Angry Brigade, rooted in the naive revolutionary optimism of a rebellious generation, ceased to exist. It had achieved nothing. **John Pimlott**

Rationale of violence

'The politicians, the leaders, the rich, the big bosses are in command... *They* control, *we, the people, suffer*... *They* have tried to make us mere functions of a production process. *They* have polluted the world with chemical waste from their factories. *They* shoved garbage from their media down our throats. *They* made us absurd sexual caricatures, all of us, men and women. *They* killed, napalmed, burned us into soap, mutilated us, raped us...

'Slowly we started understanding the *big con*. We saw that they had defined our "possibilities". They said: You can demonstrate... between police lines. You can have sex... in the normal position as a commodity; commodities are good. You can rally in defence of the TUC... the TUC "Leadership" is wise.

'They used confusing words like "public" or the "national interest". Is the public some kind of "dignified body" which we belong to, only until we go on strike? Why are we reduced then to dreaded scroungers, ruining the country's economy? Is the "National Interest" anything more than *their* interest?...

'*The Angry Brigade became a reality* when we knew that every moment of badly paid boredom in a production line was a *violent crime*... To believe that *our* struggle could be restricted to the channels provided to us by the pigs, *was the greatest con*. And we started hitting them...'

Extract from Angry Brigade Communiqué No. 7, *March 1971*

Revolution USA

Radical violence from the campus to the ghetto

The United States has the most heavily armed population in the Western world. In the 1960s there were around 90 million firearms in private hands and about 12,000 murders a year were committed nationwide. The use of arms spilled over into the political sphere: the assassinations of President John Kennedy, his brother Robert and Martin Luther King were tragic examples. Under the circumstances it is not surprising that the political agitation of the decade produced armed violence: by 1970 a radical magazine estimated that acts of 'sabotage and terrorism' were occurring at the rate of around 500 a year, aimed at multinationals, schools and universities, banks, and military installations. But most of these acts were very minor and the groups that carried them out were small and ephemeral. Only two armed organisations, the Black Panthers and Weatherman, have a serious place in the history of American radicalism.

The Black Panthers were born out of a sharp change in the black political scene in the mid 1960s. In the first half of the decade black protest had focused on a Christian, non-violent campaign for full integration into white society, concentrated in the Deep South and led by the eloquent Martin Luther King. But many blacks, like the Black Muslims of Elijah Muhammad and Malcolm X, had come to reject integration and assert black independence, while black students grew restless at the 'turning of the other cheek' to racist violence. Just as King's civil rights movement was achieving its objectives in President Johnson's liberal

For US blacks, the 1960s were a decade of ferment. General discontent manifested itself in urban riots (above, Brooklyn in flames) while at the 1968 Olympics in Mexico, athletes Tommy Smith and John Carlos (above right) gave a 'black power' salute. Out of this atmosphere emerged the Black Panthers, founded in 1966 by Bobby Seale and Huey Newton (left, left to right) and given potent publicity by Eldridge Cleaver (below).

legislation, the first of a series of city ghetto riots, in Harlem in 1964 and the Watts district of Los Angeles in 1965, reminded America that whatever legal rights blacks possessed, they remained unequal in housing, income and access to employment.

In October 1966 Huey Newton and Bobby Seale, two part-time students who had a background in tough street-gang life, formed the Black Panther Party for Self-Defense in Oakland, California. Newton, as 'minister of defense' of the new party, outranked Seale who was 'chairman'. They did not invent the name 'Black Panther' – other groups of the same title were set up elsewhere – but theirs was the one to become internationally known.

Newton and Seale set out to recruit young blacks in the ghetto to form an armed militia, primarily to defend local people against a police force whose harassment of blacks was notorious. Their initial programme was for black areas to become self-policing and self-governing, a fragmented independent black nation – although at this stage they numbered only 30 or 40 militants isolated in Oakland.

The appeal of the Panthers lay in their carefully projected image of disciplined macho violence. They ostentatiously carried guns wherever they went – even to private parties – and played for media attention. In February 1967 a group of Panthers resplendent in black berets, black leather jackets, blue turtleneck sweaters and black trousers marched into San Francisco airport carrying rifles to escort the widow

of Malcolm X off a plane. The media gave such events substantial coverage.

The Panthers were still a tiny group, but joined by the brilliant, if extreme, Eldridge Cleaver as their 'minister of information' they won nationwide status. The summer of 1967 saw some of the most violent urban riots in America's history, with troops called in to Detroit to quell black snipers and arsonists; in April 1968, after the assassination of Martin Luther King, blacks took to the streets in 80 cities. It was easy for conservatives and radicals alike to see here the beginnings of revolution, and the Panthers emerged as spokesmen and representatives of a black revolt they neither led nor controlled. The Panthers distanced themselves from black nationalism and separatism, showing a willingness to work with white radical groups and an identification with Third World revolutionaries like the Viet Cong. Their opposition to the conscription of blacks to fight 'the white man's war' linked them to the anti-Vietnam War movement. By 1968 they had dropped 'Self-Defense' from their title and were presenting themselves as part of a global revolution against American 'imperialism'. Panther branches sprang up across the United States – total membership reaching some 2000 – and in alliance with white radicals the Panthers were even able to try to field Cleaver as a presidential candidate.

The movement's magazine, *Black Panther*, indulged in an orgy of violent rhetoric, aimed chiefly at the police, whom they had christened 'the pigs'. For example, in 1967 an article urged: 'we must step up our sniping – until the last pig is dead, shot to death with his own gun and the bullets in his guts that he had meant for the people.' In fact, more Panther effort went into providing free school breakfasts, free medical services and other community work than into any violent attacks. But the FBI and city police departments were more impressed by the Panthers' rhetoric of violence and guerrilla warfare than by their pretentions to peaceful organisation. Huey Newton was wounded and arrested in October 1967 during an encounter in which a policeman was killed. In April 1968 Cleaver was arrested after a 90-minute gun-battle between police and Panthers in Oakland. Soon after, 21 Panthers were rounded up in New York on a variety of serious charges. Bobby Seale was charged with conspiracy after the August 1968 Chicago anti-war demonstration. During 1969, as part of President Nixon's law and order crackdown, 348 Panthers were arrested. In early December there were gun battles with police in Los Angeles and Chicago as Panthers resisted arrest; in the Chicago operation, it has been alleged that a Panther leader, Fred Hampton, was shot dead by police officers while he was asleep in bed. The various Panther trials became a focus for liberal concern, since there was a widespread belief the proceedings would not be fair. In fact, the courts operated properly, and a remarkably high proportion of Panthers were cleared.

A question of violence

But it was internal dissension, not police action, that broke the movement. In late 1968 Eldridge Cleaver, out on parole, fled the country, going first to Cuba and then settling in Algiers. From the safety of exile he incited the Panthers to 'go underground' into urban guerrilla warfare. But the leadership knew the mood in the ghettos was changing; after April 1968, there were to be no more ghetto riots on the scale of those of earlier years. Huey Newton pursued a policy of stepping up community activities to win popular support and extending links with other leftist groups to form a broad-based revolutionary vanguard party. Into the 1970s, membership fell and relations between Cleaver and Newton worsened. In 1970 Newton could still manage grandiose gestures: he wrote to Hanoi offering 'an undetermined number of troops to assist you in your fight against American imperialism', and called a convention to draw up a new US constitution. But in March 1971, 13 of the 21 Panthers on trial in New York were expelled from the party for advocating violence. Fighting broke out between the two factions, and the decline of the movement was complete.

The Panthers were part of a general confrontation between blacks and white authority involving many other armed groups, spontaneous rioters and individual snipers. Although they killed a number of policemen – mostly in what they called 'self-defense' actions – and obtained much of their funding by robbery and extortion, they never systematically practised terrorism, let alone guerrilla warfare. It was their violent political rhetoric and the appeal they held for white radicals and liberals that brought them fame; otherwise, their attempts to form an American revolutionary organisation were abortive and their supposed part in a global revolutionary struggle a fantasy.

But the Panthers were not the only dissidents of the time. The Weatherman group grew out of the leading white radical student organisation in the 1960s, Students for a Democratic Society (SDS), which won its spurs in the civil rights movement and then became heavily involved in the anti-war campaign. Years of political agitation and confrontation turned the SDS from a pressure group in the Democratic Party to an extreme left 'student power' movement allied to Maoists and dedicated to the overthrow of the entire American 'military-industrial complex'. In June 1969 the SDS split, the dominant faction declaring itself for a revolutionary alliance with black power groups and the Third World and aligning itself with the Panthers. It published the first Weatherman manifesto – a name taken from a line in a Bob Dylan song, 'You don't need a weatherman to know which way the wind blows' – stating that the 'struggle within the US' would play a vital part in the 'destruction of US imperialism' which would, however, largely result from US military defeat abroad. In October 1969, the Weathermen made their first notable contribution to this struggle in the 'Days of Rage', when they went on the rampage in the streets of Chicago dressed in

Below: Timothy Leary holds court in New York in 1968, at the height of unrest over the Vietnam War. Leary was an enthusiastic proponent of a counter-culture based on drugs and 'free love'. On his right is Abbie Hoffmann, author of *Revolution for the hell of it* and on his left Jerry Rubin, author of the outrageous tract *Do it!* and founder of the 'Yippies'. It was from the Utopian radicalism of this period that small groups of more violent revolutionaries such as Weatherman emerged. In 1970 the Weathermen rescued Leary from the prison in which he was serving a sentence for a drugs offence, and helped him escape to Algeria.

Above: Bernadine Dohrn, who followed Timothy Leary into an Algerian exile in 1970. A founding member of Weatherman, she was on the FBI's list of the 10 most wanted criminals, for alleged 'inter-state flight, mob action, riot and conspiracy.'

combat boots and helmets, destroying property and starting fires. In the aftermath of this riot, with most of the Weatherman leadership indicted on major charges, they took the decision to abandon all legal political activity and 'go underground'.

Unlike the Panthers, the Weathermen had no tradition of violence in their background; they came from respectable, well-off families and had mostly been 'good children' at school and home. Also unlike the blacks, they had no community to defend; it was their own society they hated. The influences on them were not only the New Left enthusiasms for Che Guevara and Ho Chi Minh, but also the hippy sub-culture of psychedelic drugs and 'free love'. They were fascinated by Charles Manson and his murdering commune, and their most spectacular action was to spring Timothy Leary, the prophet of LSD and drug culture, out of San Luis Obispo prison and arrange his escape to join Cleaver in exile in Algiers. Most of the Weathermen were sold on the cult of violence for its own sake – the theory of 'personal cleansing' through violence proposed by writer Franz Fanon. In a widely

quoted statement, Mark Rudd, perhaps the most aggressive of the group, asserted: 'It's a wonderful feeling to *hit* a pig. It must be a really wonderful feeling to *kill* a pig or blow up a building.'

The Panthers were at first enthusiastic about the Weathermen, but relations soon cooled. A Panther leader described the movement as 'anarchistic, adventuristic, chauvinistic, masochistic and Custeristic.' Certainly, with no support outside the underground of 'drop-outs', it was hard to see where Weatherman terrorism could lead. In 1970 they bombed, among other targets, the New York City police headquarters and a branch of the Bank of America, but their inexperienced home bomb-making was more dangerous to themselves than to others – in March three Weathermen were killed in an explosion that destroyed their New York 'bomb factory'.

Scattered Weatherman bomb attacks and communiqués continued into the mid 1970s, but the tide of revolt ebbed and left them stranded. The killing of four white students at Kent State University and of two black students at Jackson State College during anti-war demonstrations in May 1970 produced the most powerful wave of student protest: some 350 colleges went on strike and at 30 of them buildings were set on fire. Yet radical activists failed to capture the moment; SDS was weakened and divided, the Weathermen isolated by their terrorism, and the crisis subsided without consequence. By 1973 American troops were out of Vietnam, Mao had shaken Richard Nixon's hand, Che and Ho were long dead, and calm returned to the campuses with a new generation.

The Patty Hearst affair

The Weatherman movement was just alive enough in 1974 to salute the activities of a successor, the Symbionese Liberation Army (SLA). The SLA's claim to fame is that in February of that year they kidnapped Patty Hearst, grand-daughter of America's most famous newspaper millionaire. When Patty Hearst, having sided with her captors, was photographed taking part in an SLA bank raid, the affair became a media sensation. The core of the SLA were killed in a dramatic shoot-out with police in Los Angeles in May 1974, but Hearst and some others were not captured until September of the following year. The SLA was based on a commune of students, graduates and Vietnam veterans who had come under the influence of a black criminal, Donald DeFreeze, who called himself Cinque Mtume, the Fifth Prophet. With their ideology no more than a jumble of revolutionary slogans and half-baked mysticism, they presented a fitting caricature to close the golden years of would-be revolutionary movements in the United States.

The major effect of the evolution of black and student movements towards violence and the rhetoric of global revolution was to ensure that no radical 'third party' emerged in the US political system out of the fervour of the late 1960s. Their only contribution to 'world revolution' lay in the impact of black power and anti-war sentiment on morale and discipline in the US Army, which was certainly weakened as an agent of US government policy. Violence proved a poor tactic in a society where government legitimacy was strong and firm action by the authorities could expect widespread support. Revolution in the United States was an impossibility. **R.G. Grant**

The kidnapping and indoctrination of wealthy heiress Patty Hearst by the Symbionese Liberation Army (left, an SLA-released photograph and below a bank security picture taken during a raid) was one of the more bizarre episodes in the history of US radical violence. After her capture by the police, Patty Hearst served a prison term.

Terror from the east
The Japanese Red Army

The Japanese Red Army (later known as the United Red Army or Rengo Sekigun in Japanese) first made headlines in the world press in May 1972, when three of its members attacked passengers at Lod international airport near Tel Aviv, killing 28 people and wounding many more. It was the organisation's most 'successful' act of terrorism and the only one of major significance. The Red Army probably never numbered more than 40 or 50 active members, with 300 or 400 supporters, and it had a relatively short life.

The collapse of the revolutionary student movement in Japan in the 1960s, in the face of stern measures adopted by the Japanese police, forced the more extreme and determined elements to look abroad for support and scope for their activities. In the words of a member of the Red Army: 'Japanese society today is so rigid and dominated by the past that it is impossible for us to change it. So we are forced into violence and revolution. But in Japan today even revolution is not yet possible. So we are forced to go international if we wish to do something to change the corrupt state of the world.'

Out of this situation at the end of the 1960s the Japanese Red Army emerged, consisting of young, mainly middle-class, fanatical students, with no clearly defined ideology or organisation. As an example of the sort of person attracted by the Red Army, we can take Fusako Shigenobu, a woman then in her twenties. The Japanese police believe she played a leading part in every one of the Red Army's acts of terrorism and was primarily responsible for establishing links with the Popular Front for the Liberation of Palestine (PFLP). Daughter of a retired primary-school teacher, she studied first in a commercial college and later at a Tokyo university, where she became involved in student politics. But she always remained an eccentric, independent-minded activist, who dressed well.

used make-up and wore a hat and white gloves even for the rough and tumble of student demonstrations. Dismissing the orthodox communists as too devious and calculating, Shigenobu joined the Red Army and soon rose to a leading position.

The Red Army's first serious attack took place in March 1970, when nine of its members hijacked a Japanese airliner and forced it to take them to North Korea, where they hoped to find a base for their operations. But the communist authorities in North Korea did not give them the warm welcome they expected, with the result that they were forced to remain there, in the words of one observer, 'impotent revolutionaries under the eyes of their suspicious hosts'.

There followed a year of more internal squabbling which ended in February 1972, when the Japanese police stormed a mountain lodge 150 km (90 miles) from Tokyo, captured Tsuneo Mori, the 27-year-old leader of the United Red Army, and exposed a gruesome story of internal strife and bloodletting. Mori admitted responsibility for the murder, or execution, of 12 members of the organisation who had been sentenced to death at mock trials for having deviated from the army's policies. It was then revealed that the Red Army had been planning a series of armed attacks on leading figures in the Japanese government.

The attack at Lod marked the peak of the Red Army's terrorist campaign, although the organisation resurfaced from time to time in the 1970s. In July 1973, for example, in cooperation with the Palestinians they hijacked a Japan Airlines plane to Dubai where they blew it up. In September 1974 four members of the organisation seized 11 hostages in the

Above: Well-equipped Japanese student demonstrators prepare to take on riot police. Although the individuals may have seemed better prepared for street violence than their European counterparts, the Japanese student movement of the 1960s met the same blank wall of indifference as a prosperous society refused to take radical attitudes seriously. It was this frustration that led to the creation of terrorist groups like the Red Army.

Left and below: A Japanese airliner burns fiercely on an airstrip in Dubai after being hijacked by a joint team from the Red Army and the Popular Front for the Liberation of Palestine in July 1973. The hijackers destroyed the plane when their demands for the release of captured terrorist, Okamoto, were not met.

French embassy in The Hague and demanded a million dollars ransom and the release of Yutaka Furuya, who had been arrested by the French police when he was found to be carrying three false passports, $10,000 in counterfeit money and plans for a campaign of terrorism in western Europe. The French authorities agreed to release Furuya in exchange for the freeing of the hostages. The terrorists then returned $300,000 they had received from the French, who provided a plane to fly them to Damascus, where they were handed over to the Palestine Liberation Organisation (PLO). The government of Syria promised them safe conduct to a country of their choice. But the PLO office in Paris denied that it had any responsibility for the embassy raid.

The Red Army carried out a number of further attacks on embassies, kidnapped diplomats in Southeast Asia, and hijacked a ferry-boat in Singapore in 1974 after failing in an attempt to sabotage an oil refinery. In August 1975 Red Army terrorists stormed the American embassy in Kuala Lumpur in Malaysia, seized hostages and demanded the release of five of their colleagues under arrest in Japan. The Japanese government gave in to their demands.

Suicide commandos

In 1976 the Red Army went through a process of reorganisation and rethinking of its aims. Its leaders appeared no longer to be on close terms with the PFLP and to have decided in favour of direct action in Japan itself. By 1977 the Red Army had been reduced to a small group of fanatics who were in dire need of wider support which they began to seek outside their own dwindling ranks. This was apparent in their next major operation: the hijacking of a Japan Airlines DC-8 with 142 passengers and 14 crew aboard at Dacca airport in Bangladesh. The hijackers demanded the release of terrorists held in Japanese prisons, not all of them, as in the past, members of the Red Army. The Japanese government decided to agree to the terrorists' demands in order to prevent loss of life. But when, on 15 October 1977, a Red Army 'suicide commando' seized a bus with 15 passengers in Nagasaki the police refused to accede to the demands made, stormed the bus, killing one terrorist and capturing the others.

Compared to their allies in the Middle East, the Japanese Red Army were very unsuccessful. But whereas the Palestinian guerrillas had a concrete aim (the restoration of their homeland) with which most of the inhabitants of the numerous refugee camps around Israel could identify, all the leaders of the Red Army could offer a prosperous Japan was the remote prospect of 'changing the world'. Terrorism therefore became an end in itself. **David Floyd**

The Lod airport massacre

Left: Blood and bags in the lounge at Lod. Above: The captured terrorist, Okamoto.

At about 2200 hours on 30 May 1972, 116 passengers from Air France flight 132 filed into the customs area at Lod airport near Tel Aviv. Among them were three Japanese terrorists, Red Army supporters of the Popular Front for the Liberation of Palestine.

With passports checked and cleared, the passengers moved into the baggage area where their luggage was arriving on conveyor number three. The three terrorists, apparently innocent tourists as they mingled with the crowds, moved closer to the conveyor belt. Suddenly they leapt forward and seized their cases. In one smooth movement they unzipped them and extracted three stockless sub-machine guns, ammunition and grenades. Strangely calm in their manner, the gunmen opened fire on the roughly 300 passengers waiting in the baggage area. Panic filled the hall. One of the terrorists approached a floor-to-ceiling glass partition which separated the customs hall from the waiting area and emptied his magazine into the crowds beyond it. Then grenades were thrown wherever large groups of people had congregated, causing widespread casualties. As soon as the terrorists had emptied their magazines they reloaded and continued to fire.

One terrorist fired out towards aircraft on the runway. As he did so he stumbled and dropped a grenade. There was a loud explosion and he was killed instantly. Another guerrilla raced out onto the runway shooting at everyone in sight. As he passed an aircraft he threw a grenade between its wheels, discarded his weapon and ran off into the darkness, but an El Al mechanic successfully tackled him.

Among the blood-spattered pillars and chairs in the baggage area, the captured terrorist later identified the body of the third member of the gang. In a period of less than four minutes the attack had resulted in 28 dead and hundreds seriously wounded.

JAPAN AIR LINES

White negroes
FLQ terrorism in French Canada

The province of Quebec is the largest in area of the ten provinces of Canada and, with a population of nearly 6,500,000, it accounts for more than a quarter of Canada's total population. But Quebec is distinguished from the rest of Canada by the fact that four-fifths of its population are French-Canadian, speaking French, admiring French culture and claiming descent from the French who founded the colony of 'New France' in the 16th century.

The British formally took over in 1763, imposing British rule and law over all the provinces. The 'Quebeckers', as they are now called, resented their position and revolts against the rule of Britain and its English-speaking Canadian successors broke out from time to time through the succeeding centuries.

The provincial government of Quebec from 1944 to 1959 was aligned with the more conservative elements in Canadian political life, but an important change came about as a result of the victory of the Quebec Liberal Party in the 1959 election. The Liberals proceeded to introduce a series of reforms greatly improving the position of the French-speaking population. There remained, however, many who were not satisfied with gradual reform and who sought complete independence.

The Quebeckers' continuing resentment was founded on genuine economic grievances. A Royal Commission appointed to examine the situation reported that in 1964 more than three-quarters of the better-paid jobs in the province were filled by members of the English-speaking minority, whereas the French-speakers, who accounted for about half the total workforce, had 80 per cent of the low-paid jobs. Unemployment had long been higher in Quebec than in the rest of Canada. Only 15 per cent of local industry was owned by French Canadians, due to the predominance of US companies.

In 1963 extreme elements among the separatists began to resort to terrorism and urban guerrilla warfare to obtain their ends, forming the Front de Libération du Québec (FLQ), a loosely-knit organisation committed to a campaign of bombing, armed robbery, kidnapping and murder. The FLQ combined separatism with an extreme left-wing ideology, presenting its activities as an 'anti-colonial' struggle and part of a worldwide revolt against US power – a view given some semblance of credibility by the weighty presence of US business interests in Quebec. 'The revolution cannot, alas, be achieved without the spilling of blood,' the FLQ's leaders declared. They rejected any idea of operating through constitutional, democratic institutions: the FLQ was to be 'perfectly revolutionary', deliberately provoking open conflict with the Canadian authorities.

Most FLQ members were students or unemployed

workers under the age of 25, whose rhetoric hid a lack of any previous experience of politics or armed revolt. But some leaders brought practical skills to the organisation – like Georges Schoeters who had been in the Belgian resistance during World War II and received guerrilla-warfare training in Cuba and Algeria, and François Schirm who had seen action with the French in Indochina and Algeria. Theoretical justification for the FLQ was provided by Pierre Vallières, a journalist born in a poor district of Montreal; a renegade from the Communist Party, Vallières connected the FLQ with the theories of the international New Left.

A terrorist campaign

The first FLQ campaign began in March 1963 with bomb attacks on three army depots in Montreal, followed by other terrorist acts including planting bombs in mailboxes in a well-off English-speaking suburb. A series of arrests in June 1963 broke the original FLQ organisation, but in 1966 a new campaign was launched with the bombing of factories in support of workers involved in industrial action. Once more, arrests swiftly followed, including that of Vallières who was convicted of manslaughter and given a life sentence.

Meanwhile, pressure for an independent but non-revolutionary Quebec was growing, and it received unexpected support from France, which had traditionally done little to encourage the Quebeckers. In 1965 the French government concluded a cultural agreement with the Quebec provincial government, by-passing Ottawa, and in 1967 the French president, Charles de Gaulle, visited Montreal, promised economic aid to the province and concluded a speech to a mass meeting with the words: 'Vive le Québec! Vive le Québec libre! Vive le Canada français!' This highly provocative appeal caused consternation in Ottawa but was not followed by any effective measures from

Paris. In October 1968, however, a separatist party, the Parti Québecois, was formed by a breakaway from the Liberal Party under the leadership of René Levesque. In the election of 1970 Levesque's new party obtained 24 per cent of the vote.

Against this background of rising support for separatism and of student and labour unrest, the FLQ launched a major campaign in 1969. Targets of attack included banks and the Montreal Stock Exchange. Vigorous action by the authorities failed to stop FLQ operations, and in October 1969 the Montreal police and firemen, who had borne the brunt of the conflict, went on strike. For two days Montreal was left to the mercy of FLQ sympathisers and vandals.

In 1970, after some of its members had been trained at a Palestinian guerrilla-warfare camp, the FLQ announced a switch in policy. 'For too long the FLQ has been synonymous with bombs and useless violence.' Their policy was now to be 'selective assassination.' On 5 October they kidnapped James Cross, the British trade commissioner, and made seven demands in return for his freedom, including the release of 23 prisoners, their free passage to Algiers or Cuba, and the broadcast of an FLQ 'manifesto'. The Quebec government of Prime Minister Robert Bourassa agreed to broadcast the manifesto, which was the occasion for demonstrations of student and trade union support for the terrorists' aims, but did not release the prisoners. On 10 October another FLQ cell kidnapped Pierre Laporte, the Quebec minister of labour and immigration.

As police searches for the hostages went on, the Quebec government sought to negotiate their release, but the Federal government, on the initiative of Prime Minister Pierre Trudeau, decided to act with all the resources at its command. 'It is only weak-kneed, bleeding hearts who are afraid to take these measures,' Trudeau said. On 16 October he invoked the

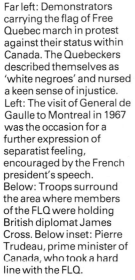

Far left: Demonstrators carrying the flag of Free Quebec march in protest against their status within Canada. The Quebeckers described themselves as 'white negroes' and nursed a keen sense of injustice.
Left: The visit of General de Gaulle to Montreal in 1967 was the occasion for a further expression of separatist feeling, encouraged by the French president's speech.
Below: Troops surround the area where members of the FLQ were holding British diplomat James Cross. Below inset: Pierre Trudeau, prime minister of Canada, who took a hard line with the FLQ.

War Measures Act, outlawing the FLQ and similar organisations and greatly increasing the power of the police. Units of the Canadian Army were sent to Montreal. In a matter of days the police had rounded up 242 people connected with separatist movements of various colours.

The FLQ struck back immediately. On 17 October 1970 it announced. 'Faced with the arrogance of the Federal government and of its valet Bourassa the FLQ has decided to act. Pierre Laporte . . . was executed at 6.18 tonight by the Dieppe cell.' Laporte's body was discovered in the boot of a car: he had been strangled.

In December, 59 days after Laporte's death, James Cross, the other captive, was saved by the determination and skill of the Canadian police. They discovered where he was being held and surrounded the building. The FLQ realised that the game was up and offered to negotiate. The talks took place in the Canadian pavilion on St Helen's Island in the middle of the St Lawrence River. The pavilion had been declared Cuban territory for the purpose of arranging the exchange. At one side of the room were the heavily-armed kidnappers, carrying primed sticks of dynamite. Cross and a British colleague stood at the other end of the room, 9 m (30 feet) away. It seemed unlikely that the encounter would end peacefully, until relatives of the kidnappers arrived and they were escorted to a Cuban plane and flown to Havana. Only then was Cross free to leave the building.

That marked the end of the FLQ's terrorist activi-

ties for some time, and revealed the bankruptcy of their strategy. They had provoked the government into emergency measures, but the Quebeckers had by and large supported Prime Minister Trudeau's uncompromising stand. The FLQ's support in the trade unions and the student body largely evaporated after the cold-blooded killing of Pierre Laporte. The 'October Days' of 1970 did not produce any lasting solution to the problems of the 'white negroes of America', as the Quebeckers have been called, but demonstrated at least that they would not support brutal terrorism against a democratic government that had the will to defend itself.   **David Floyd**

Above, inset left: Pierre Laporte, whose body was discovered in the boot of a car (above). Above, inset right: James Cross, whose whereabouts was discovered after intensive searches by the Canadian police. Indeed, efficient policework eventually led to the successful capture and arrest of three of the FLQ members connected with the Laporte murder (below).

Key Weapons

THE GALIL ASSAULT RIFLE

When the Israeli Defence Force (IDF) came into being in 1948, it was armed with whatever it could obtain, and the infantry rifle was usually the British .303in Lee-Enfield or German 7.92mm Kar 98k. In the 1950s they were replaced by the well-known FN FAL rifle in 7.62mm Nato calibre, a choice which was economically sound and which ensured that irrespective of political alignments there would always be a source of spare parts and ammunition. But after the Six-Day War of 1967 it was decided to equip the Israeli Army with a modern 5.56mm rifle, and competitive trails of several designs were held. The American M16 and Stoner 63, the Soviet AK-47, a proposal by Uziel Gal (designer of the famous Uzi sub-machine gun), a design by Israel Galil and Yakov Lior, and one or two others were all put through their paces. The field trials were exceptionally severe and none of the prototypes met the stringent requirements laid down by the IDF, but the Galil was nearest and the inventors won the annual Israeli Defence Award in 1969.

The next two or three years were taken up in modifying and retesting the rifle until in the spring of 1973 it was formally adopted as the official service rifle of the IDF, replacing the FN FAL. In addition it replaced the FN general purpose machine gun in the squad automatic role, as well as replacing the Uzi sub-machine gun in some other roles. Production, however, was slow to get under way and the Galil was not in service in any great numbers in time for the Yom Kippur War of October 1973. It has, though, seen a good deal of combat employment since then.

The Galil is a gas-operated weapon, which relies heavily on the AK-47 and its Finnish variant, the Valmet M62, since the general system of operation is identical. There is a gas cylinder above the barrel in which a piston-rod operates. Between the barrel and the cylinder is a fixed-aperture gas port, through which gas is tapped from behind the bullet to drive the piston backwards. The piston bears on the end of the bolt carrier, the upper part of which is tubular and acts as a seat for the return spring. The lower part carries the bolt, and inside this carrier is a cam slot engaging with a pin in the bolt. As the bolt carrier is driven back, so the cam slot causes the pin to move sideways, rotating the bolt to unlock it from the breech. As soon as the bolt is unlocked, the continued rearward movement of the carrier withdraws it, extracting the spent case and ejecting it. The final movement of the bolt and carrier assembly forces the firing hammer downwards until it is retained by the sear. The return spring then expands, driving the carrier forward; the bolt collects a fresh cartridge from the magazine, mounted below the receiver, and feeds it into the chamber. The bolt comes to a stop, but the carrier continues so that the cam slot now turns the bolt in the opposite direction, locking its lugs into recesses in the barrel. Pressure on the trigger then releases the hammer, which rises to strike the firing pin and begin the sequence over again.

There is a selector switch on the side of the rifle which has three settings: safe, automatic and repetition. When set at automatic, the action is as described above, but the hammer is held by an auxiliary sear until the bolt has closed and locked, whereupon the auxiliary sear is released by the movement of the carrier and the hammer comes up to fire the next round; the firer has held the trigger pressed during all this.

Previous page: Two Israeli infantrymen, armed with Galil ARM rifles, stand in front of a UN observer in Beirut. Above: Israeli troops take their ease in Lebanon; the soldier kneeling is armed with the SAR version of the Galil. Left: An Israeli soldier prepares to loose a rifle grenade from his Galil. Note the small 12-round magazine. Right: Israeli troops rest, with ARMs alongside, bipods lowered.

Additional features of the Galil include a bipod (which can also be used as a wire-cutter), a flash hider on the muzzle, and a folding shoulder-stock of tubular steel. The foresight is a post, protected by a circular hood, and the rear sight is a two-position flip aperture set for 300m (330yds) and 500m (550yds) range. In addition there are night sights: two small leaves, one above the rear sight and one behind the foresight, which can be flipped up to expose Tritium luminous spots, two at the rear and one at the front. By lining up these three dots with the target, quite reasonable shooting can be done in poor light.

There are three magazines – based on the US Stoner magazine – for 12, 35 and 50 rounds. The 12-round magazine is intended only for use with grenade-launching cartridges, while the 50-round magazine is for use when the Galil is being employed as a light machine gun. In the normal rifle-role the 35-round magazine is standard.

This basic model of the Galil is known as the ARM (assault rifle and machine gun) model, and it was soon followed by two modified versions: the AR (assault rifle) which is the same as the ARM but without the bipod; and the SAR (short assault rifle) which is the same as the AR but has a barrel 33cm (13in) long instead of the 46cm (18in) of the AR. When the shoulder-stock is folded the SAR becomes a very convenient sub-machine gun.

In the late 1970s a 7.62mm model was developed, principally for export. This is precisely the same as the 5.56mm Galil except for the larger dimensions demanded by the larger bullet. The AR/ARM version has a 53cm (21in) barrel, and the SAR has a 43cm (17in) barrel, and both use a 25-round magazine.

In 1983 a new sniper model was announced. This uses the basic Galil action, in 7.62mm Nato calibre, but there are a number of features special to the model. The bipod is mounted behind the fore-end and attached to the receiver enabling it to be easily reached and adjusted by the firer and, in addition, ensuring that the barrel is not stressed in any way. The barrel is heavier than standard, contributing to the accuracy. The mounting for the telescope sight is on the side of the receiver and is a precision-cast long-base unit giving good support to the 6×40 Nimrod telescope sight supplied as standard. Both mount and sight can be quickly dismounted and replaced without disturbing the zeroing, and any type of night sight can be fitted to the mounting. The barrel is fitted with a muzzle brake and compensator which reduces jump.

The ARM with stock open (top) and – from the reverse side – with stock closed and carrying handle folded over (above centre). Above: The 5.56mm ARM Galil weapon system – three magazines of 12, 35 and 50 rounds capacity; bayonet and scabbard; three different types of rifle grenade. The carrying handle is in the up position and the selector switch is on 'S' for safety. Alongside the US M16 and the Belgian FN FNC the Galil ARM is a leader in the field of 5.56mm assault rifles.

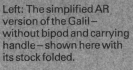

Main picture: Armed with an array of Galil assault rifles, Israeli troops parade by their national flag. The Galil proved itself to be a highly effective combat weapon during the Israeli invasion of Lebanon in 1982.

Left: The simplified AR version of the Galil — without bipod and carrying handle — shown here with its stock folded.

The short-barrelled SAR Galil with stock open (left) and folded (below left). Below: The 7.62mm sniper variant of the Galil. Besides the powerful telescopic sight, other features of this weapon include a special sharpshooter's rifle sling, a folding wooden stock with recoil pad and cheek piece, and a two-stage trigger. This model employs the standard 7.62mm Nato round.

Right: Israeli troops armed with two very different 5.56mm smallarms – the Galil ARM and the M16. Below: With APCs at the rear, Israeli troops stand guard armed with Galils.

Galil Assault Rifle

barrel — gas cylinder — front-sight assembly — night sight (folded) — gas block — piston — carrying handle — cocking handle — bolt carrier — return spring — hammer — night sight (folded) — back-sight assembly — safety catch — folding stock — flash suppressor — barbed-wire cutter — bipod (folded) — fore grip — bolt — magazine — magazine catch — trigger — sear — selector lever — grip

Galil AR/ARM Assault Rifle

Calibre 5.56mm
Length 97.9cm (38½in) with stock extended; 74.2cm (29in) with stock folded
Weight (loaded with 35-round magazine) 4.91kg (10.8lb)
Rate of fire Cyclic 650rpm; auto 105rpm; semi-auto 40rpm
Maximum effective range 500m (550 yds)
Ammunition Ball, blank, grenade-launching
Magazine 12-, 35- and 50-round box
Cartridge M193 5.56 × 45mm
Muzzle velocity 980m/s (3215fps)

Above: A group of South African infantrymen stand beside a mortar armed with R4 rifles, the locally-manufactured version of the Galil. Below: Although very similar to the Israeli Galil, the R4 has a number of different features, most notably a redesigned hand guard, a longer butt and the use of carbon-fibre.

It is possible to remove this unit and replace it with a silencer if desired. There is a two-stage trigger without provision for automatic fire. The stock is of wood, but it can still be folded forward in order to reduce the overall length for stowage or travelling. The butt is fitted with a recoil pad and cheek-piece, both of which can be adjusted to suit the firer. During trials, all shots fired at 300m (330yds) range came within a 15cm (6in) circle.

The Galil rifle has been purchased by a number of armies. One interesting adaptation has been by the

South African Army who have lengthened the butt, to better suit the larger physique of South African troops, and have replaced the tubular steel with a carbon fibre material which is stronger than steel and which does not get so hot in the high temperatures found in the African bush. This is now in full production in South Africa as the R4 rifle. The Dutch company of NWM has shown a considerable interest in the Galil and has been granted a licence to manufacture the Galil as the MN1. As with the R4, the MN1 fires the 5.56mm round.

The War of Attrition

Israel and
Egypt
locked in a
war of nerves

On the conclusion of the Six-Day War in June 1967, Israel's leaders hoped that the great territorial gains, the assertion of military supremacy, and the attainment of defensible boundaries on the Suez Canal, the Jordan River and the Golan Heights would force neighbouring Arab powers to open peace negotiations that would include recognition of the Israeli state. In fact, however, after the whirlwind series of defeats and the loss of so much territory, the Arabs were in no mood for reconciliation. At the Khartoum Summit Conference of Arab States in September 1967 a resolution was passed to the effect that there would be no recognition of Israel, no negotiations with Israel, and no peace with Israel. At the same time, the Soviet Union, whose credibility throughout the Middle East had been seriously strained by the events of the war, began re-arming Egypt and Syria with modern equipment and aircraft. For their part, the victorious Israelis saw no need to make concessions, and so the scene was set for more violence.

The first clash had already taken place on 1 July 1967, only three weeks after the war had officially ended. An Israeli patrol was ambushed on the east bank of the Canal, some 15km (10 miles) south of Port Said. The affair quickly escalated into a series of tank and artillery exchanges across the water, accompanied by air battles in which the Egyptians lost seven aircraft at no cost to the Israelis. At sea, the Israeli destroyer *Eilat* (formerly HMS *Zealous*) and two patrol boats were attacked off Romani by Egyptian torpedo boats, two of which were sunk. After a fortnight's sporadic fighting a short period of calm descended on the front.

Following the Khartoum Summit in September, however, Nasser publicly affirmed that the lull was a temporary one and would last only as long as the Egyptians wished it to. He was fully aware that Israel's limited manpower resources were its Achilles' heel and could be exploited. Israel could neither keep its reserve formations in the field for long without seriously damaging its economy, nor afford to expose its small regular army to the inevitable casualties which would result from a positional contest of attrition. It was just such a contest that Nasser intended to impose, dividing his strategy into three distinct phases: 'defensive rehabilitation', designed to restore the strength, confidence and morale of the Egyptian armed forces; 'offensive defence', intended to harry the Israelis on their own ground; and finally, a 'liberation' phase, in which the lost territory in Sinai would be recovered. His attempts to implement this policy, commencing in the autumn of 1967 and lasting intermittently until 1970, are now collectively termed the War of Attrition, although the term is often

The resumption of hostilities between Egypt and Israel, only three weeks after the end of the Six-Day War, in the form of brief exchanges of fire across the Suez Canal, ended any hopes that Egypt would recognise Israel's territorial gains. Then, the sinking of the Israeli destroyer *Eilat* (inset below) in October 1967 stimulated an Israeli bombing raid against Egyptian oil refineries (bottom, burning fiercely).

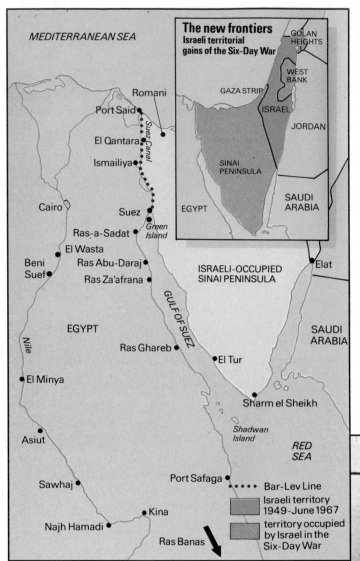

used to describe merely the most intense phase, between the spring of 1969 and the ceasefire in August 1970.

The 'defensive rehabilitation' phase began in September 1967 and involved heavy artillery duels across the Canal. The Egyptians deployed by far the greater number of weapons, although most of the Israeli guns were self-propelled and better handled. During these exchanges the towns of El Qantara, Ismailiya and Suez were virtually wrecked and some 750,000 refugees fled from the Canal area further into Egypt. For a short period the guns fell silent, but on 21 October the *Eilat*, patrolling some 24km (15 miles) off Port Said, was struck by a succession of Styx surface-to-surface missiles launched from a Komar-class missile boat anchored inside the harbour, and sank with the loss of 47 lives. This was the first occasion on which a warship had been sunk by guided weapons and the incident naturally attracted intense interest in naval circles. Four days later the Israelis took their revenge, firing such a heavy bombardment into the oil refineries at Suez that they blazed for several days, the scale of the loss being estimated by the Egyptians themselves at £36 million. This, together with the cost of continued mobilisation, the loss of revenue from the closed Canal and the collapse of the tourist industry, brought Egypt to the verge of bankruptcy and a massive injection of Soviet and

Arab funds was needed to keep the government solvent.

On 22 November the UN Security Council passed Resolution 242, the main points of which were that Israel should withdraw from the territory captured during the Six-Day War in return for Arab recognition of its sovereignty and territorial integrity. Egypt, Jordan and Israel accepted the Resolution in principle but were not prepared to implement its provisions.

Meanwhile, following the destruction of the Suez refineries, hostile activities across the Canal had tailed off into sporadic exchanges and patrol clashes, but Russian MiG-21 fighters, T55 tanks and anti-aircraft weapons continued to pour into Egypt, accompanied by thousands of Soviet advisers who re-organised and retrained the armed services. By September 1968 Nasser had 150,000 fully-equipped troops deployed along the Canal and was able to announce that the 'defensive rehabilitation' phase was complete and that the period of 'offensive defence' would begin immediately.

This phrase consisted of even heavier bombardments than hitherto, as well as commando raids across the Canal and clandestine mining of roads in Sinai. The level of casualties inflicted on the Israelis was unacceptably high, and they were out-gunned by the Egyptian artillery. Consequently they had to find an indirect way of inducing the Egyptians to lessen their attacks. They decided to demonstrate that nowhere in Egypt could be considered safe, carrying out a deep-penetration heliborne commando raid on 31 October which blew up the Nile bridges at Kina and Najh Hamadi 480km (300 miles) south of Cairo, along with a nearby electric transformer station. The raid caused widespread consternation in Egypt and the tempo of operations along the Canal promptly slackened.

The pause gave the Israelis time to look to their own defences. The support of the United States made them sure that they could match any new weaponry supplied to Egypt by the Russians–indeed, in 1969 they began to take delivery of American multi-role F-4 Phantom fighters, the most advanced aircraft of its kind in the world. But the Egyptian artillery bombardments and raids had revealed the vulnerability of Israeli positions along the Canal. Major-General Yeshayahu Gavish, the General Officer Commanding Southern Command, and Major-General Avraham Adan both examined the problem, but complete agreement as to how the Canal was to be defended was never reached. For various reasons, including shortage of manpower and the time required by reserve formations to reach the front, a policy of full forward deployment was rejected in favour of a chain of fortified observation posts and a mobile response to

any attempted Egyptian crossing, to which end lateral roads were constructed some kilometres east of the Canal. The shell-proof observation posts themselves were reinforced with rails lifted from the trans-Sinai railway and were manned by 15-strong garrisons; although commonly known as the Bar-Lev Line (after the chief of staff, Lieutenant-General Chaim Bar-Lev), the positions possessed little of the long-term defensive capability that the title suggests.

In March 1969 fighting flared again along the Canal; in one of the artillery exchanges the Egyptian chief of staff, General Abd al Muneim Riadh, was killed together with several members of his staff. Still, Nasser was determined to press forward, and on 1 May he publicly renounced the ceasefire which had ended the Six-Day War and announced the opening of the 'liberation' phase of the conflict. This was to last for the next 16 months with barely a pause, rising to new levels of intensity in a dangerous escalation. At

Commando raids were a most effective Israeli tactic. Above: Training for night action. Below: A raid into Egypt. Bottom: The attack on Shadwan Island in the Gulf of Suez, December 1969, led to the capture of prisoners and the removal of military equipment (left).

The peace process

After the Six-Day War, an intense diplomatic effort was mounted in search of a peace settlement. Some form of settlement was recognised as desirable by all parties except by the Palestinians (who stood to lose from any deal between the Arab states and Israel) and their hardline backers in Syria and Algeria. In November 1967 the UN Security Council agreed on a British compromise proposal, Resolution 242, which was accepted by Israel, Egypt, Jordan and their superpower backers, the US and the USSR. Dr Gunnar Jarring, a Swedish diplomat, was sent by the UN to negotiate with the regional governments, but his mission proved fruitless.

Unfortunately, Resolution 242 was open to differing interpretations. The Arabs held that it meant the automatic return of all their territories seized by the Israelis, but the Israelis wished to use the return of territory as a bargaining counter to win concessions. What is more, Israel had no intention of handing back all the territory it had won; those areas considered vital to the country's security would not be returned, and Israeli settlers were soon arriving in the occupied territories and showing every intention of staying.

In April 1969 four-power talks began at the UN between the US, the USSR, Britain and France to seek a new formula for agreement. The growing Soviet involvement in Egypt and the hotting-up of the War of Attrition gave the peace process a new urgency, and in December 1969 US Secretary of State William Rogers announced the 'Rogers plan', basically a fairly strict interpretation of Resolution 242, calling for the withdrawal of Israel to its pre-war borders with only minor adjustments. Israeli reaction was hostile, but the Americans continued to supply them with large quantities of modern military equipment.

As the fighting worsened, Rogers renewed his peace effort with a call for a ceasefire. To the surprise of many observers, Nasser accepted this proposal in July 1970, and on 8 August Israel and Egypt ceased operations. There was, however, to be no immediate peace agreement between the Israelis and either Egypt or Jordan.

first, however, the new phase differed little from its predecessor, with intense artillery activity, commando raids, sniping and mine warfare. By July these tactics were having a serious effect on the Israelis.

The Israelis decided that the only way to persuade the Egyptians to stop their attacks was to step up their own military activity on two levels – by carrying out even more destructive surprise raids, and by using their air force as 'flying artillery' in response to Egypt's ground artillery strength. On 19 July commandos stormed the apparently impregnable coastal artillery fort on Green Island in the Gulf of Suez, inflicting heavy losses on the garrison, and withdrew after blowing up the guns and defences. In September, General Adan planned an even more daring operation. As a prelude, on 8 September frogmen sank two Egyptian torpedo boats at anchor at Ras-a-Sadat. The following day Israeli tank landing craft crossed the Gulf of Suez and landed a small battle-group consisting of four T55 tanks and three BTR-50 APCs which had been captured during the Six-Day War. The familiar vehicles aroused no suspicions until they actually opened fire. The battlegroup was ashore for eight hours, making a 50km (30-mile) run along the coast in which it destroyed the radar installations at Ras Abu-Daraj and Ras Za'afrana, raided outposts and camps and inflicted several hundred casualties which included a number of senior officers and their Soviet advisers. By the time the Egyptians had coordinated their response the task force had re-embarked and was on its way back across the Gulf, covered by the Israeli Air Force (IAF). The psychological shock generated by the raid was immense and Nasser sustained a heart attack shortly after the news was broken to him; in addition, the Egyptian chief of staff, the head of the navy, and the commander of the Red Sea sector were all dismissed.

Carrying off the quarry

Equally spectacular was a helicopter raid which eliminated the radar complex at Ras Ghareb in December 1969. This complex contained sophisticated P12 and P15 surface-to-air missile (SAM) control and target acquisition sets, which had just arrived from Russia, and after the garrison had been neutralised the two caravans which housed these were bodily lifted out by CH-53 helicopters and flown back to Sinai. The acquisition of this top-secret equipment materially assisted Israel and the West in the development of Electronic Counter-Measures (ECM).

Effective though these raids may have been, it was the Israeli General Staff's decision in July 1969 to employ the IAF as a direct counter to the Egyptians' artillery superiority that had most impact, both immediately and in the future. The IAF quickly secured complete air superiority above the Canal and during the next six months destroyed 48 Egyptian aircraft for the loss of five of its own. Simultaneously, Egyptian gun positions, radar installations and SAM sites along the Canal were attacked with devastating results.

At this period the Egyptians relied on the SAM-2 (Guideline) for their anti-aircraft defence. This was a medium-to-high altitude missile with an operational ceiling of 25,000m (82,000 feet) which had formed part of the Egyptian armoury since before the Six-Day War, in which it had failed to score a kill. It had put up an equally poor performance in Vietnam, where a visiting IAF team had been advised by the Americans that ECM existed which neutralised the SAM-2s

radar systems, and that the missile itself was unable to follow certain evasive movements taken by its target. The IAF therefore found no difficulty in eliminating the SAM-2 screen along the Canal, and such aircraft as it lost fell victim to the conventional anti-aircraft artillery with which the Egyptians protected their missile batteries.

Shattering Egyptian confidence

Egypt now lay virtually defenceless against air attack and in January 1970 the Israelis took the perhaps unwise decision to embark on a policy of long-range bombing, deliberately selecting targets within a 40km (25-mile) radius of Cairo. The objective was to convince the Egyptian public that Israel was winning the War of Attrition; and to emphasise the fact, IAF jets repeatedly flew low over the capital, shattering windows with their sonic bangs. In desperation Nasser turned to the Soviet Union for practical and prompt assistance; this request was immediately granted. A complete Soviet air defence division began arriving in Egypt in February, bringing with it SAM-3 (Goa) low-altitude missiles, which covered part of the gap left by the SAM-2. The Russians did not believe that their hosts were capable of manning these efficiently and in effect took over the entire air defence of the country.

Their confidence restored by Soviet backing, the Egyptians resumed shelling along the Canal, and both sides continued to raid each other's positions. On 22 January 1970 the IDF had successfully assaulted the island of Shadwan, some 30km (20 miles) from Sharm el Sheikh, killing 30 Egyptian soldiers, sinking two torpedo boats, and carrying off prisoners and military equipment. In February, the Egyptians recorded noteworthy successes: their frogmen sunk a vessel in the Israeli port of Elat, the ambush of an Israeli armoured patrol on the East Bank inflicted eight casualties, and reconnaissance patrols penetrated as far as the Mitla Pass. The Egyptian Air Force also returned to the attack and carried out a series of tip-and-run raids, although it sustained losses that were not commensurate with the results achieved. There were fierce dogfights over the Canal in February and March in which some 20 Egyptian aircraft were shot down.

For their part, the Israelis were becoming increasingly aware of the Soviet presence and on 24 March the IAF mounted a major attack on the newly-installed missile sites and radar stations, putting them out of action. By Herculean efforts the Russians made good the damage in a single night, only to have their work destroyed again the following day. The bombing of targets deep inside Egypt continued.

To confront the Israeli air offensive, the Soviet build-up gathered momentum. By April there were some 15,000 Soviet personnel in Egypt, and in the middle of that month Russian pilots began to fly combat patrols in defence of central Egypt. To avoid direct confrontation with the Russians and a possible escalation of the conflict, the IAF abandoned its deep-penetration raids and confined its activities to the Canal zone, save for a foray into the Red Sea on 16 May when an Egyptian destroyer and a missile boat were sunk off Ras Banas on the Sudanese border.

The ending of bombing in central Egypt was a boost to Egyptian morale. Israeli casualties were mounting: in January 1970 only six Israelis had been killed along the Canal, but in the three months from

March to May there were some 70 Israeli dead. The Israeli response was an intensive 11-day bombing campaign against Egyptian positions along the Canal, beginning on 30 May. Over 4000 bombs were dropped in one week of the campaign.

Desperate to find an answer to Israeli command of the air, the Russians rethought their air defence strategy. Instead of siting their missiles in individual batteries along the Canal, they concentrated them in a deep defensive belt 20km (12 miles) west of the waterway. The missiles themselves were deployed in mutually supporting clusters, all of which engaged the target aircraft, low-level defence being provided by radar controlled ZSU 23-4 high-output AA guns and scores of SAM-7 (Grail) shoulder-fired infantry missiles. This reorganisation produced its first results on 30 June, when two IAF Phantoms were shot down in quick succession. Israel requested the United States to provide ECM equipment and, pending the approval of her request, developed new tactics to meet the changed situation. These involved low-level skip-bombing by several aircraft against each missile cluster, the attacks commencing on the outer edge of the cluster and working their way in towards the command and control centre. In this way two SAM-2 batteries were destroyed, but at the cost of another Phantom. During the month of July the Israelis lost a total of seven aircraft.

Aggression in the air

Throughout July it was noticed that the Russian pilots, who had hitherto played a purely defensive role, were becoming daily more aggressive, and a major air battle developed on 30 July in which five of their MiG-21Js were destroyed in exchange for one Israeli Mirage damaged. The Russians' lack of combat experience was very evident in their wooden responses and tendency to fight by the manual.

This was to be the last engagement of the war. The escalation of the fighting presented great risks for world peace. Neither the United States nor the Soviet Union wanted a confrontation, and both were ready to advise their respective client states to stop the war. On 8 August both sides accepted a ceasefire based on a plan prepared by William Rogers, the American Secretary of State, as part of a projected long-term settlement of Arab-Israeli issues. The Egyptians had suffered around 10,000 casualties in the first seven months of the year, and showed no signs of achieving their objectives; the ceasefire offered a possibility of improving their position. The Israeli government was split over the question of a ceasefire, hardliners feeling that they would be letting the Egyptians off the hook, but the majority accepted it.

The last casualty of the war was President Nasser. Worn out by the strain of the conflict, he died on 28 September 1970. Ostensibly his War of Attrition had failed in its purpose, yet it was the Israelis, the tactical victors, who found themselves in a less favourable strategic situation at the end. Many Israeli historians now believe that the policy of long-range bombing was a serious mistake, since it led directly to the installation of the Soviet air defence belt. In military terms, this was the most significant event of the war. The Egyptians soon began moving the new air defence system forward, under cover of the ceasefire, ready to support a future offensive. The full effects of this development would be demonstrated in 1973.

Bryan Perrett

The main Egyptian strengths in the War of Attrition lay in SAM missiles and artillery concentrations (left, top and below) while the Israelis relied on the power of the IAF (above, IAF F-4 Phantoms) and built the Bar-Lev Line strongpoints (right) along the Canal.

The new Palestinians

The rise of Arafat and the PLO

The disastrous outcome of the 1967 Middle East war shook the very foundations of Arab thinking on the Palestine question. The loss of the West Bank and Sinai peninsula and, not least, the virtual destruction of the Arab armies, shed a harsh light on the policy of the Arab states. Those such as Egypt's leader, Gamal Abdel Nasser, who had seen themselves as liberating Palestine from 'Zionist' rule through the unified action of the Arab nation and its conventional armies, found their approach discredited. Some Palestinian nationalists, however, had always put the Palestinian cause first, arguing that it was only through the organisation and armed struggle of the Palestinians themselves that the return to what they regarded as their homeland could be achieved; in the aftermath of the Six-Day War this viewpoint, and the technique of guerrilla warfare that it entailed, won widespread support amongst both Palestinians and other Arabs.

The roots of Palestinian nationalism lie in the 1948 Arab defeat and the resulting dispersal of Palestinians from the newly-founded state of Israel. From the refugee camps around Israel's borders and from the cities of the Arab world in which the Palestinians continued their lives, they longed for a return to their lost homeland. In some cases, this sentiment found expression in political action. In 1951 Yassir Arafat, a Jerusalem-born civil engineering student at Cairo University and president of the Palestinian Students Union, was a central figure in a group of Palestinians who believed in the one common goal of liberating Palestine through armed struggle, and who felt that ultimately the Palestinians could rely only on themselves and their own organisations to achieve it. Arafat's approach was deliberately simple and single-minded, designed to embrace all Palestinians, whatever their religious or political persuasion.

In the wake of the 1956 war, fearing Israeli reprisals, the Arab countries bordering on Israel imposed severe restrictions on Palestinian political activities on their territory. Arafat subsequently moved to Kuwait where the political atmosphere was less oppressive for Palestinians and where he could establish links with other Palestinian nationalist groups already operating in the Gulf area. In the late 1950s, he formed a new liberation group from Palestinians living in Kuwait. Known as Al-Fatah, the group published a newspaper called *Filastinuna (Our Palestine)*, and through this mouthpiece other similarly-minded activist organisations came into contact with Fatah. This led in 1962 to the amalgamation of a number of groups under the Fatah title, following a conference convened in Kuwait. Although at this time a clandestine organisation, Fatah was able to voice its ideas through *Filastinuna* in the refugee camps around Israel's borders, and the foundations were laid for its long-lasting organisational structure.

Immediately after the 1962 amalgamation, preparations began for military action against Israel. Fatah's belief in the importance of guerrilla warfare, however, brought them up against Arab opposition.

Nasser's influence in Middle East politics and Arab fears of Israeli retaliation against countries providing military aid and base camp facilities to guerrillas made Fatah's task very difficult. The only state offering concrete aid at this time was the Ba'athist regime in Syria, and by early 1964 the Fatah fedayeen (guerrillas) had been extended the use of two training camps in that country. Fatah's first commando raid against Israel was made on 31 December 1964 under the assumed name of Al-Asifah (The Storm). In the following year some 39 operations were launched, and by mid-1965 Fatah had claimed responsibility for the Asifah raids, adopting that assumed name permanently for its military arm.

The Palestinian struggle

Meanwhile, the Arab states had set up their own organisation to represent the Palestinians. Until 1964 the Arab nationalists had steadfastly rejected the idea of a separate Palestinian identity, viewing the Middle East conflict as an Arab struggle to free Arab lands from the Israelis, not as a struggle for a Palestinian state. At the 1964 Arab summit at Alexandria, however, the 13 Arab heads of state not only recognised the existence of a Palestinian entity, but also agreed to set up a Palestinian organisation dedicated to help in the overthrow of Israel through military action. The new organisation, the Palestine Liberation Organisation (PLO), was declared 'the only legitimate spokesman for all matters concerning the Palestinian people', and a regular Palestinian fighting force, to be known as the Palestinian Liberation Army (PLA), was soon recruited from among the Palestinians throughout the Arab world. Leadership of the PLO was entrusted to Ahmed Shuqairy, and at the first PLO conference in May 1964 a Palestinian National Charter and Basic Constitution were adopted, outlining the basic tenets of the Palestinian nationalist cause.

While Fatah continued to consolidate and step up the level of guerrilla activity, units of the newly-formed PLA were organised into regular army formations. However, King Hussein of Jordan, whose country had the longest border with Israel, would not

Above: Yassir Arafat, founder of the group Al-Fatah ('struggle') and, later, leader of the Palestine Liberation Organisation, the umbrella organisation that attempts to unite all Palestinian factions. Arafat's belief has always been that the Palestinians must reconquer their homeland by armed action.

Below: Watched by a small boy (in uniform), a young Fatah guerrilla charges through a flaming hoop on an obstacle course in Jordan. Below right: A Fatah assault team from a Syrian base are taken through range practice on the Golan Heights by an instructor.

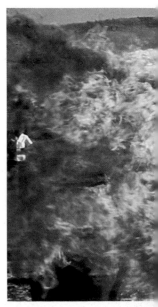

permit the PLA to deploy there nor would he allow the PLO to levy taxes on the Palestinian refugees living on the West Bank, thus cutting off a substantial source of income to the PLO. In contrast to Fatah, the PLO's political stability before the Six-Day War was severely disrupted by disputes within its own leadership.

The immediate aftermath of the Six-Day War saw a massive expansion of Palestinian guerrilla movements. Arafat's Fatah had consistently opposed the strategy of an all-out decisive conventional war against Israel and had been proved right. Arab opposition to the guerrilla strategy collapsed and Fatah mounted a new campaign to gain political and financial support from the various Arab governments, while at the same time seeking to start a guerrilla war amongst the Palestinian inhabitants of the now Israeli-occupied West Bank. Arafat established his headquarters at Nablus, setting up guerrilla networks throughout the area, while other Fatah leaders continued to tour the Middle East drumming up support. Egypt, formerly so opposed to Palestinian guerrilla activity, made arms, supplies and training facilities available to the fedayeen and links were further strengthened when, in July 1968, Arafat visited the

Below: The abject poverty of a Palestinian settlement in Lebanon. Palestinians fled to neighbouring Jordan and Lebanon and also to the Gaza Strip after the Israeli successes of 1948; there was a further exodus after the Six-Day War in 1967. Often living in squalid conditions, the millions of Palestinian refugees have created political difficulties in Lebanon and Jordan, and as their numbers increased and Israeli attitudes hardened in the 1970s, the problems of this unhappy people increased.

Soviet Union in Nasser's company. Within the Arab Nationalist Movement (ANM) – another organisation previously opposed to the Fatah guerrilla strategy – the Palestinian branch combined with a number of already existing guerrilla groups to form the Popular Front for the Liberation of Palestine (PFLP) under the ANM's Marxist leader, George Habash. Recruits poured in, and training facilities in Jordan and Syria were expanded.

On the West Bank, Arafat's attempts to consolidate a guerrilla network and sow the seeds for a local Palestinian uprising against the Israeli occupation were severely disrupted by the imposition of curfews and Israeli search operations. Although Arafat commanded a great deal of support in the refugee camps, Palestinians who had their original homes on the West Bank were more inclined towards a political solution and the application of UN Resolution 242 which called for the withdrawal of all Israeli armed forces from areas occupied in the June war. By the end of 1967, Arafat's plans were proving abortive and Fatah reverted to a strategy of hit-and-run operations.

Despite this setback, Fatah continued to gain support and recruits while at the same time making headway within the power structure of the PLO. Shuqairy's leadership of the PLO came under more and more pressure from Fatah, the PFLP and his own Executive Committee and, in December 1967, he resigned his chairmanship. A month later, Fatah convened a meeting of the various active guerrilla groups in Cairo and the Permanent Bureau, a body designed to coordinate Palestinian military action, was established. In the face of this Fatah initiative, the PLO established its own guerrilla movement, the Palestinian Liberation Front (PLF), as an off-shoot of the PLA. By July 1968, however, the Fatah faction had further consolidated its position, 38 of the 100 seats at the 4th Palestinian National Council being held by the Permanent Bureau, while the PLF/PLA faction held only 20. A further article was added to the National Charter confirming the Fatah doctrine that armed struggle was the only way to liberate Palestine and that such a struggle was an overall strategy, not just a tactical phase.

Ironically, Arafat and Fatah's political grip on the PLO had been strengthened by a considerable military setback earlier that year. On 21 March an Israeli

armoured formation with helicopter and infantry support had crossed the Jordan River from the West Bank and attacked the village of Karameh which hosted much of Fatah's organisation in Jordan. The Jordanian Army and Fatah guerrillas were forewarned of the raid and fought well, although the Israelis achieved their basic objectives and inflicted heavy casualties. Fatah's propagandists exploited the battle effectively, belittling the Jordanian contribution and the Israeli successes, and further waves of recruits joined the guerrillas. By October 1968, a Military Coordination Council was established in Amman between the PLO, Fatah and a pro-Syrian commando group known as Saiqa, and in February 1969 Arafat was elected chairman of the PLO.

As Palestinian military operations against Israel from Jordan and Lebanon continued to expand, Arafat proceeded to form the Palestinian Armed Struggle Command (PASC) to act as a military police force, and by the end of 1969 the PASC had been joined by all Palestinian guerrilla organisations with the exception of Saiqa. With Arafat as chairman, Fatah had become the dominant guerrilla group and the PLO rested firmly in its power. The PFLP, however, had boycotted the February 1969 National Council and was not fully integrated into the PLO arena until May 1970. While it was true that the Arab regimes were not happy to lose control of the PLO and see it become a fully independent political body and an active organisation, the skill of Fatah's leadership enabled it to control the PLO without unnecessarily alienating the Arab governments; Fatah considered maintaining Arab commitment to the PLO crucial to its cause.

The widespread expansion after 1967 and the Fatah take-over of the PLO, were, however, not without their problems. The PLO was essentially an umbrella organisation, embracing a number of factions, and problems of leadership and control, coupled with internal disputes, jeopardised its unity. George Habash's PFLP differed from Fatah in arguing from a radical standpoint for the creation of a revolutionary rather than a nationalist struggle in all Arab states; rejecting Fatah's policy of non-intervention in the affairs of Arab governments, it sought the overthrow of conservative Arab regimes like that of King

Palestine Liberation Organisation (PLO) main groups – 1970

Fatah (Palestine National Liberation Movement)
Founded in 1957/58 in Kuwait and led by Yassir Arafat. Al-Asifah was the military arm.

PLA (Palestine Liberation Army)
Founded in 1964 as the regular military force of the PLO and commanded by Abdel Razzaq Al-Yiha. In 1968 the Popular Liberation Forces, the PLA commando wing, was founded.

Saiqa (Vanguards of the Popular Liberation War)
Syrian-backed Ba'athist Palestinian guerrilla group founded in 1968 and led by Abu Moussa (also known as Jamian).

PFLP (Popular Front for the Liberation of Palestine)
Radical Marxist group founded in 1967/68 and led by George Habash.

PDFLP (Popular Democratic Front for the Liberation of Palestine)
Extreme left-wing offshoot of the PFLP founded in 1969 and led by Nayif Hawatmeh.

PFLP-GC (Popular Front for the Liberation of Palestine – General Command)
A PFLP commando splinter group founded in 1968 and led by Ahmad Jibril

ALF (Arab Liberation Front)
Iraqi backed Ba'athist Palestinian group founded in 1969 and led by Abd al-Wahhab al-Kayyali

Above: Under one of the international symbols of revolution – a Che Guevara poster – young Palestinians are instructed in field stripping and weapons drill on a semi-automatic weapon.

Below: Israeli paras move into the Jordanian village of Karameh, March 1968. The stiff resistance of Arafats' guerrillas to this incursion added greatly to Fatah prestige.

Top: Yassir Arafat (second from left) and President Nasser (second from right) after the meeting in which Arafat was elected leader of the PLO. Although initially Egypt had refused to give support to the creation of a separate Palestinian 'entity' the defeats of 1967 had left the Arab world looking for new ways of opposing Israel, and the PLO benefited from the search for a new approach. Above: Ahmed Shuqairy, chairman of the PLO from 1964 until December 1967. His resignation was swiftly followed by the rise of Fatah to dominance in the PLO. Above right: George Habash, the leader of the Popular Front for the Liberation of Palestine (PFLP). PFLP activities included the aircraft hijackings that captured world headlines in the late 1960s and early 1970s.

Hussein in Jordan. The PFLP was also divided: a year after its foundation in 1968, Nayif Hawatmeh, a Christian Arab enjoying close links with the Soviet bloc, seceded from the PFLP to form the Popular Democratic Front for the Liberation of Palestine (PDFLP) on the grounds that the PFLP had developed 'bourgeois tendencies', while a further PFLP splinter group, the PFLP General Command, was established under Ahmad Jibril. Yet another faction was Saiqa, formed in 1968, led by Syrian regular army officers and recruited within the Palestinian refugee camps in Syria. Old-style Nasserites, new Arab nationalists, Palestinian Ba'athists and independent Palestinian nationalists were enmeshed in a web of disagreement and inter-group rivalry within the PLO.

One of the fundamental principles of Fatah ideology regarding the relationship between the PLO and other Arab states was to avoid meddling in the host country's internal affairs and politics, but with the rapid growth of the PLO in the late 1960s and the factionalism within its ranks, this stance became increasingly difficult to maintain. As the numbers of fedayeen in Jordan and Lebanon continued to swell, so relations between the PLO and the governments of those two countries became increasingly strained. In Lebanon, the PLO found considerable support for their cause amongst the Muslim population and left-wing organisations, and the armed Palestinian presence further exacerbated existing tensions in an already divided country. Muslim grievances against the Maronite Christian minority who effectively dominated the governmental institutions of Lebanon

were fuelled, and while the PLO remained, the country's fragile political stability was increasingly jeopardised. The situation was brought to a head with the resignation of the Lebanese Muslim premier Abdullah Yafi following the retaliatory Israeli commando strike against Beirut airport in December 1968 in which 13 aircraft were blown up, and the country was plunged into political crisis. Clashes between guerrillas and the Lebanese security forces increased through 1969, but with open Muslim support for the PLO, the government was forced to negotiate. In October 1969, Arafat and the Lebanese Army commander signed the so-called Cairo agreement which regulated the guerrilla presence in Lebanon but placed the refugee camps under Palestinian control.

No such agreement, however, was forthcoming in Jordan. Faced with a guerrilla movement that had become virtually a state within a state, and provoked by the activities of the PFLP which desired a confrontation, in September 1970 King Hussein launched an offensive against the fedayeen which left an estimated 3000 Palestinians dead. The following year, the remaining guerrilla bases in Jordan were overrun by the Jordanian Army.

Despite expressions of support from many Arab leaders and a brief military intervention by Syria on the Palestinians' behalf, the events of September 1970 only served to reinforce Arafat's founding principle that in the battle for Palestine the Palestinians would have to look after themselves. By 1971 the Palestinian movement seemed in a sorry state. Chased from Jordan, it could no longer carry out an effective campaign of guerrilla raids into Israel – raids could still be effected from Lebanon, but under far less favourable conditions. To a large extent, the Arab states had brought the PLO to heel. After his ceasefire with Israel in August 1970, Nasser had closed down Palestinian radio stations in Egypt, while in Syria the new regime of Hafez al-Assad, installed at the end of the year, established tight control over the Saiqa commandos. Yet Arafat and his organisation were to prove more resilient than anyone suspected, and by 1974 the guerrilla leader would be addressing the UN General Assembly as the official spokesman of his people. **Jonathan Reed**

On 23 July 1968 a passenger flight of the Israeli airline El Al was hijacked en route to Tel Aviv from Rome and was forced to land at Algiers. The hijackers were three members of the Popular Front for the Liberation of Palestine (PFLP), and this act marked the beginning of a campaign of terrorism that was to reach its climax just over two years later on the Jordanian desert airstrip of Dawson's Field.

There were a number of reasons why the PFLP embarked on their attacks against El Al (spread later to include other commercial airlines). One motive was publicity: it was essential for the Palestinian guerrillas to keep the issue of Palestine in the forefront of world debate over the Arab-Israeli conflict, and hijacking offered the greatest possible impact on world attention that a small terrorist force could achieve. It was also easier to attack such soft targets outside Israel, since attacking objectives within Israel itself was extraordinarily difficult and dangerous. The PFLP did not regard El Al as a civilian airline, claiming that it flew military missions. Also, as a group that regarded the Palestinian struggle as part of a worldwide revolutionary conflict, the PFLP welcomed the confrontation with Western governments and conservative Arab regimes that hijacking brought with it.

Hijacks and reprisals

The July 1968 hijack established one pattern for PFLP actions: having flown the plane to a moderately friendly country, the hijackers released all the passengers except adult male Israelis, who were held hostage until Israel agreed to release 16 Arab prisoners. At Athens airport five months later, on 26 December, another model was established, when two guerrillas carried out a machine-gun and grenade attack against an El Al airliner on the ground, inflicting indiscriminate casualties. Israeli reaction was swift and decisive: on 28 December an Israeli commando group flown in by helicopter blew up 13 civilian aircraft at Beirut International Airport, claiming that Lebanon had provided the base for the Athens airport attack. The Israelis carefully avoided inflicting casualties, but their action aroused a storm of international protest and the French government, part-owners of some of the planes, banned arms sales to Israel. The PFLP were jubilant at this result.

Through 1969 and 1970 their campaign continued. El Al offices were bombed and Israelis were killed in terrorist attacks at Zurich airport (February 1969) and Munich airport (February 1970). Hijackings were extended to Western airlines. On 29 August 1969 the PFLP 'Che Guevara Commando Unit', including terrorist Leila Khaled, diverted an American TWA flight to Syria, protesting against US support for Israel and extorting the release of Arab prisoners. In February 1970 a terrorist bomb blew up a Swissair jet in flight, killing 47 passengers, this was later revealed to have been the work of an extremist breakaway group from the PFLP, the PFLP-General Command. On 22 July a Greek flight was held hostage at Athens airport until the Greek government released PFLP terrorists who had been arrested after the previous attack at Athens airport in December 1968.

But now the PFLP was planning a major coup. The situation of the Palestinian movement by September 1970 was critical. Nasser had ended the War of Attrition with Israel and closed down Palestinian radio stations when they criticised his action; in

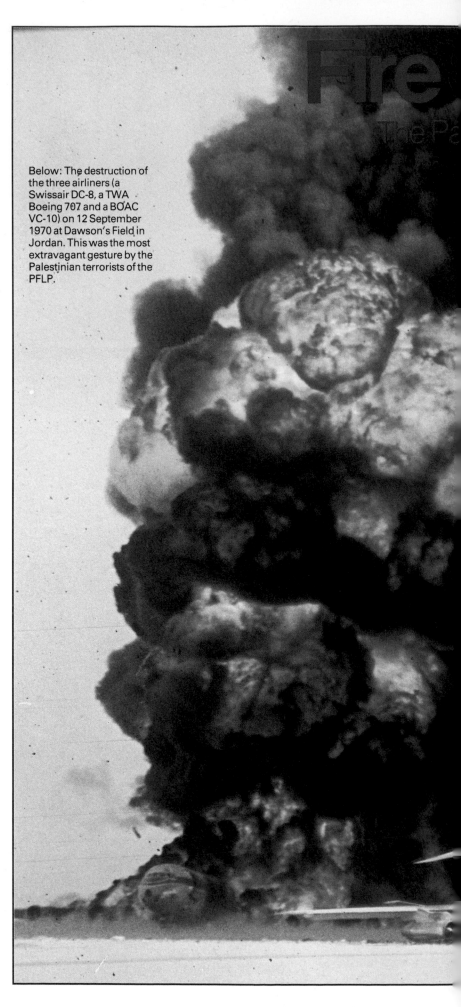

Below: The destruction of the three airliners (a Swissair DC-8, a TWA Boeing 707 and a BOAC VC-10) on 12 September 1970 at Dawson's Field in Jordan. This was the most extravagant gesture by the Palestinian terrorists of the PFLP.

Left: The El Al plane n by Palestinian Athens in Dec Below demands captured Pal xchange eld hostag PFLP terro is released

Jordan, the PFLP's main base, a confrontation was under way with King Hussein, who was also participating in the peace initiative. On 6 September the PFLP acted decisively to demonstrate its hostility to the Arab moves for peace with Israel and, possibly, in order to drive the PLO into a war with King Hussein.

On that date, three airliners bound for New York from European cities – a Swissair DC-8, a TWA Boeing 707 and a Pan Am jumbo-jet – were almost simultaneously hijacked. An attempt to seize a fourth plane, an El Al flight from Amsterdam, was foiled: one hijacker (Patrick Joseph Arguello) was shot dead and the other, Leila Khaled, was taken into custody in London. The Pan Am aircraft was flown to Cairo, where it was blown up at the airport after the passengers and crew had been moved off. The other two planes were flown to the desert airstrip of Dawson's Field, near Zerqa, in Jordan. With over 300 hostages imprisoned on the aircraft, the PFLP demanded the release of terrorists held in Britain, Switzerland, West Germany and Israel. Negotiations began through the Red Cross, and the women and children, some 127 passengers in all, were soon sent to the Jordanian capital, Amman, where they were freed. But on 9 September the crisis worsened as the PFLP hijacked another plane, a BOAC VC-10 en route from Bahrain to London, and flew that to Dawson's Field as well, with its 115 passengers and crew. The PFLP then demanded the release of Leila Khaled in exchange for the VC-10 and its human freight.

Removing the hostages

The airstrip was ringed by guerrillas who were in their turn surrounded by Jordanian troops with tanks and other armoured vehicles. But King Hussein refused to allow his army to attack, much to their disgust, and accepted for the moment this humiliation. By 12 September, after lengthy negotiations, the terrorists were still holding 54 passengers and crewmen hostage when, in the absence of the PFLP's usual leader George Habash, his deputy Dr Wadi Hadad ordered the hostages removed from the planes and carried off by bus; the three aircraft were then blown up. The Jordanian Army was forced to stand aside, for fear of harming the hostages.

Four days later the 'Black September' fighting between the Palestinians and the Jordanian Army erupted, but negotiations to free the hostages continued. On 25 September a unit of the Jordanian Army found 16 Swiss, German and British hostages in a camp deserted by the PFLP; by 29 September the other 38 had also been handed over. In return, Switzerland, Britain, West Germany and Israel all freed prisoners, including Leila Khaled who was flown out of Britain in time to attend President Nasser's funeral.

From the point of view of the PFLP, the Dawson's Field hijackings fulfilled their objectives. Arab prisoners were released, a full-scale conflict between the Palestinian guerrillas and King Hussein was precipitated, and the Palestinians were headline news throughout the world. But the war with Hussein was a disaster for the Palestinians and the publicity they received was entirely bad. Dawson's Field marked the end of one round of Palestinian terrorism on the international stage. It would continue in a slightly altered form in the 1970s.   **R. G. Grant**

Black September

The Jordanian crisis of 1970

The state of Jordan had a unique relationship to the Palestinians, for after the Israeli victory of 1948, Jordan had absorbed the West Bank area, with its resident Palestinian population and refugee camps housing Palestinians who had fled from Israel. This gave Jordan a population that was some 70 per cent Palestinian. But King Hussein, who came to the throne in 1953, relied on the support of a loyal and well-trained army and on the backing of Britain and the United States. Radical Palestinian nationalists received short shrift at the king's hands, and in the period before the 1967 war Hussein suppressed the activities of Palestinian fedayeen (guerrillas).

The loss of the West Bank and Jerusalem in 1967 was a grave blow to Hussein's authority. As refugees flooded across the Jordan River into the East Bank area and young Palestinians flocked to join the fedayeen, Hussein embraced their cause. In an expansive moment he asserted that 'one day perhaps we shall all be fedayeen'. When on 21 March 1968 a substantial Israeli force attacked Karameh, the guerrillas and the Jordanian Army fought together to resist the incursion.

The Israeli policy of carrying out raids across the border, in answer not only to fedayeen operations but also to shelling by Jordanian and Iraqi artillery, made the Palestinian refugee camps and guerrilla bases very unsafe. As a consequence, both refugees and fedayeen moved deeper inside Jordan to more secure sites, including parts of the Jordanian capital Amman. The bases nearer the border were reserved for the actual launching of commando raids into Israel.

But relations with King Hussein's government worsened steadily. The streets of Amman and other East Bank towns were thronged with heavily-armed Palestinians, setting up roadblocks, ignoring the army and taunting the police. Already in November 1968 clashes had led to the shelling of Palestinian camps by the army, and in February 1970 there was serious fighting. As head of the Palestine Liberation Organisation (PLO), Yassir Arafat, who had always followed a policy of non-intervention in the affairs of Arab states, opposed any attempt to unseat the king; Hussein was also keen to avoid open conflict. The more adventurous of the fedayeen and, most notably, George Habash's Popular Front for the Liberation of Palestine (PFLP), were hostile to Arafat's policy of restraint. In June 1970 the PFLP seized the Intercontinental Hotel in Amman and held 80 guests hostage, but Hussein refused to respond to the provocation. Yet he was himself under pressure from the army to take a stronger line. On 9 July the king narrowly escaped with his life in a fedayeen ambush not far from Amman. Time was clearly running out.

In June 1970 the United States had privately informed Hussein that the Americans or the Israelis would intervene in his defence if the Syrians or the Iraqis moved to support the Palestinians in an armed conflict. With this backing, the king prepared for a possible showdown by removing army officers suspected of favouring the Palestinian cause. Meanwhile the PFLP, outraged by the moves of both Egypt and Jordan towards peace with Israel, had planned a decisive intervention.

After another assassination attempt against the king on 1 September, the PFLP on 6 September carried out the Dawson's Field hijackings. The army was incensed by Hussein's failure to act and an artillery column marched on Amman, only to be intercepted and turned back by the king himself. Inquiring after the reason for a brassière fluttering from a wireless aerial, the king was told, 'It's because you have turned us all into women.' Hussein was under great pressure from other Arab leaders to go easy with the PLO, and Arafat denounced the Dawson's Field hijackings, expelling the PFLP from his organisation. However, on 15 September the king's closest confidants made it plain to him that further inaction would lose him the support of the army. By that night the king had decided to bring the Palesti-

Above: PFLP fighters brandish their weapons, including a Soviet-made RPG-7 rocket launcher. Right: King Hussein (centre) who was forced by pressure from his army to strike at the Palestinians. When he had taken the decision, well equipped Jordanian troops (below left, using a US recoilless rifle and below right with a British Saladin armoured car) swiftly cleared the streets of Amman, in spite of resistance from Palestinian guerrillas (below).

nians to heel, appointing a military government under Field-Marshal Habes el Majali, and imposing martial law. The Palestinians took these actions as a declaration of war; Arafat summoned his central committee to an emergency meeting and appointed Brigadier Yahya, who commanded the Palestine Liberation Army (PLA) brigade in Syria, as his chief of staff.

The Jordanian Army was 65,000 strong, organised into one armoured, one mechanised and two infantry divisions. The Royal Jordanian Air Force had two Hunter squadrons, one F-104 interceptor squadron, and some transport planes and helicopters. The Palestinians could field a well-armed force of 25,000 full-time troops and about 76,000 militia; their main strength was concentrated in Amman and Irbid, Jordan's second city, which had been virtually taken over by the fedayeen. In addition there was a PLA brigade attached to the Iraqi Expeditionary Force of two divisions (one armoured) which was deployed between Zerqa, 24km (15 miles) north of Amman, and Ramtha on the Syrian frontier. No one knew how the Iraqis would react to an attack on the Palestinians but they obviously posed a considerable threat. Meanwhile, ominous troop movements were reported in Syria, a state that had no love for King Hussein and his Hashemite dynasty.

The Jordanian general staff reckoned it would take from two to three days to deal with the fedayeen in Amman, after which attention could be turned to Irbid. At dawn on 17 September Amman's citizens

woke to the sound of tanks clanking through the streets as the 1st Infantry and 4th Mechanised Divisions moved against the Palestinians on Jebel Wahadat and Jebel el Webdeh, both heavily built-up residential areas of the capital. Resistance proved to be much fiercer than anticipated, the Jordanians discovering that in street-fighting well-armed and determined infantry are more than a match for tanks. Each house became a stronghold from which the defenders had to be winkled out in hand-to-hand fighting. Not until the morning of 20 September was the army beginning to get on top in Amman – and by then the centre of attention had switched to the north.

The Iraqis had not intervened, much to the Jordanians' relief, but the PLA brigade attached to them had joined in the battle at Zerqa. Farther north still the Jordanian 2nd Infantry Division, supported by the 40th Armoured Brigade (Centurions with 105mm guns), was threatened by the Syrian 5th Infantry Division concentrating across the border. At 0500 hours on 20 September Syrian Forces crossed into Jordan with more than 200 Soviet T55 tanks, many manned by PLA personnel attached to the Syrian Army. The Jordanians fought back gallantly, inflicting heavy casualties on the Syrian armour, but they were vastly outnumbered. By nightfall they had been forced to withdraw to a defensive line south of the vital Ramtha-Jarash/Irbid-Mafraq crossroads which fell into Syrian hands. Only a much weakened armoured brigade and some widely dispersed infantry

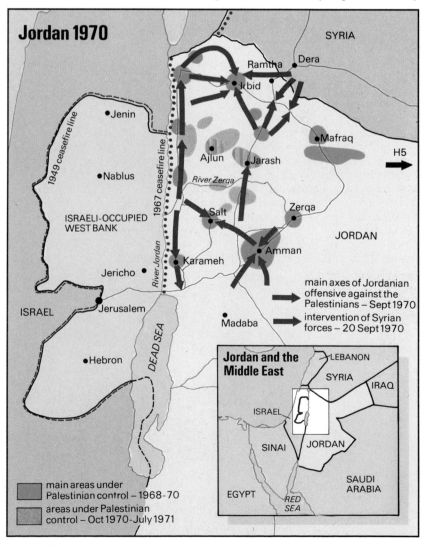

stood between the Syrians and a link-up with the Palestinians to the south and west (and possibly also with the Iraqis).

In response to the Syrian intervention, the United States alerted the Sixth Fleet and carried out some very visible troop movements. They made it plain to the Soviet Union that they expected them to restrain their Syrian clients. At the same time, Israel started preparations for military intervention. In fact, the Syrian action had been initiated without the approval of the Syrian defence minister Hafez al-Assad. Possibly under Soviet pressure, Assad refused to use the Syrian Air Force to provide the advance with air cover. As a result, the Syrian ground forces were hopelessly exposed when Jordanian Hunters flew into the battle. On the king's orders the Hunter squadrons had been moved from Mafraq to a base at H5, 120km (75 miles) to the east, the reason being Hussein's fear that the Iraqis, who had already fired on a reconnaissance mission, might try to seize the planes. Early in the morning of 21 September the Hunters came rocketing and machine-gunning out of the sky, their targets the Syrian tanks and trucks. The Syrian 5th Division attempted to fight its way forward but was held by the Jordanians who possessed the high ground. By nightfall it was clear that the Syrians had shot their bolt and orders were issued for a Jordanian counter-attack at dawn the next day. There proved to be no need for this. The Syrians withdrew during the night, leaving behind them 62 crippled tanks and 60 APCs; they lost 600 men killed and wounded.

Meanwhile Nasser and other Arab heads of government were trying to intervene, notably President Nimeiri of the Sudan who at great personal risk managed to meet with Arafat in Amman on 25 September. The outcome of that meeting was the agreement of terms which included the requirement that the fedayeen should move out of Amman and the cities, and that their guerrilla activities should be restricted to the border with Israel. Nasser then invited Hussein to Cairo for a meeting with the other Arab heads of government and with Arafat. On 27 September the meeting took place with both Hussein and Arafat reportedly carrying side-arms, but by the end Nasser had even persuaded them to shake hands. Twenty-four hours later Nasser was dead from a heart attack and a new era in Arab politics had begun.

Fedayeen who did not accept Arafat's compromise moves still held out in Irbid, but with the Syrians out of the way the Jordanian Army could give them its full attention. After a week of determined resistance all but a few isolated groups had capitulated. The end of the fighting left the army with some 600 killed and 1500 wounded; the fedayeen had lost many more. There had been many Palestinian sympathisers in the army and there were in fact 5000 desertions. But the vast majority had remained loyal to the king, to the surprise of Arafat and his advisers.

The Cairo meeting left the fedayeen free, in principle, to pursue their guerrilla activities against Israel from bases near the border, but in 1971 the king moved to finish with them. In April he forced the remaining guerrillas to leave Amman and on 13 July launched a final offensive against their mountain camps. Some 5000 fedayeen put up stiff resistance around Ras el Agra, towering 1100m (3500 feet) above the valley of the River Zerqa, but after four days of battle during which little quarter was given, they were defeated. Jordan would no longer be a base for the PLO guerrillas. **James Lunt**

Below: The Cairo meeting of 27 September 1970, convened by President Nasser, that led to the end of the fighting in Jordan. The publication of photographs of Yassir Arafat shaking hands with King Hussein provoked fury within the Palestinian camp. The meeting had been prepared by the activity of various Arab heads of state (including President Nimeiri of the Sudan) and was conducted in an atmosphere of great tension – both Arafat and Hussein were reported to have carried pistols. The resolution of the fighting was Nasser's last act in Middle Eastern affairs, for he died on 28 September.

Key Weapons

WESTERN STRATEGIC MISSILES

part 1

Of all the nuclear delivery systems in use today, the most fearsome must be the range of land and sub-marine-launched strategic ballistic missiles. Measuring their destructive power in thousands of tons of TNT and capable of travelling over global distances at barely imaginable speeds, such weapons are almost beyond comprehension, but are the key element in the fragile balance of power between East and West.

Within the framework of the Western Alliance, three countries, America, France and Great Britain, have developed such weapons. Of these three programmes, that of the USA, almost inevitably, is the largest, beginning during the mid-1950s with two designs, the Thor and the Jupiter. The first of these was a product of the Douglas Company and entered service in 1958. Standing 19.8m (65ft) high and weighing approximately 49,900kg (110,000lb) at lift-off, Thor was capable of delivering a nuclear warhead at ranges of up to 2780km (1725 miles). Power was provided by a 68,027kg (150,000lb) thrust Rocketdyne MB-3 liquid-fuelled motor and all

such weapons were sited in eastern England between 1958 and 1963.

The location of the Thor batteries in the UK was a consequence of the type's limited range: it could not hit a Soviet target if launched from the United States. Because of the sensitive political nature of nuclear weapons and the 'special relationship' between the two countries, the missiles were operated by the RAF under a 'dual-key' system which allowed the British to initiate the launch and the Americans to arm the warhead.

No such sensitivity constrained the use of the Jupiter which was deployed in USAF bases in Turkey and Italy from 1958, the Turkish weapons being withdrawn as part of the settlement of the Cuban missile crisis of 1962. Jupiter, developed by the US Army Ballistic Missile Agency, had a length of 17.7m (58ft) and a performance similar to that of the Thor. In all, some 60 such missiles were deployed operationally.

Both Thor and Jupiter had relatively short ranges, a

Previous page: A Minuteman III powers upward following its launch from the Vandenburg airbase, California. Below far left: A Thor IRBM is launched, February 1958, while the modified British variant stands on the launch pad (inset). Below left: A Jupiter rocket is prepared for launch.

General Dynamics CGM-16D Atlas-D

Type Land-based strategic missile
Dimensions Length between 23.11m (75ft 10in) and 25.15m (82ft 6in) dependent on type of nose-cone installed
Weight Launch 120,200kg (265,000lb)
Powerplant 1×25,855kg (57,000lb) thrust liquid-fuelled Rocketdyne LR105-3 sustainer; 2×68,040kg (150,000lb) thrust liquid-fuelled Rocketdyne LR89-3 boosters; 2×450kg (1000lb) thrust liquid-fuelled Rocketdyne LR101 verniers
Range 14,500km (9000 miles) plus
Guidance Inertial
Warhead Nuclear

fact not lost on the US military. Indeed, even before they became operational, strenuous efforts were made to produce a truly intercontinental weapon. Such work bore fruit in 1957 with the first test launch of the General Dynamics Atlas. Powered by liquid-fuelled Rocketdyne motors, Atlas entered service between 1959–60 and was produced in three versions, the CGM-16D, CGM-16E and HGM-16F. The 16D was the original model with the E having more powerful booster motors and the F being designed for storage in a nuclear-hardened silo. Although capable of ranges in excess of 14,500km (9000 miles) the Atlas's above-ground launch system left it vulnerable to a counter-strike and its 'reaction time' – that is, the time taken to launch the missile from the moment of firing-authorisation – was an uncomfortably long 15 minutes.

The lengthy launch sequence was shared by the Martin-designed Titan missile which began trials in 1959. Originally developed as a back-up to the Atlas programme, the Titan differed from the General Dynamics weapon in being a two-stage missile. Known as the HGM-25A, the Titan I entered service in April 1962 and equipped six nine-missile squadrons until de-activated in 1965 (the 126 operational Atlas weapons being taken out of service at the same time).

The second Titan model, the LGM-25C, appeared in 1962 and differed radically from its predecessor in that it was launched directly from its protective silo and had a reaction time of about one minute. A total of 54 Titan IIs were originally deployed – two of which were lost in nuclear accidents at their launch sites in 1978 and 1980 respectively – and some 40-odd of the original number remain operational and carry an up-dated guidance system. They are expected to remain in service until the end of the 1980s.

The problems inherent in using liquid propellants – handling, surface launch sites and slow reaction times – were overcome in the next strategic missile to enter USAF service, the Boeing LGM-30 Minuteman, which used solid fuel to feed the motors in its three

Below: An Atlas ICBM blasts off from its launch pad. An important advance over its predecessors, such as the Thor and the Jupiter, the Atlas had an intercontinental range which placed the Soviet Union within striking distance of launch sites in the United States.

Right: A Titan I is test launched from Cape Canaveral in 1964. Although initially developed to act as a back-up for the Atlas ICBM, the Titan had the advantage of being a two-stage missile, a technical advance that represented the future path of missile development.

Below: The Titan assembly line; stage 1 and 2 vehicles wait in line in various phases of assembly. A completed stage 1 vehicle can be seen in the background, shrouded and prepared for shipment to Cape Canaveral, with its stage 2 directly behind.

Martin-Marietta LGM-25C Titan II

Type Land-based strategic missile
Dimensions Length 31.4m (103ft)
Weight Launch 149,690kg (330,000lb)
Powerplant 2×98,000kg (216,090lb) thrust
liquid-fuelled Aerojet LR87-AJ-5s (first stage);
1×45,500kg (100,328lb) thrust liquid-fuelled Aerojet
LR91-AJ-5 (second stage)
Range 15,000km (9315 miles)
Guidance Inertial
Warhead Mk6 10-megaton nuclear, housed in a
General Electric Mk6 re-entry vehicle

stages. The use of this form of propellant allowed the weapon to be stored ready for action over long periods and for it to be silo-launched within 32 seconds of a firing-authorisation. Solid fuel rockets were to prove a major advance in missile technology.

Minuteman entered service as the LGM-30A in 1963 and equipped five Strategic Air Command Missile Wings. A second model, the LGM-30F, was deployed in 1966 and featured an increase in range coupled with a vastly more accurate guidance system capable of choosing between any one of eight pre-designated targets whilst in flight. The final and most important version, the LGM-30G, was introduced in 1970 and incorporated a warhead 'bus' containing three separate nuclear packages (known as MIRVs – multiple independent re-entry vehicles) each capable of attacking a different target.

The USAF currently operates six Minuteman II/III Wings (the 44th, 90th, 91st, 321st, 341st and 351st), the LGM-30A Minuteman I no longer being in service. Minuteman will remain an important part of the US's nuclear arsenal into the 1990s, by which time it will be partnered by America's newest weapon, the MGM-118 Peacekeeper.

Boeing LGM-30G Minuteman III

Type Land-based strategic missile
Dimensions Length 18.20m (59ft 9in)
Weight Launch 34,500kg (76,085lb)
Powerplant 1×91,000kg (200,655lb) thrust
solid-fuelled Thiokol TU-120 (first stage);
1×27,500kg (60,638lb) thrust solid-fuelled Aerojet
SR18-AJ-1 (second stage); 1×15,500kg (34, 178lb)
thrust solid-fuelled Aerojet SR73-MJ-1 (third stage)
Range 14,000km (8700 miles)
Guidance Inertial
Warhead Three General Electric Mk12 MIRVs, each
carrying a 165-kiloton nuclear device

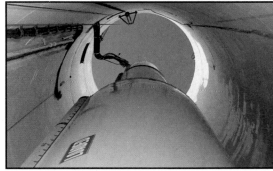

Opposite page far left: A Titan II is launched from the John F. Kennedy Space Center, Cape Canaveral. The 100 foot-plus missile can deliver a nuclear payload of around 165 tons and has a maximum range of 15,000km (9315 miles). Opposite page left: The massive Titan III blasts off from its launch pad. Top: A Minuteman I is prepared for launch at Cape Canaveral. Above: The view from a Minuteman II silo, complete with loaded missile. Main picture: A Minuteman III blasts skyward, its first-stage motor still burning furiously. Left: Six (unarmed) Minuteman III MIRVs approach targets near Kwajelein Atoll in the western Pacific Ocean.

Originally known as the MX, Peacekeeper began life in 1974 when design requests for a third-generation strategic missile were issued by the administration of President Gerald Ford. Martin-Marietta won the contract but the weapon's actual production remained in doubt during the remainder of the decade as political arguments raged about its cost and how it was to be launched. At least three launch options were considered, even including dropping the missile out of a transport aircraft such as the C-5.

Intended for service in the late 1980s, MGM-118 is a four-stage, solid and liquid-fuelled weapon carrying 10 MIRVs. The first three stages are used to power the fourth-stage warhead bus to a height of around 116km (72 miles). Equipped with a liquid-fuel manoeuvring motor, the bus launches the MIRVs individually before plunging back into the atmosphere. The MIRVs themselves are of the General Electric Mk12A type (also used on some Minuteman IIIs) and each carries a W-78 nuclear warhead with a yield of 335 kilotons. Some idea of the power of this weapon can be gained when it is realised that each W-78 is 16 times more powerful than the atomic bomb which destroyed Hiroshima.

Martin-Marietta MGM-118 Peacekeeper

Type Land-based strategic missile
Dimensions Length 21.6m (70ft 10in)
Weight Launch 88,450kg (195,000lb)
Powerplant 1 solid-fuelled Thiokol type (first stage); 1 solid-fuelled Aerojet type (second stage); 1 solid-fuelled Hercules type (third stage); 1 liquid-fuelled Rockwell type (warhead bus)
Range 14,000km (8700 miles)
Guidance Inertial
Warhead Ten General Electric Mk12A MIRVs, each carrying a 335-kiloton W-78 nuclear device

Top: The deceptively simple exterior of a Minuteman ICBM silo, with – in the insets – a missile-control officer checking the 'ready status' of his missile (left) and a silo entrance door (right).
Above: A fifth nuclear warhead is carefully lowered into position on the deployment module of a Peacekeeper ICBM.
Left: A Peacekeeper is assembled at Martin-Marietta's Denver aerospace complex.

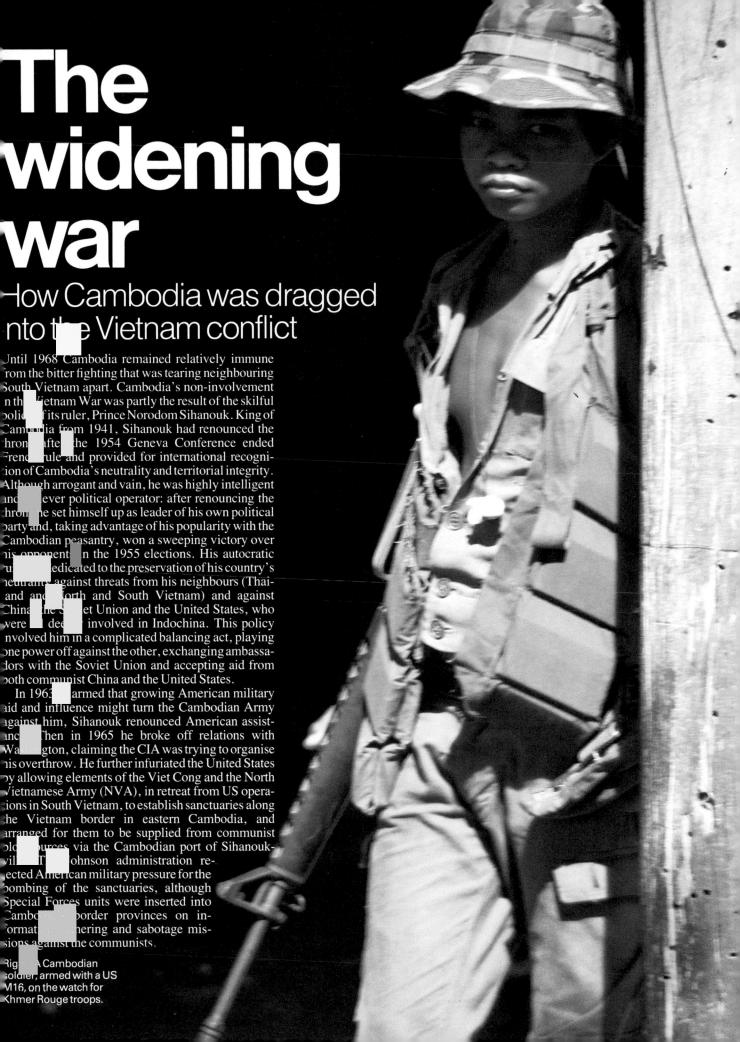

The widening war

How Cambodia was dragged into the Vietnam conflict

Until 1968 Cambodia remained relatively immune from the bitter fighting that was tearing neighbouring South Vietnam apart. Cambodia's non-involvement in the Vietnam War was partly the result of the skilful policy of its ruler, Prince Norodom Sihanouk. King of Cambodia from 1941, Sihanouk had renounced the throne after the 1954 Geneva Conference ended French rule and provided for international recognition of Cambodia's neutrality and territorial integrity. Although arrogant and vain, he was highly intelligent and a clever political operator: after renouncing the throne he set himself up as leader of his own political party and, taking advantage of his popularity with the Cambodian peasantry, won a sweeping victory over his opponents in the 1955 elections. His autocratic rule was dedicated to the preservation of his country's neutrality against threats from his neighbours (Thailand and North and South Vietnam) and against China, the Soviet Union and the United States, who were all deeply involved in Indochina. This policy involved him in a complicated balancing act, playing one power off against the other, exchanging ambassadors with the Soviet Union and accepting aid from both communist China and the United States.

In 1963, alarmed that growing American military aid and influence might turn the Cambodian Army against him, Sihanouk renounced American assistance. Then in 1965 he broke off relations with Washington, claiming the CIA was trying to organise his overthrow. He further infuriated the United States by allowing elements of the Viet Cong and the North Vietnamese Army (NVA), in retreat from US operations in South Vietnam, to establish sanctuaries along the Vietnam border in eastern Cambodia, and arranged for them to be supplied from communist bloc sources via the Cambodian port of Sihanoukville. The Johnson administration rejected American military pressure for the bombing of the sanctuaries, although Special Forces units were inserted into Cambodia's border provinces on information-gathering and sabotage missions against the communists.

Right: A Cambodian soldier, armed with a US M16, on the watch for Khmer Rouge troops.

The lightly armed units of Khmer Rouge guerrillas (below, patrol and leader armed with an RPG7 move through forest) proved an elusive target for Cambodian Army units (bottom, Cambodian troops, mounted in a US M113 APC, patrol areas along the Mekong).

After 1967 Sihanouk decided to realign Cambodia's foreign policy in a pro-American direction. His realignment was prompted by increasing economic difficulties, which necessitated a resumption of US aid. Sihanouk was also increasingly concerned about the threat to Cambodia's independence posed by the steady build-up of Viet Cong and NVA forces in eastern Cambodia. He stepped up the repression of communist and left-wing elements, and this demonstration of his anti-communist credentials enabled him to secure the restoration of diplomatic relations with the United States in July 1969.

But Cambodia's comparative insulation from the Vietnam War was coming to an end. President Richard Nixon, inaugurated in January 1969, and his influential national security adviser, Dr Henry Kissinger, were anxious to withdraw American ground forces from Vietnam. As US Army strength in the South gradually declined, the Nixon administration began to rely increasingly on air power both to shore up the South Vietnamese Army and to demonstrate US determination to uphold the status quo in Vietnam, in the hope of forcing Hanoi to abandon the struggle. Nixon was able to take advantage of the more favourable atmosphere in Phnom Penh towards the United States by authorising joint US and South Vietnamese Air Force attacks on the sanctuaries in eastern Cambodia. Sihanouk had no alternative but to acquiesce.

Bombing the communists

The immediate pretext for the bombing was provided by US Army claims to have detected the presence of a Vietnamese communist command and control headquarters, known as the Central Office for South Vietnam (COSVN), in the Cambodian border areas. Army chiefs feared that this presaged an imminent communist offensive in South Vietnam. In March 1969 Nixon authorised heavy bombing of the sanctuaries in the belief that this would destroy COSVN and the communist forces in the area, thus removing a serious threat to South Vietnam and Cambodia. Fearing an outcry in the United States if the bombing of supposedly neutral Cambodia became public knowledge, he kept the operation a closely guarded secret. B-52s pounded eastern Cambodia from March 1969

to early 1970 – some 3630 missions were flown – but apart from destroying Cambodian villages, the bombing appeared to have minimal effect. The Vietnamese communists escaped heavy casualties by withdrawing further into the interior of Cambodia, and Cambodian peasants fled from the war zone to the relative security of the towns along the Mekong.

These developments exacerbated Cambodia's already acute economic plight as production of vital rice and rubber declined catastrophically. Economic hardship sharpened discontent in the towns, a situation easily exploited by Sihanouk's political rivals. On 19 March 1970 Marshal Lon Nol, a former minister of defence and current prime minister in Sihanouk's government, took advantage of Sihanouk's absence in Europe to overthrow the prince and assume dictatorial powers. It was widely rumoured that the CIA funded the coup. Certainly it was welcomed by the US government, which immediately recognised the new regime in the expectation that it would be more consistent in its anti-communism than Sihanouk had been.

Sihanouk had been widely criticised because of the involvement of members of his family in shady financial deals, and many of the ruling groups in Cambodia had felt that he was losing control of events. Nevertheless, his widespread popularity in the countryside made him a force to be reckoned with, even in exile.

Sihanouk went into exile in Peking, where he placed himself at the head of a National United Front Party for Kampuchea (Cambodia) which included the Cambodian communists – the Khmer Rouge – and soon became dominated by them. The Khmer Rouge had engaged in a small-scale and unsuccessful guerrilla campaign against Sihanouk since 1954, but the events of the late 1960s had enabled them to expand in size with the help of the Viet Cong. After Sihanouk's crackdown against the communists in 1967 the Khmer Rouge had received a welcome influx of new recruits, especially left-wing intellectuals, escaping from Sihanouk's political police – men like Saleth Sar (later known as Pol Pot) who gradually assumed leadership of the Khmer Rouge and brought to it a renewed sense of mission and enthusiasm. Now Sihanouk called for a mass uprising against Lon Nol and the Cambodian peasantry rallied to his cause – and hence to the Khmer Rouge with whom he was now identified. By the end of March 1970 the Khmer Rouge controlled about 30 per cent of the land area of Cambodia.

Halting the invasion

Partly to shore up Lon Nol's new regime, President Nixon authorised a joint US and South Vietnamese ground invasion of eastern Cambodia. The main object of the incursion, however, was the capturing of COSVN and the crushing of Vietnamese communist forces in the area. While the invasion, which was launched on 30 April 1970, disrupted Vietnamese communist supply routes, it made little impact on the communist forces. It did, however, cause an outcry in the United States, forcing Nixon to order his forces to halt 40km (25 miles) inside Cambodia, and to promise Congress that all US forces would be withdrawn from Cambodia by 30 June 1970. The invasion had the same result as the 1969 bombing raids, pushing the communists deeper inside Cambodia. The hard-pressed Lon Nol government appealed to the United

States for immediate assistance, and Nixon hastily complied, despite increasing Congressional opposition to the Cambodian adventure. Extensive US military aid was provided to enable Lon Nol to modernise and expand his army from less than 100,000 to 200,000 men, and the B-52 bombing was resumed, this time against any likely communist targets inside Cambodia.

The events of 1969 and 1970 seriously destabilised Cambodia and dragged it deeper into the expanding Indochina War. After 1970 the increasing destruction of the countryside and the continuing flight of Cambodian refugees into Phnom Penh and the remaining government-held provincial capitals led to the complete collapse of the economy; Lon Nol became entirely dependent on US financial assistance. To make matters worse, Lon Nol and his army leaders were both corrupt and incompetent. Army officers sold US arms to the Khmer Rouge, while even more fell into the hands of the insurgents in 1971 and 1972 as a result of Lon Nol's decision, under pressure from the US, to commit his increasingly demoralised army to futile offensives against the communists. As a result the Cambodian Army suffered a number of humiliating and costly defeats. By 1972 the Khmer Rouge was in control of about 65 per cent of the country. Nothing daunted, Lon Nol thrust aside the remaining vestiges of internal opposition, taking over complete control of what territory was left to him in Cambodia by getting himself elected president. His doomed regime, sustained by American aid, was to struggle on until April 1975.

Michael Dockrill

Prince Sihanouk (top) whose political skills had allowed him to retain control of his country during the 1950s and 1960s was ousted by his prime minister, Marshal Lon Nol (above, centre), in March 1970 while abroad. Ironically, Sihanouk's call for a mass uprising against Lon Nol helped rally the peasants to the Khmer Rouge – the communist force which Sihanouk had attempted to eliminate during his time in power.

Parrot's Beak and Fish Hook

The incursions into Cambodia

The fall from power of Prince Norodom Sihanouk in March 1970 fundamentally altered the relationship between Cambodia and the war in neighbouring Vietnam. The Cambodian border areas had long been the site of Vietnamese communist bases and supply networks, and from March 1969 a massive B-52 bombing campaign had been launched against the communist sanctuaries, but under the Prince's rule Cambodia clung tenuously to its neutrality. The new government of Lon Nol, however, was dedicated to driving out the communists and appealed for American help. US military commanders in South Vietnam were very keen to be allowed to cross the border and had begun contingency plans for an incursion in January 1970. As Lon Nol and the communists came into conflict – with Lon Nol getting much the worst of it – the US administration determined to intervene.

On 14 April 1970 units of the Army of the Republic of Vietnam (ARVN) made a limited sweep across the border, and ten days later the US government instructed the US Army to prepare a combined South Vietnamese and American effort to begin on 30 April. To the military leaders and their troops the crossing of the border did not pose any new problems; they were already operating in similar terrain against the same enemy just inside South Vietnam. But President Nixon and his advisers knew that the incursion would be seen as a major widening of the war and that opposition would be intense. They braced themselves to ride the storm of protest that would break.

There were to be two main axes to the operation, one a drive into the 'Parrot's Beak' salient and the other an assault on the 'Fish Hook'. The Parrot's Beak invasion was entrusted to Lieutenant-General Do Cao Tri, commander of III Corps, ARVN, and would be carried out by South Vietnamese ground forces with US advisers and US air and artillery support. The Fish Hook attack was to be a combined US Army/ARVN operation under Brigadier-General Robert Shoemaker of the 1st Air Cavalry Division. The objectives were to inflict casualties on enemy forces – believed to consist of some 45,000 troops of the North Vietnamese Army (NVA) 7th Division, the Viet Cong 5th Division and the Viet Cong 9th Division – to disrupt enemy logistics, and to locate and destroy the Central Office for South Vietnam (COSVN), the communist command headquarters.

General Tri established an operational command post at Tay Ninh, and from there on 29 April he ordered his force of some 12,000 men into the Parrot's Beak. This was a flat, fertile region offering reasonable conditions for conventional ground operations. The ARVN armoured cavalry in M113 armoured personnel carriers and M41 light tanks pushed for-

ward up Route 1 with supporting infantry, calling in strikes by US fighter bombers and helicopter gunships to overcome opposition. In fact, they encountered relatively light resistance: within three days the ARVN force reached the limit of its operational area and began a series of sweeps in search of communist troops and supplies.

Further to the north, the Fish Hook incursion had started a day late, on 1 May. The Fish Hook region was quite different from the Parrot's Beak, being densely forested, difficult terrain. General Shoemaker had decided on a 'hammer and anvil' operation, in which units of the ARVN 3rd Airborne Brigade would be flown into blocking positions to the north of the presumed enemy concentrations while US and ARVN ground forces advanced from the south, west and east. After overnight bombing by B-52s, at dawn an artillery barrage and tactical air strikes hammered the attack zone. Then the ARVN airborne troops were heli-lifted into three landing zones which had been cleared in the jungle by the dropping of 6800kg (15,000lb) bombs fused to detonate just above ground level. At the same time, the 3rd Brigade of the US 1st Cavalry, supported by tanks and mechanised infantry, the US 11th Armored Cavalry Regiment and the ARVN 1st Armored Cavalry Regiment advanced across the border. There was little resistance, but the number of enemy located was correspondingly disappointing. Most casualties were inflicted by gunships harrying small units of communists fleeing to the west and north. On 3 May the town of Mimot was occupied and on 6 May Snoul was taken. Near there, the Americans uncovered a large complex of supply depots, training facilities and living accommodation deserted by the communists. 'The City', as it became known, had served the NVA 7th Division; much attention was devoted to the destruction of the complex and to ferrying any useful supplies back to South Vietnam.

By mid-May the 1st and 2nd Brigades of the 1st Air Cavalry had joined in the operation, which developed into a lengthy search for communist supply dumps and bases within the 32km (20 mile) limit imposed on the depth of incursion into Cambodia. There were numerous small-scale encounters with the enemy, but most communist troops had withdrawn further from the border. Following a politically-imposed limit on the US incursion, the Fish Hook operation ended on 30 June, the withdrawal of forces being carried out efficiently and in good order. ARVN activity in the Parrot's Beak and further south along the Mekong River continued into July.

The military balance sheet of the Cambodian incur-

Blackboard operations at home (top) as Nixon explains the Cambodian incursions to the US public.

The Cambodian incursions

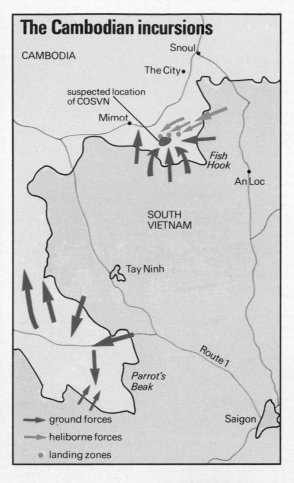

CAMBODIA

Snoul

The City•

suspected location
of COSVN

Mimot•

Fish Hook

An Loc•

SOUTH
VIETNAM

Tay Ninh

Route 1

Parrot's Beak

Saigon

➤ ground forces
➤ heliborne forces
• landing zones

Above and below: The hard fighting winkling out the Viet Cong from within Cambodia.

sions was favourable to the South Vietnamese and the Americans. The US Army claimed that almost 5000 communists had been killed; US casualties were given as 338 killed and 1525 wounded. Great quantities of communist equipment were seized and their ability to operate into South Vietnam was, at least temporarily, seriously impaired. But COSVN – if it existed – was not found, and driving the NVA and Viet Cong deeper into Cambodia certainly did nothing to improve Lon Nol's security.

A political disaster

Politically, the invasion of Cambodia was a disaster. A wave of opposition to the widening of the war broke out as soon as it was announced. Across America students occupied faculty buildings, and there was a new virulence to the demonstrations. On 4 May, at Kent State University, Ohio, the National Guard shot four students dead and wounded 11 others. Almost every college in the country closed in protest, and the White House was besieged by demonstrators. In Congress reaction to the incursions was also generally hostile. President Nixon was given a 30 June deadline, by which time all US troops had to be withdrawn from Cambodia. Moreover, the Gulf of Tonkin Resolution, which had given the president a free hand to fight the war, was repealed. Henceforth the president would have to seek Congressional approval for any ground operations outside South Vietnam – approval which would not be forthcoming.

Under mounting pressure, President Nixon promised to speed up US troop withdrawals. Thus the final effect of the Cambodian operation was to limit still further American options in the Vietnam conflict, increasing the urgency of Vietnamization and of the search for a negotiated basis for American withdrawal. **Edward Trowbridge**

Lam Son 719

Attacking the Ho Chi Minh Trail in Laos

In late 1970 intelligence reports concerning North Vietnamese activity on the Ho Chi Minh Trail convinced US commanders that a major offensive against South Vietnam's northern provinces was being prepared for the following spring. The US Army had long been keen to launch a ground attack against the Trail in Laos; in 1967 General Westmoreland had envisaged the use of 60,000 troops to cut the Trail. But under the Johnson administration the idea of an incursion by ground forces into neutral Laos was consistently rejected by the politicians, and interdiction of the communist supply route was restricted to extensive bombing, the deployment of sensors, and some secret Special Forces' operations. As he had shown by authorising the Cambodian incursion earlier in 1970, however, President Nixon would not impose the same limits as his predecessor, and in December he agreed that planning should begin for a South Vietnamese invasion of Laos backed by US air and artillery support – the use of American ground forces beyond South Vietnam's borders having being strictly ruled out by Congress.

The operation was destined to be the first severe test of Vietnamization, since the Army of the Republic of Vietnam (ARVN) would have to enter combat in hostile territory without even the assistance of US advisers; it was to be the first time for a decade that the ARVN had fought without advisers present. Command of the ARVN side of the operation – code-named Lam Son 719 after the site of a Vietnamese victory over the Chinese in the 15th century – was allotted to Lieutenant-General Hoang Xuan Lam, commander of I Corps, ARVN. The US contribution – code-named Dewey Canyon – was placed under Lieutenant-General James W. Sutherland, commanding US XXIV Corps. Planning went ahead at top speed, and on 18 January 1971 official authorisation was given for operations to begin on 30 January.

The target of the incursion was the North Vietnamese Base Area 604, centred on the town of Tchepone some 22km (35 miles) inside Laos. Because of weather conditions along the Trail, it was suspected that the month of February would see the maximum concentration of communist supplies and equipment in the Base Area. The prime aim of Lam Son 719 was to destroy supplies and the logistics

Below: While a gun team check range and elevation (foreground) on an artillery piece, a Sikorsky 'flying crane' prepares to land a 155mm howitzer. During the incursion into Laos, over 10,000 US troops were involved in providing ground support and cross-border artillery barrages.

infrastructure, along with inflicting casualties on the North Vietnamese Army (NVA). The incursion was also intended to stop the flow of material southwards by cutting the Trail, but this would only be temporary since the South Vietnamese did not intend to stay.

South Vietnamese forces allotted to the operation comprised the 1st Infantry Division, the 1st Airborne Division, the Marine Division, three Ranger battalions, the 1st Armored Brigade and three armoured cavalry squadrons. These were more or less the best troops the ARVN could field, but they numbered only some 17,000 men, compared with the 60,000 US troops General Westmoreland had considered necessary when planning an earlier invasion. Still, the scale of US support was generous: 2000 fixed-wing aircraft, over 600 helicopters, and some 10,000 troops on the ground providing cross-border artillery support and operating along Route 9 inside South Vietnam. The US Army contribution involved units of XXIV Corps Headquarters, the 101st Airborne Division (Airmobile), the 5th Infantry Division (Mechanized) and the 23rd Infantry Division (Americal). The crucial aviation task force providing airmobility was based on 101st Airborne Division's aviation component augmented by air cavalry units from other formations.

The area of the incursion lay within the North Vietnamese 70B Corps area. Formations in this part of Laos included the NVA 304th, 308th and 320th Infantry Divisions, two artillery regiments and an armoured regiment. The North Vietnamese were well prepared for a possible incursion, with extensive anti-aircraft defences deployed in mutually supporting batteries; there may have been 19 anti-aircraft battalions stationed in Base Area 604. The heavily forested mountain terrain offered few natural sites for landing zones (LZs), and the NVA had identified and defended most of these positions. The weather in February was unreliable and could be expected to interrupt US air operations with mist and low cloud.

At midnight on 30 January the Americans and South Vietnamese moved into action. Initial operations were carried out in Quang Tri Province, preparing the ground for the incursion. The 1st Brigade of the US 5th Infantry Division and ARVN forces re-occupied the abandoned US base at Khe Sanh which was to serve as a forward staging area for helicopters and a forward artillery base, while other US and ARVN troops set about clearing Route 9 of mines and ambushes up to the Laotian border. The communists at once interpreted these activities as harbingers of an offensive, but efforts were made to confuse them as to the actual target of the coming incursion: artillery of the 101st Airborne Division shelled targets in Base Area 611, to the south of Base Area 604, and the ARVN 1st Infantry Division made a diversionary advance towards the demilitarised zone (DMZ). Suspecting that an invasion of Laos was on the way, not only the North Vietnamese but also peace groups in the United States and even the American-backed neutralist government of Laos denounced the operation in advance.

On 8 February at 1000 hours, the ARVN 1st Armored Brigade rolled across the Laotian border, heading up Route 9 towards Tchepone. To the north of the road, on the right flank of the advance, the three Ranger battalions established two hilltop firebases. Units of the ARVN 1st Airborne Division were flown deeper into Laos, setting up two more firebases on the same right flank and landing at the village of Aloui on Route 9, where they met up with the 1st Armored

Brigade on 10 February. On the left flank, the ARVN 1st Infantry Division was heli-lifted onto the escarpment which towers 300m (1000ft) above the Xe Pon River to the south of Route 9. The South Vietnamese Marines were held in reserve near Khe Sanh.

During these first days of the incursion, opposition was relatively light, but the NVA 70B Corps quickly began to muster a vigorous response. The Corps' own forces were soon concentrated on the area of the incursion and reinforcements were rushed from North Vietnam and other parts of Laos. As the communist units pressed down from the north, the Airborne and Ranger firebases on the right flank of the South Vietnamese advance came under heavy pressure. Artillery, sapper and infantry attacks wore down the ARVN defenders, who depended on helicopter resupply and close air support for their survival. But the weight of anti-aircraft fire brought to bear by the NVA began to take its toll on the US 'Huey Slicks' and Cobras. The North Vietnamese fully exploited the well-tried technique of 'hugging' their enemy – getting in so near that close air support could not be used for fear of inflicting casualties on one's own side. Low cloud, mist and the smoke of artillery barrages frequently made the helicopter pilots' task more difficult. Flying in mountainous terrain, they found themselves forced to follow routes that were soon recognised by the NVA who covered them with anti-aircraft fire. The lack of US advisers on the ground to coordinate airstrikes limited the effectiveness of the usual lavish US airpower.

Firebases under pressure

By 22 February the two Ranger firebases had become untenable, and the defenders were moved back to positions nearer the South Vietnam border. They had sustained heavy casualties – some 300 dead or wounded – although they claimed 639 North Vietnamese killed. The two firebases manned by the 1st Airborne Division, Objective 30 and Objective 31, remained under pressure. On 25 February the 500

Above: Officers of the ARVN 1st Airborne Division discuss the deployment of their men on Objective 31. The firebase quickly attracted the attentions of the NVA and on 25 February a communist offensive involving 20 tanks and 2000 infantry was launched against the firebase. Twice repulsed, the attackers overran the base at the third attempt and forced the ARVN defenders to withdraw.

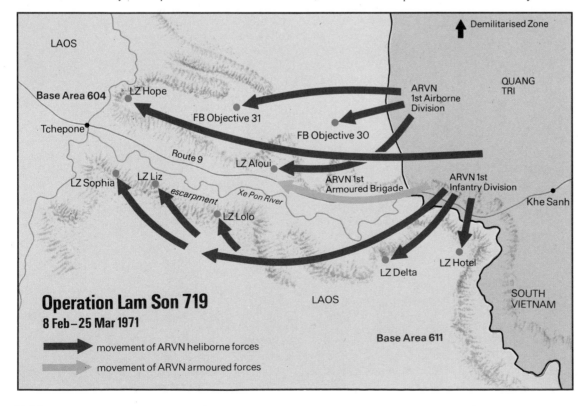

Operation Lam Son 719

8 Feb – 25 Mar 1971

→ movement of ARVN heliborne forces

→ movement of ARVN armoured forces

paratroopers defending Objective 31 were attacked by 20 PT76 tanks and 200 infantry in daylight. Assisted by heavy US air strikes the paratroopers twice repelled the attackers, but the third attempt overran the base. Some 120 South Vietnamese were taken prisoner, although NVA casualties may have numbered 1000.

The ARVN advance had now bogged down. The South Vietnamese armour on Route 9 was exposed on its right flank and subjected to harassment by ambushes and mines. Realising that the planned drive up Route 9 to Tchepone was not going to succeed, on 1 March General Lam ordered a change of tactics. The Airborne and armoured forces were put in defensive positions, while the 1st Infantry Division was flown forward in a series of heliborne moves along the southern escarpment. By 5 March they had established three LZs – Lolo, Liz, and Sophia – as they leapfrogged towards Tchepone. The stage was then set for the largest, longest-range heliborne assault of the Vietnam War. After a concentrated B-52 bombing strike to soften up the attack zone, two ARVN infantry battalions were flown 77km (48 miles) from Khe Sanh to landing zone Hope just to the northeast of Tchepone by an armada of helicopters. Tchepone was quickly seized; there was little resistance.

Scramble to survive

On 8 March General Sutherland pronounced the operation a complete success, quoting the quantities of supplies captured and the number of enemy killed. But the planned withdrawal which began on 10 March soon took on the air of a rout. Under pressure from a powerful NVA counter-offensive, the South Vietnamese had to be extracted from their forward positions and flown back to Quang Tri Province. Afraid of being left behind, many ARVN troops panicked, scrambling to fill helicopters and even travelling balanced perilously on the helicopter skids. The ARVN ground forces that had to fight their way back down Route 9 suffered heavy losses. On 22 March, ARVN Marines who had taken over defence of firebase Delta on the escarpment were barely evacuated in time to avoid being overrun. This was the last dramatic engagement of the operation; by 25 March

the remaining ARVN forces were back in Vietnam. Khe Sanh was evacuated two weeks later.

As so often in Vietnam, the argument over who had won and what had been achieved continued long after the fighting had stopped. South Vietnam's President Thieu boldly held a Lam Son victory parade in Saigon, but the dominant impression was one of defeat. Opponents of the war in the United States described Lam Son as a 'nightmare' and 'a massive misjudgement', while even South Vietnam's vice-president, Nguyen Cao Ky, called it a 'failure'.

The statistics paint a confused picture. ARVN casualties were certainly heavy, with possibly 2000 dead and 5500 wounded out of a total force of 17,000. Many units disintegrated; others precariously held together. More critically, this was the cream of the ARVN that had been decimated. US losses totalled 176 aircrew killed and around 2000 wounded. There were 107 helicopters destroyed, and most of those deployed sustained damage. Estimates of NVA casualties are speculative, especially since they include a rough figure for those supposed killed by more than 46,000 tons of bombs dropped by B-52s, but the communists certainly suffered badly. According to some calculations they may have lost as many as 14,000 dead, but other sources estimate the entire NVA force involved in the fighting as no more than 18,000; no solid information is to be had. The South Vietnamese claimed to have captured or destroyed over 4000 individual weapons, 2000 crew-served weapons and 20,000 tons of ammunition.

If the North Vietnamese had indeed intended to launch a major offensive in 1971, then Lam Son 719 can be said to have prevented it; the offensive did not actually come until the spring of the following year. But it is equally possible that Hanoi had no such intention. Activity on the Ho Chi Minh Trail was only temporarily disrupted, and intelligence reports indicated that two months after the incursion Tchepone had been largely reconstructed. As a test of Vietnamization, Lam Son gave mixed results; even with the most extensive US air support, an ARVN force without US advisers had proved decidedly shaky when the going got hot. **Edward Trowbridge**

Above: Two NVA soldiers keep heads down as they advance up a hillside. The rapid NVA counterattacks against the flanks of the ARVN incursion slowed the initial stages of Lam Son 719. Intense close air support and extensive use of helicopters was necessary to regain momentum.

Breakdown

The collapse of US morale in Vietnam

In June 1971 an article in the *Detroit News* claimed that the US Army in Vietnam was 'in a state of approaching collapse, with individual units avoiding or having refused combat, murdering their officers and non-commissioned officers, drug-ridden, and dispirited where not near-mutinous'. A subsequent official report by Lieutenant-General W.J. McCaffrey had to admit that 'mission accomplishment' had declined since 1969 although the erosion of discipline was described as having reached a 'serious' rather than a 'critical' level. US morale had been good between 1965 and 1967 but it had certainly entered a transitional stage by 1969 and all but disintegrated from 1970 onwards. Indeed, one controversial account of the war published in the United States in 1981 has claimed that no American unit in Vietnam was wholly usable by 1972–73.

There is little doubt that all the main indicators of morale and discipline paint the same disturbing picture. One example is the rate of desertion. Between 1965 and 1971 army desertion showed a staggering increase of 468 per cent, reaching a peak of 73.5 desertions per 1000 men during 1971 (the comparable figure at the end of the Korean War in 1953 was 22.3 per 1000). In terms of actual numbers, this meant that in 1970 some 27,000 men deserted, not counting those who went absent-without-leave but subsequently returned to unit.

Another significant indicator was the level of drugs usage. Drug abuse affected US armed forces worldwide but in Vietnam drugs were readily available since they constituted an essential component of South Vietnam's economy. In 1967 the reported incidence of marijuana usage among army personnel in Vietnam was marginally lower than the army's average worldwide, but by 1969 it was calculated, on the basis of self-reporting, that between a half and a third of American other ranks in Vietnam were using marijuana and between 5 and 10 per cent were at least occasional users of heroin. This situation continued to worsen: drug arrests rose from 8440 in 1969 to 11,058 in 1970, when a Drug Abuse Task Force had come into action. In 1971 a Department of Defense study revealed that over half of army personnel had used marijuana, just under a third had used psychedelic drugs, and over a quarter had experience of hard drugs such as opium and heroin. The use of hard drugs was particularly worrying with a total of 7026 offenders arrested in 1971, representing a seven-fold increase at a time when overall troop strength was actually declining. In all some 600,000 American servicemen may have acquired a drugs habit in Vietnam, although evidence suggests that drugs were not widely used during combat itself.

A far more damaging sign of the fragility of discipline and morale was the increasing number of 'fragging' incidents in which American officers, NCOs or men were murdered by their fellow servicemen.

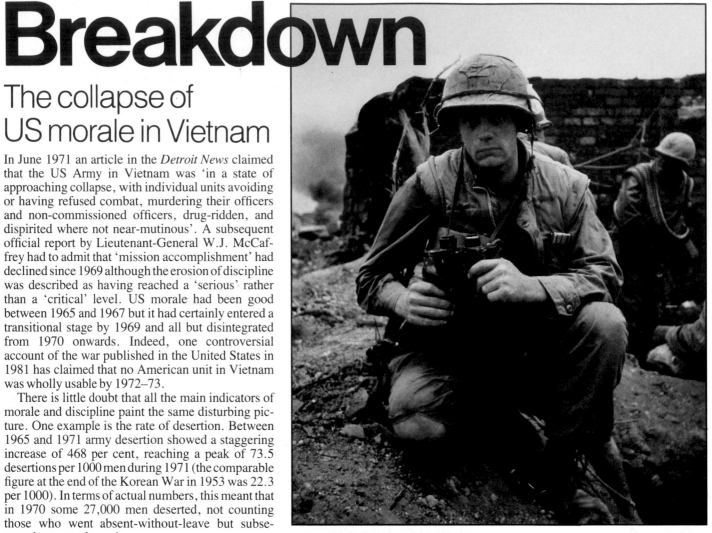

The collapse of US morale in Vietnam was a gradual process, and had various causes. Battlefield stress (left, the strain of fighting for Hue in February 1968 is shown clearly on the face of this GI) was a relatively minor element and up to 1969 the fighting ability of the average soldier was not seriously impaired. Then, however, there was a rapid slide. The use of drugs (below) increased greatly, and the more unpalatable side-effects of the US presence in Vietnam, such as the growth in prostitution (bottom, US troops are accosted in the streets of Saigon) became more obvious. The overall result was that servicemen were quite prepared to make their disenchantment with the war obvious – like the soldier below left whose helmet is an eloquent testimony to his feelings.

Official figures record 788 fragging incidents between 1969 and 1972 resulting in 88 deaths and 714 injuries, but it is possible that as few as 10 per cent of incidents were recorded and that over 1000 officers and men were actually killed in this fashion. Fraggings were not usually the result of an individual vendetta but the planned action of a group of men. Although about half the recorded attacks were on officers and NCOs, fraggings could also result from racial tensions or 'dope hassles'. A related problem was 'combat refusal'. The only official figures are those for 'insubordination, mutiny and other acts' which show 330 convictions between 1968 and 1970. However, it has been claimed that there were 35 'individual refusals' in the crack 1st Air Cavalry Division alone during 1970. Also in many cases negotiations took place between officers and men ('talking it out') over whether to carry out orders issued for individual operations. An officer who insisted on the execution of a combat patrol or an assault which led to heavy casualties amongst his men might find himself a prime target for fragging, either as a form of 'revenge attack' or as self-defence on the part of soldiers who feared the over-keen officer would soon lead them to death or mutilation. After the bloody battle for Hamburger Hill during the 1969 A Shau Valley operation, a soldiers' underground newspaper offered a $10,000 reward for anyone who would kill the officer who had ordered the attack – though he did survive his tour of duty.

Disciplinary problems were exacerbated by the racial tension imported into the army in Vietnam from conflicts back home. The civil rights movement, ghetto riots and the various black power movements – the Black Panthers, the Black Muslims, and so on – had created a mood of aggressive black self-assertion against white authority. It was a widely-held view amongst black Americans that Vietnam was the White Man's war, and that they had no business fighting it. Under combat conditions such attitudes tended to evaporate – blacks and whites integrated in the cause of common survival – but out of combat many blacks practised a self-imposed segregation. Black troops developed greater loyalty to one another than to the army, symbolising their racial consciousness by black power salutes and the adoption of distinctive social customs. It has been claimed that black troops had their own enclave in Saigon which was a 'no-go' area for US military police. Many isolated acts of indiscipline occurred. In one incident in October 1971, for example, 14 black servicemen barricaded themselves inside a bunker at 'Whiskey Mountain' base, after they had been refused permission to attend a civil rights memorial service. In 1968–69, when blacks totalled 9.1 per cent of the US forces in Vietnam, some 58 per cent of all those in army stockades for disciplinary purposes were blacks.

Dealing on the black market

Crime was not, of course, confined to black personnel. Corruption is alleged to have provided the Viet Cong with more material aid in terms of equipment than either China or the Soviet Union. In 1967 there were only 64 courts martial for currency violations and black marketeering but in 1968 this figure rose to 471. Courts martial generally swelled from a total of 814 in 1965 to a staggering 9922 in 1969.

A symptom of the general decline of discipline was the growing number of war crimes perpetrated against Vietnamese civilians by American servicemen, the most serious of which was the My Lai massacre of March 1968. There were 241 official allegations of war crimes by army personnel, the large majority dating from 1968 onwards. Of these a total of 78 were substantiated, although only 31 men were ever convicted on resulting charges. A further 201 army personnel were convicted of other serious crimes against civilians, mostly for homicide or rape. In the nature of things – as the story of the My Lai cover-up shows – many war crimes must have gone unreported. On the other hand, it must be recognised that there was something of a war crimes 'industry'; such bodies as Vietnam Veterans Against the War in the United States and the Bertrand Russell War Crimes Tribunal in Stockholm were devoted to uncovering American atrocities.

Although there was clearly much incidental brutality, the American record was probably no worse in this respect than many other armies under similar circumstances. In many areas they found themselves fighting amongst a basically hostile population, where civilians and enemy guerrillas were virtually indistinguishable. Mines and booby-traps caused US patrols terrible casualties, with no indication of who had laid them; nothing could be more tempting than to take revenge at random on a local village, almost certainly inhabited by Viet Cong sympathisers if not by actual part-time combatants. Some officers were

Massacre at My Lai

The events at My Lai occurred as a result of a wider 'search and destroy' operation being conducted by battalion-sized Task Force Barker (Lieutenant-Colonel F. Barker) under the direction of the 11th Infantry Brigade (Colonel O.K. Henderson) of the 23rd Infantry (Americal) Division (Major-General S.W. Koster). Task Force Barker itself consisted of three companies from different battalions of which two – B (Bravo) Company of 4/3rd Infantry, and C (Charlie) Company of 1/20th Infantry commanded by Captain E.L. Medina – would take part in the operation. The task of C Company was to clear My Lai-4, a sub-hamlet of My Lai which was itself a hamlet of Son My village in the Son Tinh District of Quang Ngai Province.

The area was a known location of the formidable Viet Cong 48th Local Force Battalion and American units operating in its vicinity had suffered numerous casualties without ever closing with the enemy. Heavy opposition and casualties were expected and Henderson had said he was determined to eliminate the Viet Cong 'once and for all'. In anticipation of heavy losses, no warning was to be given to the village, as was permitted in such circumstances under the Rules of Engagement. It was expected, however, that all civilians would have left for market by the time of the operation and that only Viet Cong would remain. Precise orders do not appear to have been issued but it was generally accepted that in his briefing Medina 'left little or no doubt in the minds of a significant number of men in his company that all persons remaining in the My Lai-4 area at the time of combat assault were enemy and that C Company's mission was to destroy the enemy'. It was also intended to burn the hamlet, destroy crops and kill livestock.

When the first helicopters touched down at 0730 on 16 March 1968 there was confusion over whether they were being fired on although, in fact, no fire was received. The Company cleared the hamlet and during the operation at least two large groups of civilians were killed in cold blood, one group of 70 people being massacred in a ditch. Only three Viet Cong actually seem to have been among those killed. There were some rape-killings and at least one gang rape. The subsequent Peers enquiry made a 'conservative' estimate of 172–200 civilians killed, although the army's Criminal Investigation Department calculated 347 and certainly well over 400 were killed in Son My as a whole – B Company was responsible for similar murders at the hamlet of My Khe-4. The enquiry pointed to a number of contributing factors including an unfamiliarity with the laws of war, the 'gook syndrome' – the belief that the civilians were all VC sympathisers and might have laid mines and booby traps themselves – the expectation of heavy losses against a

On the orders of Captain Ernest Medina (right), Lieutenant William Calley (above right) led a unit of US troops into the village of My Lai during a search and sweep operation. The result of the operation was the massacre of local villagers that shocked the world (above, some of the bodies).

formidable opponent, the lack of specific orders and, above all, the inexperience of younger officers and the permissive attitude that had developed at all command levels in the division.

The attempt to conceal what had occurred succeeded until an ex-GI turned reporter, Ronald Ridenhour, began, in April 1969, to investigate allegations of a massacre at 'Pinkville'. This then led to investigation by the military authorities and the establishment of the Peers enquiry in November 1969. The fact that Medina had reported 90 Viet Cong dead but had requested no fire support and had received no casualties beyond one case of a self-inflicted wound should have aroused suspicion. Similarly, both Barker and Henderson had flown low enough over My Lai during the operation to have seen something amiss, while Koster knew from other sources that at least 28 civilians had been killed but did not press an investigation at the time. Peers named 30 individuals as guilty of omission or commission concerning My Lai. However, of the 16 men charged only five were court-martialled and only Lieutenant William J. Calley found guilty. Medina was acquitted through flawed instructions given to the jury by the judge while Peers subsequently remarked that the dismissal of charges against Henderson, Koster and others was 'most difficult to understand'. Others guilty of offences in relation to My Lai were never brought to trial.

Calley was found guilty on three counts of premeditated murder of 22 civilians and one count of assault with intent to murder a child. He was sentenced to life imprisonment with hard labour at the conclusion of his court martial in March 1971. In face of considerable support for Calley, who appeared something of a scapegoat, President Nixon agreed to review the sentence. Although numerous appeals subsequently failed, Calley's sentence was reduced to 20 years in August 1971 and to 10 years in April 1974. He was finally released on parole in November 1974.

only too willing to accept civilian dead as Viet Cong in order to boost their units' 'body-count'. In general, it cannot be said that the Americans showed particular sensitivity towards Vietnamese civilians even in relatively friendly urban areas, although contact was often close: there were at least 10,000 illegitimate children by American fathers by the end of 1968.

The decline in morale and discipline in Vietnam corresponded to the time of troop withdrawals and falling combat casualties. Between 1968 and 1971 the number of American deaths in Vietnam fell by 85 per cent. Thus it was clearly not the strains of combat that led to disintegration, nor was it due to any shortcomings in living conditions. By comparison with their predecessors in other wars the US servicemen in Vietnam enjoyed considerable luxury. At base they were likely to have the use of swimming pools, beaches, air-conditioned recreation facilities, and good quality food.

Some officers attributed the disintegration of the army to anti-war propaganda emanating from the United States or even the general effect of a 'permissive' society. Certainly, each fresh intake of draftees or regular soldiers transferred from home postings brought with it the latest developments in social attitudes, ideas and customs. It was not only blacks who carried with them a hostility to authority and doubts about the war that had been bred at home. A sizeable proportion of the young white draftees had some experience of the drug culture or youth revolt that was pervading the main urban centres across the United States. Many observers described a general breakdown of social cohesion and discipline in Amer-

ica at this time, of which the army's disintegration could equally have been a reflection.

More specifically, US servicemen were influenced to a degree by anti-war attitudes emanating from back home. They read newspapers from home in which the war was frequently criticised, and there was also a plethora of underground newspapers in circulation, most of them short-lived, which were often highly subversive in content. Organisations appeared within the forces such as the Trotskyite 'American Servicemen's Union', 'Resisters in the Army' and the 'Movement for a Democratic Military', but they do not seem to have had a membership of much over 10,000 by 1971 and clearly failed to create any mass anti-war movement within the army. There was, however, a pervasive sense that the war was not being supported back home, and a widespread impression that the Vietnam involvement had been a mistake, a disaster, or an outright defeat. Up to 1967 morale had been sustained under harsh combat conditions by confidence in the power and efficiency of the American military machine and by trust that the US was once more doing its idealistic duty in the defence of freedom and democracy. After 1968 the Americans faced withdrawal without victory, and the justifications for the war had worn very thin. Inevitably, the army's self-belief suffered.

Draftees and lifers

These pressures brought out tensions within the army as an institution, playing on three crucial weaknesses in its cohesion. The first was a split between conscripts or 'draftees' and professional career soldiers or 'lifers'. The career soldiers often had a choice of arm of service denied the conscript and, as they often chose a non-combat arm, lifers tended to suffer lighter casualties than draftees. In 1969, for example, draftees represented 39 per cent of the army personnel in Vietnam but suffered 62 per cent of the casualties. Re-enlistment as a lifer also invariably meant allocation to a non-combat role.

The second factor was the rotation policy which, to some extent, was forced upon the army through the refusal of the administration to mobilise reserves for the war. In Korea, those serving in rear echelon units had invariably served a longer term than those in combat units but in Vietnam a standard 12-month tour was instituted for all. As approximately four-fifths of personnel served in support units and only one-fifth in combat units, this tended to generate resentment on the part of those at the front against those at the rear. Another result of the rotation policy was that every individual had a definite Date of Expected Return (DEROS) which put a personal terminal limit to endurance. It was generally accepted that a soldier would be 'dutifully commitful' from months two to eight, after his initial settling-down period, and would reach a peak of efficiency and commitment at month nine. Thereafter, as the DEROS approached, individuals would be increasingly intent only on personal survival. Obviously, as the US troop withdrawals got under way, this attitude was generalised: the whole army was, so to speak, in the last period of its tour of duty, and everybody's mind was concentrated on getting back safe and sound. No one wanted to be the last soldier killed in Vietnam.

Another unfortunate effect of rotation was the constant state of flux or 'turbulence' within units as men came and went, a problem which could only have

Below: Even though he is leading a combat patrol, First Lieutenant Jesse Rosen wears a black armband to show sympathy with anti-war demonstrations taking place in the USA. This form of protest by a serving officer engaged in combat would be almost inconceivable in any other army of the modern world and demonstrates the nature of the problems within the US Army during the final years of its Vietnam involvement.

Above and top: Although there was never any doubt as to their combat abilities, the most serious problems in Vietnam were with black troops. In 1968-69, 58 per cent of all those in army stockades for disciplinary purposes were black. Black power organisations such as the Black Panthers, commanded much sympathy among black soldiers in Vietnam, although there were rarely any threats of widespread political action within the armed forces.

been solved by strong leadership; crucially, this was often lacking. There was undoubtedly a widespread failure on the part of officers to exercise leadership. It was not assisted by the fact that while enlisted men did a 12-month tour, officers were required only to complete a six-month combat tour. Ostensibly this was so that they would not 'burn out' but, in reality, the army had had no combat commands since 1953 and it was intended to ensure that as many officers as possible should experience command in action. This was sensible as far as it went, but it only increased 'turbulence', one GI reported having five platoon and four company commanders during his 12-month tour in Vietnam. In the prestigious II Field Force, command averaged only seven and a half months for general officers. Worse still, the combat tour became a recognised route to promotion: over 90 per cent of second-lieutenants, first-lieutenants and captains got promotion as a result of a Vietnam tour. Promotion was, however, dependent upon demonstrable short-term results, and officers increasingly became intent on 'ticket punching' with often little regard for the welfare of the men temporarily under their command. The inflation of the notorious 'body-count' was one symptom, while the extraordinary inflation of medals

and awards was another: one brigadier-general even had to be stripped of an unearned Silver Star. In fact, awards for bravery increased as the incidence of combat declined. While the American army in Vietnam was over-officered by previous standards, the ratio of officers to men rising from 1:11.9 in World War II to 1:6.5 in Vietnam, the rate of officer casualties declined. Yet although not visible at the front, officers were seemingly highly visible in the rear; senior officers were involved in both scandals and black marketeering. Both the deputy chief of staff for personnel and administration and the provost marshal general were entangled in corruption charges during the war.

The declining quality of the officer corps was highlighted by Lieutenant-General Peers in a memorandum accompanying his official enquiry report on the My Lai incident in March 1970. As a result the Army War College was commissioned to produce a report, 'The Study on Military Professionalism', which was published in June 1970. The report found that the army had departed from its former emphasis on the officer as 'gladiator' to one of 'manager'. Officers were now showing signs of selfish promotion-orientated behaviour, dishonest reporting of 'status statistics', disloyalty to subordinates, technical and managerial incompetence and an inadequate grasp of communication. Far from being a result of Vietnam or contemporary social pressures, the failures were internally generated. As a result there was to be a new emphasis on teaching ethics and leadership to American officers.

To a large extent, then, Vietnam only exacerbated existing problems within the army and the decline in morale and discipline was related to the character and integrity of the officer corps rather than the strains of combat. Disintegration came at a time of disengagement from Vietnam and therefore its contribution to the American failure is hard to assess. Clearly, however, from 1969 the outcome of the war would depend upon the speed and effectiveness of Vietnamization rather than the efficiency of the increasingly unreliable American units, where it was a case of 'the unwilling led by the unqualified, doing the unnecessary for the ungrateful.' **Ian Beckett**

STRATEGIC MISSILES
part 2

Alongside the USAF's ground-launched missiles, the US Navy operates a similar arsenal of submarine-launched strategic weapons. The first of these, the Lockheed UGM-27A Polaris A-1, became operational in November 1960 aboard the USS *George Washington*, the first of a class of five similarly-armed vessels. Polaris A-1 was rapidly replaced (from 1962) by the A-2 which offered an increased range. The final version, the A-3, appeared in 1964 and it is this weapon which has been supplied to the Royal Navy to arm its four Resolution-class submarines.

Today the Royal Navy remains the only Polaris operator, the US Navy having withdrawn the type in 1981 and replaced it with the Lockheed UGM-73A Poseidon C3. The 64 British weapons have always carried locally-manufactured warheads and today are believed to be equipped with MIRVs (multiple independently-targetted re-entry vehicles) – developed under the 1973 Chevaline programme – which are able to carry six 40-kiloton nuclear devices each.

In keeping with the 'MIRVing' of the USAF's strategic weapons, the Poseidon (which became operational in 1971) was designed from the outset to carry a payload of ten MIRVs. Essentially an enlarged, more capable Polaris, the UGM-73A has armed 31 vessels of the Benjamin Franklin and Lafayette classes, 19 of which remain in service. During its service life, Poseidon has been up-dated and the remaining 304 operational rounds carry 14 MIRVs each armed with a 50-kiloton warhead.

The US Navy's latest strategic missile, the Lockheed-built Trident, entered service in October 1979 aboard a converted Poseidon submarine. Two versions of the weapon have appeared, the UGM-93A Trident I C4 and the Trident II D5. Like all Lockheed's previous submarine-launched missiles, Trident I is a solid fuel powered weapon and carries seven MIRVs each armed with a 100-kiloton W-76 warhead. Presently, 12 Benjamin Franklin-class submarines have been modified to carry it and the weapon

Previous page: The first launch of the Trident missile on the 18 January 1977. Below: The two-stage Polaris missile. Work on this weapon began in the mid-1950s and the original A-1 missile became operational in 1960, providing the West with the most advanced nuclear delivery system then available. Opposite page: A Polaris A-3 is prepared for a test firing (left) and blasts skyward following a submarine launch (right).

forms the initial armament of the new Ohio-class vessels, the first of which was commissioned in November 1981.

Trident II differs from the UGM-93A in using a more powerful propellant, carrying ten MIRVs each with a 335-kiloton warhead and having an extremely accurate guidance system. Trident II will be carried by the Ohio-class submarines in the US Navy and it is the weapon chosen to replace Polaris in Royal Navy service. The current British plan is to build four new submarines, each carrying 16 missiles, with a service entry date in the mid-1990s.

Britain has made large-scale use of American strategic missiles but has never operated a weapon of local origin. This is not to say, however, that such a missile has never been built. Indeed, as early as 1955 a specification for a British ballistic missile was drawn-up which evolved into the Blue Streak. Developed by Hawker Siddeley, the British weapon employed two Rolls-Royce liquid-fuelled motors offering a total

Lockheed UGM-27C Polaris A-3 (US Navy version)

Type Submarine-launched strategic missile
Dimensions Length 9.85m (32ft 4in)
Weight Launch 15,900kg (35,060lb)
Powerplant 1×36,000kg (79,380lb) thrust solid-fuelled Aerojet type (first stage); 1×solid-fuelled Hercules type (second stage)
Range 4000km (2484 miles)
Guidance Inertial
Warhead Three independently targetable vehicles each carrying a 200-kiloton nuclear device

Right: The Trident's advantage over previous submarine-launched missiles is its greater range, larger warhead and increased accuracy.
Below: The launch of a Poseidon C3 missile. Poseidon was developed from Polaris and its improved accuracy and greater payload provided an eight-fold increase in effectiveness over Polaris.

thrust of 123,000kg (274,000lb) and was envisaged as having a range of 4022km (2500 miles) with a nuclear warhead. Unlike the American first-generation weapons, such as the Atlas, Blue Streak was intended to be silo-launched and it was the cost of such a system, combined with the increasingly obvious advantages of solid-fuel missiles, which finally led to the cancellation of the project in April 1960.

More successful in developing an independent strategic system were the French who currently operate two nine-round squadrons of land-based weapons and six missile-armed submarines. The land-based

Lockheed UGM-73A Poseidon C3

Type Submarine-launched strategic missile
Dimensions Length 10.36m (33ft 11in)
Weight Launch 29,500kg (65,048lb)
Powerplant 2×solid-fuelled Hercules types (first and second stages)
Range 4600km (2857 miles)
Guidance Inertial
Warhead Ten or 14 MIRVs each carrying a 50-kiloton nuclear device

Right: A Trident is launched from the submarine USS *Francis Scott Key*. Far right: A French two-stage S3 is fired from the launch pad. Possessing a range of 3150km (1957 miles) it is capable of hitting targets in the Soviet Union but in turn is highly vulnerable to Soviet pre-emptive strikes.
Below: Britain's nuclear deterrent consists of Polaris-armed submarines which are far more effective than silo-launched missiles such as the abortive British Blue Streak (inset), cancelled in 1960.

Lockheed UGM-93A Trident I C4

Type Submarine-launched strategic missile
Dimensions Length 10.36m (33ft 11in)
Weight Launch 32,000kg (70,560lb)
Powerplant 3×solid-fuelled Hercules types (first, second and third stages)
Range 7000km (4347 miles)
Guidance Inertial
Warhead Seven MIRVs each carrying a 100-kiloton W-76 nuclear device

system became operational in 1971 when the first Aérospatiale SSBS S2 was delivered. A solid-fuel, two-stage weapon, the S2 was capable of delivering a 150-kiloton nuclear warhead over a range of 2750km (1708 miles). Work on a replacement for this weapon began in 1973 and the first example of the new model, the S3, entered service in 1980. Again a solid-fuelled missile, the S3 carries a 1.2-megaton warhead over a range of 3150km (1957 miles) and is believed to have a reaction time of three-and-a-half minutes.

France's submarine-launched system became operational in 1971 with the commissioning of the

Redoutable carrying 16 Aérospatiale MSBS M1 missiles. Like its land-based counterparts, the M1 was a two-stage, solid-fuel weapon with a range of 2593km (1610 miles). The M1 was replaced by the M2 which offered a range of 3148km (1955 miles) and finally the M20 which entered service in 1977 and carries a one-megaton warhead over a range of approximately 3000km (1864 miles). The French Navy is working on the M4 missile which has three stages and is designed to carry seven MIRVs, each with a 150-kiloton warhead, over a range of 4500km (2795 miles).

Quite what value the French 'independent' nuclear deterrent would have in the event of an all-out nuclear war remains debatable, especially when compared to the vast arsenals of the USA and the Soviet Union. But if nothing else, France's nuclear programme is a sop to national pride and in the event of nuclear war could be usefully deployed in support of US nuclear strikes. And certainly, the French seem determined to continue their strategic missile programme.

Aérospatiale SSBS S3

Type Land-based strategic missile
Dimensions Length 13.8m (45ft 3in)
Weight Launch 25,800kg (56,880lb)
Powerplant 1×55,000kg (121,275lb) thrust
solid-fuelled Aérospatiale/SEP P16 (first stage); 1×
32,000kg (70,560lb) thrust solid-fuelled
Aérospatiale/SEP P6 (second stage)
Range 3150km (1957 miles)
Guidance Inertial
Warhead 1.2 megaton nuclear housed in a re-entry
vehicle

Aérospatiale MSBS M20

Type Submarine-launched strategic missile
Dimensions Length 10.4m (34ft)
Weight 20,000kg (44,120lb)
Powerplant 1×45,027kg (99,207lb) thrust
solid-fuelled Aérospatiale/SEP P10 (first stage);
1×32,019kg (70,592lb) solid-fuelled
Aérospatiale/SEP 6 (second stage)
Range 3000km (1864 miles)
Guidance Inertial
Warhead One megaton

Below: The French M4 missile is launched from the experimental submarine *Gymnote* as part of a trials programme begun in 1980. Inset: A scale model of the M4 is lowered into its tube aboard the *Gymnote*. The M4 is the successor to the M20 missile which equips five submarines, each capable of holding sixteen missiles.

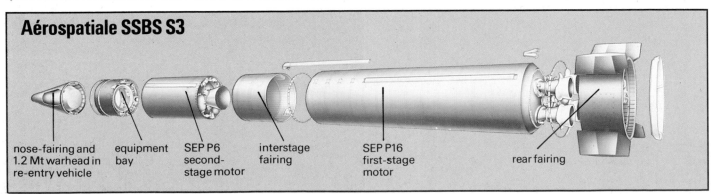

Aérospatiale SSBS S3

nose-fairing and
1.2 Mt warhead in
re-entry vehicle

equipment
bay

SEP P6
second-
stage motor

interstage
fairing

SEP P16
first-stage
motor

rear fairing

Civil rights and sectarian violence

Northern Ireland 1967-69

Northern Ireland was born out of the reluctance of Protestants in Ireland's northern province of Ulster to come under the control of a Catholic government in Dublin and their desire to maintain the 'Union' with Great Britain. In 1921 six of Ulster's counties became Northern Ireland, remaining part of the United Kingdom under the rule of the British government, but with its own parliament and prime minister at Stormont. The borders of Northern Ireland are drawn in such a way as to guarantee the Protestants political primacy and they consequently assumed a permanent hold on power at Stormont. Violent conflict between Catholics and Protestants occurred sporadically through the years. Many of the Catholic minority were 'Nationalists', desiring the unification of Ireland under the Dublin government; the Irish Republican Army (IRA), both south and north of the border, until the 1960s advocated an armed campaign to unify Ireland. The policing of the province was in the hands of the Protestant-dominated Royal Ulster Constabul-

ary (RUC), whose duties included border defence and who were armed as a paramilitary body rather than a civilian police force; if necessary, the RUC could call on the B Specials, a militia (wholly composed of Protestants) which acted as a local police reserve. The Protestant hold on political power led to discrimination against Catholics in such areas as housing and employment. Even in a predominantly Catholic area such as Londonderry the 'gerrymandering' of electoral boundaries could ensure a Protestant majority on the local council, which would then defend Protestant interests.

Still, the early and mid-1960s were comparatively good years in Northern Ireland. An IRA campaign begun in 1956 had petered out by 1962, and it seemed that the 'physical force' tradition of Irish nationalism had fallen into abeyance. By the middle years of the decade there had been a marked relaxation of security throughout the province, especially in the border areas. RUC barracks, which had been fortified with

Above: Critical moments in Northern Ireland. RUC men look on helplessly as rioters take over areas of Londonderry after the 'Apprentice Boys of Derry' march of 12 August 1969. It was the inability of the RUC to cope with the situation in Londonderry that led directly to the deployment of British soldiers on the streets of the province of Northern Ireland. The events of August 1969 were a distinct break. The civil authorities had admitted that they could no longer keep order on the streets of the province.

rewarded by granting concessions to the 'disloyal' Catholics.

While O'Neill raised apprehension among many Protestants, he stimulated rising expectations within the Catholic community. These were increasingly expressed in terms of civil rights agitation. One of the chief Catholic grievances concerned housing. The effective start of the Northern Ireland troubles can be dated to June 1968 when Austin Currie, a young Nationalist MP in the Stormont parliament, drew attention to council-housing discrimination in Dungannon, County Tyrone. The issue prompted the Northern Ireland Civil Rights Association (NICRA) to organise its first civil rights protest march.

NICRA was another manifestation of the rising expectations. It was founded early in 1967 and drew support from a broad spectrum of opinion, including old-fashioned Catholic Nationalists, trades unionists, republicans and liberal Unionists. Its aims included reform of the local government franchise so as to provide one-man-one-vote in council elections; the redrawing of 'gerrymandered' electoral boundaries; and the establishment of machinery to prevent discrimination by public bodies.

IRA involvement

Among the founders of NICRA were undoubtedly a number of IRA sympathisers. The involvement of the IRA in an avowedly non-violent organisation reflected a shift in IRA tactics away from relying on a guerrilla or terror campaign to a more political approach, which combined Marxist aims with the more traditional Nationalist aspirations. But the involvement of any IRA men at NICRA demonstrations persuaded suspicious Protestants that the civil rights agitation was no more than an IRA plot to bring down the state.

The first civil rights march was held in Dungannon on 24 August 1968. It was a striking success. It attracted some 4000 people, including Bernadette Devlin and Gerry Fitt MP (now Lord Fitt). Despite the presence of over a thousand counter-demonstrators, some of them mobilised by a 'Loyalist' paramilitary group called the Ulster Protestant Volunteers, the march went off peacefully. For the civil rights supporters it raised optimistic hopes that the key to reform lay in non-sectarian and non-violent action.

There were immediate calls for further marches. Under the NICRA banner a number of mainly radical groups organised a march in Londonderry on 5 October. In order to symbolise NICRA's claim to be non-sectarian, the march was planned to traverse both Protestant and Catholic districts of the city. But local Unionist groups strongly objected and the minister of home affairs banned part of the route. Nevertheless, the marchers, who included Fitt and three backbench British Labour MPs, went ahead along the original route. When the RUC attempted to stop it, rioting broke out and continued all night. Eleven police and 72 civilians were injured.

Despite the violence, the 5 October march boosted support for the civil rights campaign. The Derry Citizens' Action Committee, one of whose leaders was an ex-teacher called John Hume, was set up to coordinate future protests. In Belfast, students at Queen's University – both Catholic and Protestant – combined to form the 'People's Democracy' (PD) and began a series of marches throughout the province – a local expression of the worldwide student unrest in

Ian Paisley (left) was a hard-line Unionist while Bernadette Devlin (below) was a fiery civil rights leader. Early marches (bottom right, August 1968) were relatively peaceful, but at the Burntollet Bridge confrontation in January 1969 (above and right), violence was predominant.

sand-bags and barbed wire, were returned to normal and the B Specials were largely demobilised.

In economic and social terms these were also years of improvement, although unemployment in Northern Ireland remained at three or four times the United Kingdom average. The postwar development of the Welfare State – in terms of social legislation Northern Ireland went 'step by step' with Great Britain – had led to a bettering of living standards. Together with the expansion of grant-aided higher education, the improving economic situation stimulated the growth of a significant Catholic middle class. This group within the half-million strong Northern Ireland Catholic population was increasingly prepared to question, if not also to challenge, the long-standing dominance of the province's one million Protestants.

But there was also a degree of political liberalisation within the predominantly Unionist Protestant community. In 1963 Captain Terence O'Neill succeeded Viscount Brookborough as prime minister of Northern Ireland. Although an Old Etonian landowner who had served with the Irish Guards during World War II, O'Neill deliberately set out to be a reformer. He encouraged cross-border contacts with the Irish Republic and sought to improve community relations, hoping to draw the new Catholic middle class more fully into the public life of the province.

For some Protestants, however, even O'Neill's gradualist reform was far too revolutionary. One man in particular, Ian Paisley, came to epitomise the traditional Protestant Unionist reaction to the 'modernisation' of the 1960s. Paisley, founder of his own Free Presbyterian Church in the early 1950s, first came into political prominence in 1963 when he led a march to the Belfast City Hall in protest at the lowering of the Union Flag to mark the death of Pope John XXIII. In his opposition to the civil rights campaign of 1968–69, he played on lower-class Protestant fears that their steadfast loyalty to the Unionist Party and the British system was being

1968. In their turn these provoked 'Paisleyite' counter-demonstrations and they frequently culminated in rioting. In November Captain O'Neill announced some moderate reform proposals concerning council housing and local government. Although these were welcomed by NICRA, the PD declared itself totally unsatisfied and planned a New Year march from Belfast to Londonderry.

The by-now inevitable counter-protest was organised. On Saturday 4 January 1969 the marchers were brutally attacked by Protestant extremists – some of them members of the B Specials – at Burntollet Bridge near Londonderry. When the march finally reached the city more violence erupted. There was, moreover, as the official Cameron Commission inquiry into the events later put it, an 'unfortunate and temporary breakdown of discipline' among the RUC, some of whom made malicious attacks on people and property in the predominantly Catholic Bogside area of Londonderry. The local people reacted with barricades and the declaration of 'Free Derry', which lasted for a week.

Following the January rioting, there was a continuous series of marches and counter-marches, often ending in riots. Particularly serious were those in Londonderry on 19–20 April, in the course of which some RUC men again committed 'acts of grave misconduct' (Cameron Commission), leaving one

innocent Catholic fatally injured. In the week that followed, a number of explosions interrupted the Belfast water supply. These, the first bombs of the present troubles, were at the time widely attributed to the IRA, but it has since been established that they were planted by a Protestant paramilitary group seeking to remove Captain O'Neill from power. Their immediate result was to bring British troops into action for the first time, as members of the local British garrison were used to protect key installations.

The rise in disorder

Although he had won a Stormont general election in February, O'Neill's pursuit of reform and conciliation in the face of the rioting had lost him the support of his Unionist colleagues, and at the end of April he resigned, to be replaced by Major James Chichester-Clark, another Old Etonian and former Irish Guardsman. For a while after O'Neill's resignation there was a pause in the apparently inexorable rise in disorder. The new prime minister promised to implement the O'Neill reforms and also announced an amnesty for all offences connected with demonstrations. Among those released from prison was Ian Paisley, gaoled in March 1969 for his part in a counter-demonstration the previous November.

The early summer of 1969 was a period of relative tranquillity, but tensions rose as the summer 'marching season' approached. Many Protestants believed that they had to reassert themselves after seeing concessions made to the mainly Catholic (and therefore 'disloyal') civil rights movement. The two chief Protestant festivals are on 12 July and 12 August. On the first the 100,000-strong Orange Order celebrates the victory of William III (of Orange) over the Catholic James II at the Battle of the Boyne in 1690 with marches all over Ulster. On 12 August comes the more exclusive 'Apprentice Boys of Derry' march to mark the 'no surrender' action of the 13 apprentices who slammed the city gates on King James's army in 1689. In 1969 the July demonstrations were violent enough, and the Derry march was to be followed by two days of very serious rioting, which would lead directly to the start of the British Army's peacekeeping role in Northern Ireland. **Keith Jeffery**

Summer of strife

In 1969 there was an even fiercer determination than usual behind the organisation of the Protestant Orange marches of 12 July and 12 August. Rioting and violent confrontation were hardly new to Northern Ireland but since the fighting of 5 October 1968 they had attracted the attention of the international media and of Westminster politicians. So far the initiative had been with the civil rights marchers who had proved that there was a powerful swell of dissident opinion in Ulster. The Protestant Loyalists felt that they needed to mount a massive demonstration of support for their own values and the Stormont government. At the same time the increasing disorder persuaded Catholics and radicals that they stood a real chance of stopping the Orange marches. Moderate leaders on both sides feared the possible consequences of the marches, but it was politically impossible for a Protestant Stormont government to ban them – and a ban would inevitably have been largely ignored.

The events of 12 July, although limited by later standards, proved quite as bad as had been feared. There was widespread rioting and on 13 July one man was killed in ugly clashes at Dungiven. The 2500-strong British Army garrison in Ulster under Lieutenant-General Sir Ian Freeland was almost called into

action: a unit went on 'stand-by' in case things got out of hand in Londonderry. In the event, the troops were not needed but anxiety about the 12 August Apprentice Boys parade through Londonderry mounted. As usual the parade would pass close to the Catholic Bogside district. Despite their recent experience of harassment from club-wielding Royal Ulster Constabulary (RUC) men the previous April, the Bogsiders were far from cowed. On 20 July a Derry Citizens Defence Association was formed; although many residents were understandably worried at the prospect of further Protestant attacks, the association was more interested in attack than defence. Extensive preparations were made for trouble: stocks of petrol bombs and stones were built up, first-aid facilities and communications prepared, and plans for barricades finalised. For their part, the Protestants seemed ready to fight it out with the Bogsiders. An appeal from Prime Minister Chichester-Clark to the organisers, asking them voluntarily to call off the parade, was turned down. There was plenty of notice of an impending crisis – further serious disturbances had occurred in Belfast on 3 August – but the Northern Ireland government had neither the resources nor the will to face it.

Above: Sectarian feelings run high in the streets of Belfast, in August 1969, as a Protestant crowd mobilises against the Catholics.

1969: the British Army is deployed in Northern Ireland

Below: Wearing a protective helmet and gas mask, a constable of the RUC fires a canister of riot gas on the battle-scarred streets of Londonderry.

The principal force for the maintenance of order was the RUC which numbered only 3400 men and was already overstretched by its internal security role. As a largely, but not exclusively, Protestant force (some 11 per cent Catholic) it rarely concerned itself with Protestant excesses, but it was now apparently not even able to contain Catholic disorders. The only men available to back up the RUC were the B Specials – over 8000 Protestants widely regarded as bigoted psychopaths by the Catholic population. The Stormont government itself may have been nervous of the B Specials and wary of the possibility that they might perpetrate a headline-catching massacre, so the decision to mobilise them was half-hearted. They were not to be allowed to draw their arms but were to be issued only with batons. Besides this they were to be kept away from the urban Catholic enclaves and deployed only in Protestant areas or the countryside. Under those circumstances they could not do much harm but could hardly be of much help to the RUC (in fact, once the trouble started the B Specials were used with virtually no restrictions). The small British garrison remained ready to be called in, but only if all police resources were exhausted.

The Apprentice Boys parade set off as planned on 12 August in Derry with its usual bands and banners, but major trouble hit the march when it reached Waterloo Place. Showers of missiles fell on the RUC men who were between the marchers and the Bogside, and clashes spread to Guildhall Square, William Street and Rossville Street. The Bogside was now enclosed in barricades; as the RUC rushed the Rossville Street barricades they were attacked by petrol bombs from the top of high-rise flats. Despite the use of CS gas and Protestant support – official from the B Specials, unofficial from rioters – the RUC could not regain control of 'Free Derry'. By 14 August the RUC were exhausted. Rioting Catholics and Protestants fought on the streets, fires were started; finally the Stormont government had no choice but to ask the British government for troops to restore order in the city. Well aware of the situation, General Freeland already had troops in readiness at 'Sea Eagle' base near Londonderry. Soldiers of 1st Battalion, Prince of Wales' Own were in Londonderry by 1700 hours on 14 August. Exhaustion and relief combined to urge the Bogsiders into welcoming the troops with cups of tea and every indication of cooperation. But elsewhere the British soldiers were to have a more difficult reception.

The violence in Belfast

The events in Londonderry had sparked off incidents in other towns – there was trouble in Dungannon, Armagh and Coalisland. But by far the worst violence came in Belfast. The news from Londonderry on 12 August had confirmed the worst fears of both Catholics and Protestants. Many Catholics were convinced that the RUC, the B Specials and Protestant extremists were planning to carry out a 'pogrom' in Catholic areas; the Protestants believed the Catholics were attempting an insurrection, spearheaded by the IRA. These distorted perceptions led to overreaction which turned local rioting into a major crisis.

Trouble in Belfast broke out in three areas: Divis Street, Crumlin Road and the Ardoyne. Although some civilians on both sides possessed and used firearms, the RUC were primarily responsible for escalating the violence. When disturbances by small numbers of Catholic protesters broke out on 13 August, the RUC immediately moved Shorland armoured cars onto the streets. The following night – as the British troops were settling down for the first time in Londonderry – the situation in Belfast went completely out of hand. RUC men drove their Shorlands into the Catholic enclaves spraying fire from their Bren guns at supposed snipers and killing at least three demonstrably innocent bystanders. Protestant mobs ranged through the streets setting fire to blocks of Catholic houses, and the atmosphere was tense with the threat of a bloodbath.

On 15 August the British Home Secretary, James Callaghan, announced that British troops would immediately be deployed in Belfast. Although understandable under the circumstances, this decision did not please General Freeland who knew that the force at his disposal was inadequate in numbers and insufficiently informed of the situation. Although the first reinforcements, 3rd Battalion, The Light Infantry, arrived in Northern Ireland that evening, the army was still unable to prevent another night's rioting. When British troops first reached Belfast they were deployed in Divis Street which was not the boundary between Catholic and Protestant areas but the middle

The B Specials

The B Specials only partly earned their black reputation. There is no doubt that they were a highly partisan force with dubious standards of discipline and restraint, but their infamy has been exaggerated in Republican folklore. This distortion is the direct result of their troubled origins.

They were born as a result of the wish of the Protestant community to bear arms in the struggle against republicanism in Ireland. The Ulster Volunteer Force (UVF), raised in 1912, took up arms illegally in defiance of the British government but, at the height of the anti-IRA campaign of 1920, it was obvious that the hard-pressed police needed some reinforcement. When three auxiliary police forces were raised – the A, B and C Specials – there was little attempt to disguise the fact that they were recruited from the men who formed the UVF.

The violence which attended the birth of the state of Northern Ireland was prolonged and a curfew was enforced in Belfast from 1920 to 1924. At the end of this time the IRA threat had receded but, although the categories A and C Specials were dropped, the B Specials were 'retained against the risk of further outbreaks of subversive activities'. This remnant numbered about 25,000 men who were to be officially known as the Ulster Special Constabulary. Their official numbers had dwindled to 8285 by 1969 but they never lost their old title of B Specials or the reputation won by their heavy-handed repression of opposition in 1922.

In many ways the B Specials were more akin to a territorial army unit than a special constabulary. In times of emergency their main duties were to guard key installations and set up road blocks and they had armoured cars and rifles to assist them in this – not the sort of weaponry which is useful for police work. The darker side of their organisation was reflected by the fact that there were no medical or educational tests for members, they were exclusively Protestant, and they were controlled by the Stormont government rather than Westminster. In effect they were a peculiarly Northern Irish institution with all the indigenous failings of bigotry and bias. In the troubles of August 1969 the part the Specials played in Protestant attacks on Catholics led directly to their disbandment. Many former B Specials found a place in the new Ulster Defence Regiment set up in 1970, although the new organisation turned down a large number of ex-Specials who applied.

of a Catholic area. While they separated Catholic from Catholic, rioting raged unchecked in the Clonard, Crumlin and Ardoyne. It was only on the evening of 16 August that relative calm was restored amid more press photographs of Catholic women taking mugs of tea to delighted soldiers. This occasioned the prophetic query of the young Bernadette Devlin: 'You're giving them tea now. What'll you be giving them in six months?' Her insight was impressive not only because she foresaw future enmity between soldiers and Republicans but because she expected the army to be on the streets for some considerable time.

Barricades and gun-running

This was not the way the soldiers expected things to turn out. They were not blind to the prospect of future trouble and made efforts to prevent gun-running to either side. A battalion of infantry with helicopters and a squadron of lancers with armoured cars put up road blocks and searched cars in the west to contain the IRA threat, while SAS men haunted the roads of counties Antrim and Down to foil Protestant arms cargoes. In general though, it was felt that the trouble was dying down and would be resolved quickly.

In the cities both sides had secured themselves behind impressive barricades and there were army posts between them to prevent further clashes. The soldiers enjoyed so much goodwill that they were able to achieve the removal of the barricades by negotiation in September and in Belfast set up the peace line, but the absence of an adequate police force was a major obstacle. The Catholics would not accept RUC policing in their areas and also called for the disbandment of the B Specials.

The British government was meanwhile pressing for a programme of reform in Northern Ireland which

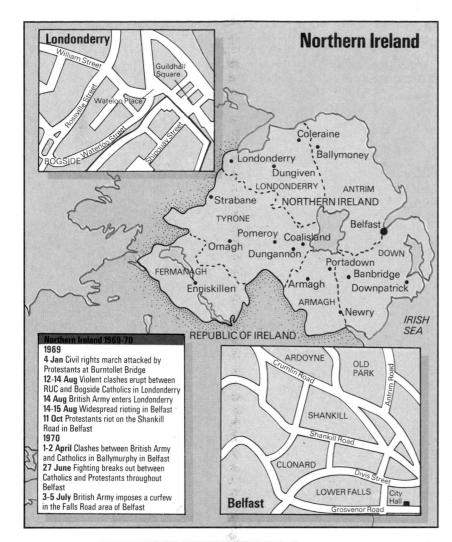

Northern Ireland

Londonderry

William Street
Rossville Street
Waterloo Place
Guildhall Square
Waterloo Street
Shipquay Street
BOGSIDE

Coleraine
Ballymoney
Londonderry
Dungiven
LONDONDERRY
ANTRIM
Strabane
NORTHERN IRELAND
TYRONE
Pomeroy
Coalisland
Belfast
Omagh
Dungannon
DOWN
Portadown
Banbridge
FERMANAGH
Armagh
Downpatrick
Enniskillen
ARMAGH
Newry
REPUBLIC OF IRELAND
IRISH SEA

Northern Ireland 1969-70
1969
4 Jan Civil rights march attacked by Protestants at Burntollet Bridge
12-14 Aug Violent clashes erupt between RUC and Bogside Catholics in Londonderry
14 Aug British Army enters Londonderry
14-15 Aug Widespread rioting in Belfast
11 Oct Protestants riot on the Shankill Road in Belfast
1970
1-2 April Clashes between British Army and Catholics in Ballymurphy in Belfast
27 June Fighting breaks out between Catholics and Protestants throughout Belfast
3-5 July British Army imposes a curfew in the Falls Road area of Belfast

ARDOYNE
OLD PARK
Crumlin Road
Antrim Road
SHANKILL
Shankill Road
CLONARD
Divis Street
LOWER FALLS
City Hall
Grosvenor Road
Belfast

Far left: British troops dash into action. Left: Conventional responses to crowd violence were often inadequate – RUC men had little protection against petrol bombs. Below: British troops were, initially at least, popular with the Catholics.

they felt would remove Catholic grievances and thus get to the root of the troubles. In October the Hunt Report made its recommendations for the future of Northern Ireland's security forces: the RUC were to be disarmed and reorganised, and the B Specials were to be disbanded. The Specials would be replaced by the Ulster Defence Regiment (UDR), a militia controlled from Westminster. These moves confirmed a widely-held belief among the Protestants that the British government – and the British Army – were on the side of the Catholics. To show their displeasure with Hunt's conclusions, Protestants rioted on the Shankill Road on the night of 11 October. Ironically, they succeeded in shooting the first RUC man to die in the troubles. The army responded vigorously to the Protestant riot: after holding their fire for 90 minutes during which over 20 soldiers were injured, the troops opened fire. Two Protestants were killed, and many were injured as army riot squads took the initiative. This was the last serious action of 1969.

Time for tea?

It was obvious that it would take some time until the native security forces had been reconstructed along less partisan lines and, during the interval, the British Army would have to hold the ring. At the time the soldiers did not view this prospect with much alarm. They were still popular with the Catholics, who still regaled them with tea – even if the Protestants were not so keen, and Ian Paisley had described the army as 'like the SS'. But the position was slowly deteriorating. The very success of the troops with the local population created its own problems: the arrival of thousands of uniformed young men had a marked effect on susceptible Catholic girls, but the resulting friendships and marriages caused resentment amongst Catholic men and excited religious disapproval of 'mixed' marriages and lax morals. More importantly, political reform was slow to take effect and showed no signs of altering the Protestant monopoly of power. At the same time rioting spluttered on, with the occasional crude nail-bomb and low-velocity gunfire to worry the army into arms searches in Catholic areas. It would not be long before the Catholics started to perceive the British Army as the main prop of the hated Stormont government, and the time for tea would be over. **P.J. Banyard**

Chronology 1966-70

EUROPE & NORTH AMERICA

1966
March
7　France announces military withdrawal from Nato.
29　Soviet Union Leonid Brezhnev appointed secretary-general of the Soviet Communist Party.
September
16　United Kingdom First Polaris submarine, HMS *Resolution*, launched.

1967
January
27　Soviet Union, United Kingdom and United States sign Outer Space Treaty banning the placing of weapons of mass destruction in space.
March
29　France First nuclear submarine, *Le Redoutable*, launched.
April
21　Greece Right-wing army officers seize power, led by Colonel George Papadopoulos.

1968
January
5　Czechoslovakia Antonín Novotný resigns as first secretary of the Czechoslovak Communist Party and is replaced by Alexander Dubček.
16　United Kingdom Government announces all British bases east of Suez to be closed by 1971.
May
3-30　France Student disturbances in Paris develop into violent confrontation between riot police and demonstrators followed by a nationwide workers' strike.
July
29　Czechoslovakia Brezhnev and most of Soviet Politburo meet Dubček and other Czechoslovak leaders at frontier town of Čierna nad Tisou.
August
20　Czechoslovakia Armies of the Soviet Union and four Warsaw Pact countries invade, occupying Prague and major cities.
29　United States 'Police riot' in Chicago against anti-Vietnam War demonstrators.
October
16　Czechoslovakia Treaty signed with Soviet Union providing for the 'temporary' stationing of Soviet troops in the country.
November
5　United States Richard Nixon elected president.
12　Poland Brezhnev enunciates 'Brezhnev Doctrine' on intervention in socialist countries.

1969
January
4　Northern Ireland Civil rights march attacked by Protestants at Burntollet Bridge near Londonderry.
March
2　Soviet Union Armed clashes with Chinese on River Ussuri.
April
17　Czechoslovakia Alexander Dubček replaced as first secretary of Communist Party by Gustáv Husák.
28　France President de Gaulle resigns.
July
12-14　Northern Ireland Rioting in many towns after Orange parades.
August
12　Northern Ireland Apprentice Boys' march sets off serious rioting in Londonderry.
14-15　Northern Ireland British troops deployed in Belfast and Londonderry to stop rioting.
September
28　West Germany Willy Brandt elected chancellor.

October
28　West Germany Brandt declares need to open relations with East Germany.
November
15　United States 'Moratorium' nationwide anti-Vietnam War demonstrations.
17　Soviet Union and United States begin Strategic Arms Limitation Talks (SALT).

1970
May
7　United States Four students shot dead at Kent State University by members of Ohio National Guard during demonstration against invasion of Cambodia.
July
3-5　Northern Ireland Army imposes curfew on Catholic Lower Falls district of Belfast after heavy riots.
August
12　West Germany and Soviet Union sign treaties guaranteeing frontiers and renouncing the use of force.
October
17　Canada FLQ assassinate Pierre Laporte, minister of labour and immigration.
December
15-20　Poland Widespread civil disorder leaves 300 dead; Edward Gierek replaces Gomulka as first secretary of Polish Communist Party.

SOUTHEAST ASIA

1966
March
12　Indonesia General Suharto seizes power in military coup, reducing Sukarno to a figurehead.
April
12　Vietnam First use of B-52s over North Vietnam by US Air Force.
June
29　Vietnam US Air Force attacks oil installations near Hanoi and Haiphong for the first time.
August
11　Indonesia Treaty signed in Djakarta ending hostilities with Malaysia.
December
31　Vietnam Total US strength in South Vietnam now 385,000.

1967
January
8　Vietnam Operation Cedar Falls begins north of Saigon.
February
22　Vietnam Operation Junction City begins in Tay Ninh Province.
March
22　Thailand US Air Force granted permission for bomber bases.
September
3　Vietnam General Nguyen Van Thieu elected president of South Vietnam.
December
31　Vietnam Total US strength in South Vietnam now 486,000.

1968
January
22　Vietnam Siege of Khe Sanh (To April 7).
30　Vietnam Communists launch Tet offensive throughout South Vietnam (To February 29).
February
7　Vietnam Fall of Special Forces camp at Lang Vei (first use of North Vietnamese Army tanks).
March
16　Vietnam My Lai massacre of some 400 villagers.

27　Indonesia Suharto appointed president.
31　Vietnam US President Johnson restricts bombing of North Vietnam and announces he will not seek re-election.
April
1-15　Vietnam Operation Pegasus relieves Marines besieged at Khe Sanh.
May
13　Vietnam US and North Vietnamese officials meet in Paris.
October
31　Vietnam President Johnson orders cessation of all air, naval and ground bombardment against North Vietnam in an effort to promote peace talks.
December
31　Vietnam Total US strength in South Vietnam now 474,000.

1969
January
25　Vietnam First serious peace talks in Paris.
March
18　Cambodia US Air Force begins secret B-52 bombing raids.
July
8　Vietnam US troop withdrawals begin.
September
3　Vietnam Death of President Ho Chi Minh in Hanoi.
December
31　Vietnam Total US strength in South Vietnam now 474,000.

1970
February
2　Laos Communists recapture Plain of Jars.
March
18　Cambodia General Lon Nol seizes power from Prince Norodom Sihanouk.
April
30　Cambodia US and South Vietnamese forces launch invasion of border areas.
November
21　Vietnam Son Tay raid attempts to free US POWs in North Vietnam.
December
31　Vietnam Total US strength in South Vietnam now 335,800.

SOUTH ASIA

1966
January
10　India and Pakistan agree at Tashkent to withdraw troops from frontier confrontation.

1967
September
11-14　India Clashes with Chinese forces on Sikkim-Tibet frontier.

1969
March
25　Pakistan Ayub Khan resigns following increasing unrest and hands over to General Agha Mohammed Yahya Khan, C-in-C of the army.

EAST ASIA

1966
October
3　China Cultural Revolution emerges with open battle against Liu Shao.

1967
June
17 **China** explodes first H-bomb.

1968
January
23 **North Korea** USS *Pueblo* seized by North Korean gunboats.
December
22 **North Korea** Crew of Pueblo released.
October
China Meeting of Communist Party Central Committee effectively declares the end of the Cultural Revolution.

1969
March
2-15 **China** Clashes with Soviet troops on Manchurian frontier.

MIDDLE EAST
1966
February
23 **Syria** Dissident army officers led by General Salal Jedid overthrow Prime Minister Salal al Bitar.

1966
May
16 **Egypt** Nasser demands immediate withdrawal of UN peacekeeping force from Sinai.
22 **Egypt** Nasser installs garrison at Sharm el Sheikh and closes the Strait of Tiran.
30 **Jordan and Egypt** sign defence treaty.
31 **Jordan** Iraqi troops move to Jordan.
June
5 **Israel** Israeli Air Force destroys most of Egyptian Air Force in pre-emptive strike, and Israeli Army invades Sinai; fighting begins between Israelis and Jordan and Iraq.
6 **Israel** Gaza surrenders to Israeli Army; fierce fighting in Sinai and on Jordanian front.
7 **Israel** Units of Israeli Army seize Sharm el Sheikh; other units reach Suez Canal. Ceasefire with Jordan leaves Israel in control of West Bank.
8 **Israel** Israeli fighter-bombers and MTBs attack and damage USS *Liberty*.
9 **Israel** Offensive launched against Syrian positions on Golan Heights.
10 **Israel** Ceasefire on Syrian front; end of the Six-Day War.
20 **Aden** Mutinies by police at Champion Lines and in Crater district inflict casualties on British troops.
July
4 **Aden** Crater district retaken by Argyll and Sutherland Highlanders.
October
21 **Israel** Israeli destroyer *Eilat* sunk by Egyptian Styx missiles.
November
5 **Yemen** President Abdullah el Salal overthrown by dissident republicans.
29 **Aden** Last British troops withdraw, South Yemen becomes independent the following day.

1968
March
21 **Jordan** Israeli attack on Palestinian guerrilla base at Karameh beaten back.
July
17 **Iraq** Army officers seize power under General Ahmed Hassan al Bakr.

1969
July
20 **Israel** adopts strategy of aerial attack to counter Egyptian artillery in War of Attrition.

1970
January
7 **Israel** extends air war against Egypt to deep penetration raids near Cairo.

July
23 **Oman** Qaboos bin Said seizes power from his father.
August
8 **Israel and Egypt** agree to ceasefire; end of the War of Attrition.
September
6 **Jordan** PFLP guerrillas hijack airliners to Dawson's Field.
17-26 **Jordan** King Hussein attacks Palestinian guerrillas, inflicting heavy casualties; Syrian forces invade in support of Palestinians, but are repulsed.
27 **Jordan** King Hussein and Yassir Arafat meet in Cairo and agree an end to the fighting.
28 **Egypt** President Nasser dies; Anwar Sadat succeeds to power.
November
13 **Syria** General Hafez el-Assad seizes power.

CENTRAL AMERICA
1967
July
11 **Anguilla** Gains independence and seeks renewed association with Britain.

1968
August
18 **Guatemala** Guerrillas kill US ambassador.
October
11 **Panama** Military coup d'etat overthrows President Arnulfo Arias.

1969
March
19 **Anguilla** Britain sends occupation force to maintain order.
June
24-28 **El Salvador** Armed conflict with Honduras (the 'Football War').
December
15 **Panama** General Torrijos seizes power in military coup.

SOUTH AMERICA
1966
May
26 **Guyana** Britain grants independence but leaves garrison.
June
28 **Argentina** Military coup removes President Arturo Illia.
November
7 **Bolivia** Ernesto ('Che') Guevara arrives and organises guerrilla activity.

1967
October
8-16 **Bolivia** Military forces track down and kill Guevara and his men.

1968
October
3 **Peru** General Juan Velasco Alvarado, army chief of staff, takes power.

1969
September
4 **Brazil** US ambassador kidnapped by urban guerrillas in Rio de Janeiro.
26 **Bolivia** Military coup installs General Torres in power.

1970
June
8 **Argentina** General Levingston becomes president following coup.
August
10 **Uruguay** Tupamaros urban guerrillas kill US police adviser.
October
6-7 **Bolivia** Coup and counter-coup leave General Torres as president.

AFRICA
1966
January
1 **Central African Republic** Colonel Jean-Bedel Bokassa seizes power in military coup.
3 **Upper Volta** Colonel Lamizana, army chief of staff, seizes power.
15 **Nigeria** General Ironsi seizes power and forms military government.
February
24 **Ghana** Armed forces led by Colonel Joseph Ankrah take power in Nkrumah's absence abroad.
March
3 **Uganda** Mutesa deposed as president by Prime Minister Milton Obote.
July
29 **Nigeria** Colonel Yakubu Gowon takes power after assassination of General Ironsi.
September
30 **Botswana** Former British colony of Bechuanaland gains independence.
October
4 **Lesotho** Former British protectorate of Basutoland gains independence.
27 **South Africa** UN ends mandate to rule South West Africa.
November
28 **Burundi** Colonel Michel Micombero deposes king and makes himself president.

1967
January
13 **Togo** Colonel Etienne Eyadema takes power in bloodless coup.
May
30 **Nigeria** Colonel Ojukwu proclaims the Eastern Region the independent state of Biafra.
July
7 **Nigeria** Federal government launches campaign against Biafra.
November
16 **Central African Republic** French troops airlifted in to support Bokassa.
December
17 **Dahomey** Military coup.

1968
May
9 **Rhodesia** UN Security Council imposes trade embargo.
18 **Nigeria** Federal forces take Port Harcourt, cutting off Biafra from outside world.
September
4 **Congo (French)** Major Marien Ngouabi seizes power.
November
19 **Mali** Military coup led by Lieutenant Moussa Traore.

1969
May
25 **Sudan** Colonel Nimeiri seizes power in military coup.
September
1 **Libya** Army officers led by Muammar Gadaffi overthrow King Idris.
October
21 **Somalia** Bloodless coup installs government of Major-General Mohammed Siyad Barre.
December
10 **Dahomey** Military coup.

1970
January
12 **Nigeria** Biafra surrenders and Ojukwu flees abroad.
21 **Libya** French government sells Libya 100 Mirage III fighters.
March
2 **Rhodesia** proclaimed a republic.
July
23 **South Africa** UN Security Council imposes arms embargo.

Baton rounds and barricades

Riot control in Northern Ireland

The reason British troops found themselves on the streets of Belfast and Londonderry in August 1969 was the failure of the police to cope with rioting crowds. Yet the British Army itself was ill-prepared to face the problem of civilian street disorders, especially in a sensitive area of the United Kingdom where tough methods would not be acceptable.

In their first encounters with rioters in 1969, the troops were protected only by a standard steel helmet, a small steel shield and some form of flack jacket – none of which prevented injuries being sustained from the rain of bottles and bricks they faced. Fortunately, in the early days rioting was sporadic and relatively light, but the need for more protection was immediately realised. Since the face was the most vulnerable area, the first major advance was the use of a plastic visor. At first these were only partially effective, but the development of a special plastic called 'Makrolon' – a spin-off from the US space programme – made the visors resistant to any thrown missile. Soon troops were being issued with full-length Makrolon shields.

Armoured vehicles like the ubiquitous Pig (the one-ton Humber armoured car) could be used in limited numbers during riots, but some protection had to be provided for other army vehicles. Hinged steel grilles were fixed to the windows of Land Rovers and lorries, But Makrolon was again called into play to construct a removable hard skin for these soft-skinned vehicles. Army units differed in their attitude to this

protection, some preferring to keep the speed of all-round response offered by an open Land Rover, but no-one would want to drive such a vehicle into a crowd when petrol bombers were active.

As well as developing protection, the army had to devise techniques for catching rioters and dispersing crowds. It was generally agreed that the excessive use of force – and especially undisciplined firing – by the Royal Ulster Constabulary (RUC) had largely contributed to the escalation of the disturbances in the

Below: Troops train a dye-filled water cannon on demonstrators. Bottom left: A blood-spattered rioter is led away. Bottom right: Troops armed only with batons and shields and CS gas face violent crowds. Right: A snatch squad grabs a rioter as irate women are held at bay.

The plastic bullet (above) replaced rubber rounds.

summer of 1969. The army therefore followed a broad policy of restraint; yet this threatened to leave them subject to attack with no means of response.

Three methods of clearing crowds used by the RUC were also employed by the army: wooden batons, water cannon and CS gas. It was to CS gas that they most often resorted, either fired from a hand gun or thrown as a grenade (methods for projecting the gas at longer range were developed later). CS gas was certainly an effective substance, faster-acting and stronger in its impact than conventional tear gas (CN gas), but rioters soon discovered that a handkerchief soaked in vinegar and water offered protection against the effects of nausea and vomiting. The gas also required a favourble wind if it was to be effective. Finally, and most important, it was indiscriminate, tending to affect all local inhabitants.

What the army really needed was to be able to get at the rioters and arrest them, but the missile-throwing youngsters who were in the forefront of any trouble proved very difficult to catch. Since a fully-equipped soldier was too weighed down to have any chance of catching a fleeing lightly-clad youth, the army quickly developed the now-famous 'snatch-squads'. These specially-trained groups of soldiers, carrying only shields and batons, were kept out of sight behind the front line of troops. At a moment when the rioters had advanced far enough, the snatch-squad would sprint forward from the rear and attempt to seize as many as possible. Given, however, that the rioters were usually fleet of foot and could count on the cooperation of the local inhabitants for concealment, only a small number were ever caught.

'Paddy pushers' and water cannon

Despite the introduction of a number of ingenious concepts to expand existing resources – such as dyes to be mixed with the water in water cannon so that rioters caught in the jet could be identified later, or the 'paddy pusher', an armoured bulldozer with a massive shield fitted instead of a bulldozer blade, used for pushing back crowds – the army's strongest desire was to have some way of using guns to disperse and deter the troublemakers. In the colonies, a policy had sometimes been pursued of identifying and shooting 'ringleaders' to quell disturbances, but in Northern Ireland this was seen as clearly unacceptable. From April 1970 the army announced that bomb-throwers would be shot, but even this decision was rarely acted on. Renouncing also the idea of firing over the heads of crowds or shooting to wound, the army was left with the use of fire only in response to being fired on itself.

Faced with this limitation on the use of standard fire, the army turned to the rubber bullet; it was to prove highly controversial. The rubber baton round was fired from a riot gun or a signal gun, aimed low to hit the legs or body. The impact of the round was such as to cause pain and discomfort without serious injury at a distance of around 30m (100ft). But it had several disadvantages: it could be dangerous at shorter ranges; what is more, the rubber bullet was extremely inaccurate. A combination of these two factors led to notorious incidents, in one of which a woman standing at the window of her house was blinded.

At the end of August 1972 the rubber bullet was replaced by the plastic bullet, which had a similar impact but was appreciably more accurate. Yet although this permitted soldiers to hit rioters with precision, it could not prevent the possibility of the occasional serious injury or even death, especially when young children were in the field of fire. As a result, the plastic bullet has achieved much of the notoriety of its predecessor.

As the war of sniping and bombing grew in Northern Ireland through 1971 and 1972, riot control ceased to be the army's prime task. Despite the casualties suffered, many soldiers undoubtedly felt more at home when the difficulties and frustrations of a policing role were replaced by open firefights for which they were better trained and psychologically prepared.   **Graham Brewer**

The Falls Road Curfew

Army tactics and Catholic attitudes, 1970

In September 1969 the British Army set up a 'peace line' between the Catholic Falls Road and Protestant Shankill Road areas of Belfast. Originally a temporary measure to give both sides security, it soon became a fixed landmark of the divided city, with its rusted corrugated iron, sandbags and barbed wire overtopped by observation posts. The line dramatically symbolised the army's position in Northern Ireland – between the two sides, facing both ways.

As they waited for the politicians in Westminster and Stormont to tackle the province's problems, the army did its best to evolve procedures to reduce tension. The most important tactic was to establish contact with the leaders of the warring communities. Local commanders took pains to discover the men considered to exercise some authority in their area and consulted them or negotiated with them as far as possible. These contacts were invaluable but also controversial, since many of the community leaders on the Catholic side were well-known Nationalists or even members of the IRA. The army came under great pressure from Unionists to limit such contacts; on the other side, the inevitable cooperation of the army with the RUC and the Protestant-dominated legal and political system slowly undermined its reputation with the Catholic minority.

In the autumn of 1969 the army's major confrontation had been with the Protestants, but by early 1970 relations with the Catholics were worsening and the breakaway Provisional IRA were arming themselves.

The pace of political reform was slow and did not meet their expectations. Extreme Nationalists from the start viewed the British Army as an 'occupying force' preventing the 'liberation' of Northern Ireland from British rule and the unification of Ireland. But it took months of political prevarication and the shock of confrontation with strong security measures to turn the bulk of the minority population against the army.

On 1 April 1970 came the first serious clashes between Catholics and the army. A group of Junior Orangemen were attacked by a stone-throwing Catholic crowd near the Ballymurphy estate and 70 soldiers of 1st Battalion, Royal Scots intervened to protect the Protestants. The following day it took 600 troops with five Saracen armoured cars to control the rioting. Over 100 CS canisters were fired and by the time the disturbances had calmed down 35 of the security forces and 40 rioters had been injured. The army had at last found itself in the same position as the RUC in 1969: defending the Protestants and thus regarded by the Catholics as a hostile force. In the wake of the riots the ministry of defence announced that more troops would be sent to the province, and the commander of the Northern Ireland garrison, Lieutenant-General Sir Ian Freeland, warned that people throwing petrol bombs were liable to be shot.

As summer approached, all the signs were bad; politicians and army leaders were sure that the Orange marches would, as in the previous year, result in violence. Their attention was focussed on the 12 July

Above: Armed with a sub-machine gun (magazine loaded) a military policeman rides shotgun atop a Land Rover as a motorised patrol moves through the streets of Belfast. The escalation of hostilities inevitably forced the army to adopt the role vacated by the RUC – that of protecting the Protestant establishment, and thus appearing as a hostile force to the Catholics.

march as a probable starting point and three battalions of reinforcements were earmarked to be sent to Ulster in the first week of July. Unfortunately, trouble flared before it was expected. On 27 June an Orange march provoked rioting between Protestants and Catholics on the Springfield Road, and this soon spread to other areas of Belfast. In Ballymurphy an RUC post was temporarily occupied by rioters. But the most serious development was the emergence of gunmen into action for the first time since October 1969. Protestants and Catholics engaged in exchanges of fire in the Ardoyne and Short Strand districts. The army was overstretched and incapable of separating the two sides. By dawn the following day five civilians had been shot dead and two more later died of their wounds. Some of those killed or injured in the shooting were certainly gunmen themselves, including Provisional IRA leader Billy McKee who was

seriously wounded. Also on that night, incendiary attacks damaged a number of shops in central Belfast and there was looting on the Crumlin Road. The following day army engineers began to seal off Catholic and Protestant streets along the Crumlin Road to create a new 'peace line'.

The events of 27 June seemed to reveal the inadequacy of army tactics to contain disorder. The Stormont government and its Unionist supporters had long been urging the army to take a tougher line with the Catholics, and the presence of a newly-elected Conservative government in Westminster more favourably disposed to their views, gave them renewed confidence. The British Army knew that a shortage of troops had been crucial to their failure to limit the fighting – three battalions of reinforcements were to arrive in the first week of July – but General Freeland agreed that a demonstration of force by the

The unusual nature of the operations in Northern Ireland had two quite different and contrasting faces. While on the one hand troops found themselves readily accepted by the local population (above, British troops enjoy a night out with Irish girls), their task of policing Catholic areas and the occasional injuries sustained by innocent bystanders (above right, a small boy, hit by a rubber bullet, is rushed to a first aid post) gradually made them the target for recrimination and hostility, until by the time of the Falls Road curfew (July 1970) relations with the Catholic population had radically deteriorated.

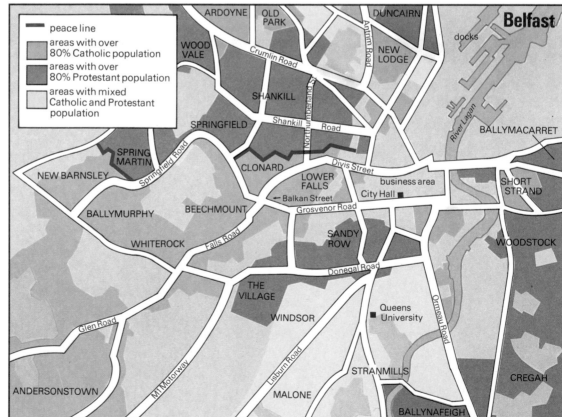

army might prevent further trouble. This decision, arrived at on 1 July, ran counter to the policy previously pursued, which had emphasised the maintenance of good relations with local communities and the avoidance where possible of heavy-handed measures that might provoke a hostile response.

On the afternoon of 3 July, acting on a tip-off, a unit of the Royal Scots sealed off Balkan Street in the Catholic Lower Falls area and, accompanied by police, searched a house in which 12 pistols, a sub-machine gun, and quantities of explosives and ammunition were discovered. The arms belonged to the Official IRA, which had strong roots in the Lower Falls. As the soldiers attempted to leave the scene, they were jostled by angry crowds, and in the confusion a man was crushed by an armoured car. Soon, a platoon and a company of the Royal Scots were effectively besieged by missile-throwing crowds at two separate points.

More troops were quickly sent in to support the units under attack, including a company of the Glosters and a company of 2nd Battalion, The Queen's Regiment. Large quantities of CS gas were fired, creating confusion and inciting an angry response from many residents as yet uninvolved in the disturbance. Within an hour of the original arms search petrol bombs, nail bombs and even hand grenades were being thrown at troops. Buses and other vehicles were commandeered to form barricades and the Official IRA began to organise snipers, talking wildly of taking on the British Army. By 2000 hours troops had formed a cordon around the Lower Falls. They had already suffered serious casualties when five men of 1st Battalion, Royal Regiment of Fusiliers, were hit by grenade fragments in Northumberland Street.

A show of strength

On previous occasions a decision might have been taken to hold back and try to calm the situation, but under the newly agreed policy a show of strength was required, the order was given to restore army control of the Lower Falls. At 2020 hours the first units were sent in to dismantle the barricades. There followed a night of intense, if confused fighting. CS gas was fired liberally into the area as troops advanced, met by a rain of petrol and gelignite bombs. Sniper fire became

heavy in places, especially after the announcement of a curfew at 2200 hours. By daylight the following morning 13 soldiers had received bullet wounds and a number of petrol bombers and a sniper had been reported shot. It was later alleged, however, that the army had used their firearms with too great a freedom – in all they probably fired over 1000 rounds. Among the units used were elements of the Black Watch and the Life Guards who had just stepped off the ferry from England and were totally unacclimatised to Belfast conditions. The five people, all civilians, who died as a result of the fighting – four of gunshot wounds and one killed by a military vehicle – were probably in fact innocent observers (one was a Polish photographer).

Humiliation of the innocent

The curfew was maintained for 36 hours, with a two-hour interruption for shopping. During that time troops conducted a systematic house-to-house search of the whole area. In all over 100 firearms, 20,000 rounds of ammunition, plus explosives and incendiary devices were uncovered, but the effect on relations with the Catholic population was disastrous. Inevitably, the thorough searching of a house by soldiers untrained for the task caused considerable damage to property, often little short of ransacking. For every innocent Catholic searched it was a humiliation and an indignity. Like the use of CS gas, the curfew and house-to-house search were security techniques which affected everyone, moderate or radical, innocent or guilty. The exercise unquestionably created vast support for Catholic extremists. After the curfew was lifted, the army made the mistake of driving two Unionist ministers on a tour of the Lower Falls, confirming the suspicion of the local population that the army operation had been carried out against the Catholics on behalf of their Protestant enemies.

After the Lower Falls curfew relative calm descended for the rest of 1970, but under the surface trouble was growing. Increasingly hostile to the army, Catholics were joining the Provisional IRA in droves. In early February 1971 the storm broke; on 6 February Gunner Robert Curtis became the first British soldier to be killed in the Northern Ireland crisis.

Brian Markworthy

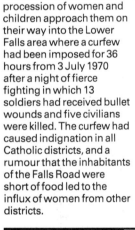

Below: Troops, armed with 7.62mm rifles, look on as a procession of women and children approach them on their way into the Lower Falls area where a curfew had been imposed for 36 hours from 3 July 1970 after a night of fierce fighting in which 13 soldiers had received bullet wounds and five civilians were killed. The curfew had caused indignation in all Catholic districts, and a rumour that the inhabitants of the Falls Road were short of food led to the influx of women from other districts.

THE AMX13 SERIES

The design, development and production of any new armoured fighting vehicle (AFV) is a lengthy and expensive process and one of the keys to a tank's long-term success is the vehicle's ability to provide a sound working platform for a number of other weapon systems and specialised battlefield equipment. Successful designs such as the US M48 series and the German Leopard I have provided the basis for a great many weapon types, from self-propelled and anti-aircraft guns to specialist engineering vehicles and flame throwers. The economic advantages of exploiting a tried and tested chassis in as many service roles as possible are enormous. In this respect the French AMX13 light tank is an excellent example: developed in the early 1950s, it has given birth to many variants and has seen service in some 25 countries.

Immediately after World War II, in line with government policy to re-equip with all-French vehicles and guns, the French Army's AFV design and development centre – the Atelier des Constructions d'Issy-les-Moulineaux (AMX) – was set to work on a programme for three new vehicles; these were the AMX50 heavy tank, the Panhard EBR-75 heavy armoured car and the AMX13 light tank. The original specification required the AMX13 to be airportable, although this was subsequently abandoned, and it was intended that the tank be primarily employed as a tank destroyer and reconnaissance vehicle. Work on the design went ahead quickly and by 1949 the first prototype was complete. Three years later the AMX13 went into production at the Atelier de Construction Roanne where it was produced until the early 1960s, when the Roanne works switched to construction of the AMX30 main battle tank (MBT) and the AMX13 was transferred to the Creusot-Loire factory at Châlon-sur-Saône.

One of the most interesting and unique features of the AMX13's design is its two-piece oscillating turret. The lower part of the turret is fitted to the turret ring in the normal way, while the upper part, which houses the main armament, is mounted on two trunnions allowing it to pivot and elevate and depress through 18 degrees. Since the whole top part of the turret moves up and down with the main armament fixed within it, this has allowed for the installation of a breech-aligned automatic loader in the turret bustle, and the gun is fed by two revolving magazines with a

Previous page: An Israeli light tank of Colonel Amnon Reshef's AMX13 battalion rolls through Gaza on 6 June 1967, the second day of the Six-Day War. Reshef's AMX13s provided the crucial armoured support for Colonel Raphael Eitan's paratroop brigade in the hard-fought battle for control of the Gaza Strip. Top: An early prototype of the AMX13 ploughs through a sea of mud while on trial with the French Army. The early models were fitted with a 75mm main gun while the current standard AMX13 (above) mounts a 90mm fixed main armament in an FL-12 oscillating turret. Right: An Israeli 75mm AMX13 on reconnaissance enters a deserted town in the Sinai during a lull in the fighting in the Six-Day War.

AMX13 Light Tank

Crew 3
Dimensions Length (gun included) 6.36m (20ft 10in); width 2.5m (8ft 2in); height 2.3m (7ft 6in)
Weight Combat loaded 15,000kg (33,070lb)
Ground pressure 0.76kg/cm^2 (10.8lb/in^2)
Engine SOFAM 8GxB eight-cylinder water-cooled petrol engine developing 250hp at 3200rpm

Performance Maximum road speed 60km/h (37mph); range (road) 350km (218 miles); vertical obstacle 0.65m (2ft 2in); trench 1.6m (5ft 3in); gradient 60 per cent; fording 0.6m (2ft)

Armour Conventional 40mm (1½in) maximum
Armament One 90mm gun; two 7.5mm or 7.62mm machine guns – one co-axial with the main armament, the other mounted on the commander's cupola; four smoke dischargers, two on each side of the turret

full capacity of 12 rounds. Although this provides a very high rate of fire for the first twelve shots, it has a serious drawback on the battlefield in that the magazines have to be replenished from outside the vehicle. The first service type, the AMX13 Model 51, was fitted with the FL-10 turret mounting a 75mm gun, but in the mid-1950s a variant was produced for use in Algeria with a shortened 75mm armament housed in a slightly modified FL-11 turret. The current standard AMX13 is an upgunned 90mm version fitted with an FL-12 turret while the export model, the AMX13 Model 58, mounts a 105mm main gun. In the current 90mm model, 32 rounds of fin-stabilised HE (high-explosive), HEAT (high-explosive anti-tank), smoke and canister ammunition are carried and the main gun, with a muzzle velocity of 950mps (3117fps), can penetrate up to 320mm (12½in) of armour. Secondary armament can consist of two 7.5mm or 7.62mm machine guns, one mounted co-axially with the 90mm gun, and the other, which is optional, on the commander's cupola. Four smoke dischargers, two on either side of the turret, are also provided.

In line with modern developments in anti-tank weaponry, the AMX13 can also be fitted with ATGWs (anti-tank guided weapons), further enhancing its role as a tank destroyer. While retaining its 75mm gun, the anti-tank missile version of the AMX13 Model 51 mounts four SS-11 ATGWs in pairs on the turret front and can engage long-range targets up to an effective range of 3000m (3280yds). The French have also experimented with a model mounting six HOT (*haut-subsonique optiquement téléquidé*) ATGWs, although this was only taken to prototype and never adopted by the French Army.

Despite its offensive capabilities the AMX13 light

As new and more sophisticated anti-tank weaponry became available, the French experimented with two different types of missile, the HOT system (top) and the SS-11 (above centre). After trials the HOT-armed version was scrapped while the SS-11 AMX13 was adopted for service by the French Army. Above: An AMX13 armed with a 105mm main gun, a version specifically produced for the export market. Left: A knocked-out Israeli AMX13 in the Sinai. While the AMX13 provides high performance and cross-country agility, its thin armour gives little protection against a direct hit.

Left: The AMX13-DCA anti-aircraft variant which mounts two 30mm cannon on the basic tank chassis. Below: The Dutch Army have further modified the AMX-VCI APC model to accommodate the American TOW anti-tank missile system. Bottom: A French Army AMX 155mm Mk F3 self-propelled howitzer. Two spades at the rear anchor the chassis while firing.

tank is a highly vulnerable vehicle. The hull, which is of all-welded steel construction to a maximum thickness of 40mm (1½in), although well sloped, provides little protection when up against high-velocity anti-tank rounds and guided missiles. To compensate for this, the AMX13's designers concentrated on keeping its size to a minimum and maximising its battlefield mobility. Along the same lines as the Soviet T64 and T72 MBTs, the introduction of an automatic loading system dispensed with the need for a fourth crew member, thereby reducing the size of the turret. Crew space is kept to a minimum and the maximum height of an AMX13 crewman is limited to 1.72m (5ft 8in). The crew consists of a driver seated in the front of the hull with the engine to his right, while the other two members, the commander and gunner, occupy the turret space to the left and right of the main armament. The AMX13 is powered by the Renault-built SOFAM 8 GXB petrol engine which, with the tank's low combat weight of 15,000kg (33,070lb) and its rugged torsion-bar suspension, gives it a high level of cross-country performance, even though its maximum road speed is only 60km/h (37mph). There are five road wheels on either side with the drive sprocket at the front and the idler at the rear; either two, three or four track return rollers are fitted.

Although the AMX13 remains in service with a number of countries' armed forces, it is by modern standards a relatively unsophisticated machine. The early production models had no night-vision equipment although most were subsequently retrofitted with infra-red driving lights and, in some cases, turret-mounted infra-red searchlights. Passive night-vision gear and a laser rangefinder are now available. The AMX13 light tank version also lacks NBC

Left: A battery of AMX 105mm Mk 61 SPGs on manoeuvres with the French Army. Below: The AMX-VCI armoured personnel carrier which utilised an extended version of the AMX13 chassis and also provided the basis for a number of variants. Firing ports are provided at the sides and rear of the vehicle and the turret mounts a 7.62mm machine gun.

(nuclear, biological and chemical) protection and no provision is made for amphibious use although it can ford water obstacles of up to 0.6m (2ft) in depth without preparation.

Apart from its light-tank role, the AMX13's robust chassis and powerful engine have also provided the basis for a great many other combat and support vehicles. The most extensive exploitation has been in the production of a group of vehicles centred around the AMX-VCI APC which features the same eight-cylinder SOFAM engine mounted in a slightly leng-thened version of the AMX13 chassis. When the original AMX-VCI APC went into production in 1957 it carried ten infantrymen in addition to a three-man crew, but since then a number of different vehicles have been developed from this basic design. These include a version mounting a 20mm cannon turret, 81mm and 120mm AMX-VTT/PM mortar carriers, the VTT/PC command vehicle, the AMX-VCG pioneer vehicle, the VTT/TB unarmed ambulance and a battery command vehicle for use with artillery. Several missile-armed models have also been produced carrying ENTAC and SS-11 missiles, while an anti-aircraft version armed with two Roland surface-to-air missiles has been developed for trials. The Dutch Army has further modified the APC to accommodate the US TOW anti-tank system. Further variants for carrying cargo, supplies and artillery ammunition have also been manufactured.

Apart from the APC variants, the AMX13 has also provided the basis for two SPGs (self-propelled guns) and an anti-aircraft cannon system. The first of the SPG versions, the Mk 61 or Model A, appeared at the same time as the light tank and consists of an OB 105-61-AU 105mm howitzer mounted on a modified

Below: The AMX13 *char de dépannage* armoured recovery vehicle carries a crew of three and is fitted with a 15-tonne capacity winch and a five-tonne A-frame. Below centre: An AMX-VCG pioneer vehicle uses its A-frame and dozer blade to shift timber for the construction of a makeshift bridge. Bottom: An AMX13 *poseur de pont* swings its scissors bridge out over a river.

AMX chassis. Weighing 16,000kg (35,274lb) loaded, it can fire a shell to a range of 15,000m (16,400yds), carries 56 rounds of ammunition and is served by a crew of five. The second SPG version, which came into service in the 1960s, is the 155mm Mk F3. This vehicle mounts the OB 155-50-BF gun and can fire the French Mk 56 and US M107 HE shells, the Brandt rocket-assisted projectile, as well as smoke and flare rounds. The Mk F3 is supported in combat by the AMX-VCI APC which carries the remaining six of the eight-man crew and further supplies of ammunition. It is also used in conjunction with the AMX-VCI battery command vehicle.

For anti-aircraft defence, the French Army is equipped with the AMX13-DCA which mounts two 30mm Hispano-Suiza HSS 831A cannon in a cast-armour turret on an AMX13 chassis. The guns can be fired at a cyclic rate of fire of some 600rpm from each barrel and have an effective range of 3000m (10,000ft). The AMX13-DCA also features the RD 515 Oeil Noir 1 (Black Eye) radar system which can detect targets to a range of 12km (7½ miles) at an altitude of 3000m (10,000ft).

The AMX13 series also includes two engineering vehicles, the *char de dépannage* Model 55 ARV (armoured recovery vehicle) and the *poseur de pont* or AMX13 bridgelayer. The ARV is fitted with two winches, an A-frame, various pieces of lighting equipment and tools for repair work. Armament consists of one 7.5mm or 7.62mm machine gun and smoke dischargers. The bridgelaying version mounts a scissors-type bridge on a modified AMX chassis and can span obstacles of up to 7.15m (23ft 3in).

It has been estimated that over 4500 AMX13 vehicles have been produced and while in the early 1980s it remained the standard light tank in service with the French Army, many of its variants have been replaced with more sophisticated equipment. Although the APC series was subsequently provided with NBC fit, it was replaced by the diesel-powered AMX-10P mechanised infantry combat vehicle family which is fully amphibious. The Mk 61 and Mk F3 SPG variants were also phased out in favour of the new French 155mm GCT guns which are based on the heavier AMX30 chassis and feature an automatic loader and fully-enclosed NBC protection.

The AMX13 series was very much a product of its generation, designed to meet the military requirements of the time. The light tank saw action with the Israeli armoured forces in both the 1956 Sinai campaign and the 1967 Middle East War but has since been retired, the Israeli command favouring the deployment of heavier and better protected MBTs. But in countries without the stringent up-to-date defence requirements of Israel, the AMX13 still has a role to play and is deployed in a number of Central and South American countries including Chile, Argentina, Peru, Ecuador and El Salvador, as well as with the armed forces of India, Indonesia, Morocco, Tunisia and Saudi Arabia.

The sticking point in Sino-Soviet relations was the question of the Chinese possession of nuclear weapons. Worried by Chinese belligerence and unwilling to accept China as a military equal, the Soviet leaders went back on the secret agreement of 1957 by which they had promised to supply their eastern neighbour with the means to develop nuclear capability. The Chinese made rapid strides even without Soviet aid, however: by 1964 they had exploded atomic weapons and in 1967 came the first nuclear tests – exultantly displayed for TV audiences worldwide (left).

Nuclear bombs and paper tigers

The Sino-Soviet split

Left: Demonstrators outside the Soviet embassy in Peking, expressing an ostensibly popular disgust with Soviet revisionism and failure to keep to the true path of socialism. Mass demonstrations, the symbolic burning of flags and public denunciation of the ideological errors of the Russians were all part of the elaborate code in which Sino-Soviet relations were couched from the mid-1960s onwards.

The collapse of the alliance between the Soviet Union and China and the public disagreement between the two major communist powers was one of the most important developments in modern international relations. What had appeared to be a firm and lasting alliance between the two great nations dominating Eurasia simply broke up in its infancy, having lasted no more than a decade. From about 1965 the USSR and China were in a state of open hostility which at one point took the form of armed clashes on their common frontier. A shared ideology of Marxist-Leninism, and a commitment to world revolution and the defeat of Western 'imperialism' did not prove strong enough to overcome rivalry between two great nations.

At first Western observers were inclined to minimise the significance of the rift in Sino-Soviet relations and to believe that, if not ideology, then common interests and a shared hostility to the West would prove stronger than national rivalry. There were even those who believed that the quarrel between Peking and Moscow was a pretence, intended to deceive the West. But the conflict continued and has now lasted for nearly a quarter of a century. Although there have been moves by both Russians and Chinese to improve relations, the prospects of a serious reconciliation appear today to be as remote as ever.

Relations between the Soviet Union and communist China appeared to be strong enough at the outset. Within months of establishing the communist regime in Peking in October 1949 the communist leader Mao Tse-tung went to Moscow and concluded with Stalin a 30-year treaty of 'friendship, alliance and mutual assistance' and obtained a credit of $300 million with which to purchase industrial equipment from Russia. After Stalin's death in 1953 the extent of Soviet economic aid to China was increased and plans were made for an improvement in rail links between the two countries. Even more significant was the agreement concluded by the Chinese and Soviet governments in 1955 providing for joint atomic research 'for peaceful purposes', the supply by the Russians of the necessary raw materials and equipment and the training of Chinese scientists in nuclear physics. A further, secret, agreement was signed in October 1957 – its existence was revealed only in 1963 – by which the Soviet Union undertook to supply the scientific information and technical material necessary to enable the Chinese to manufacture their own nuclear weapons.

During the Korean War (1950-53) the Soviet Union provided China with substantial military aid and became the principal supplier of the Chinese armed forces. When the Soviet leadership was considering whether or not to use force to suppress the national revolt in Hungary in 1956 they sought the advice and approval of the Chinese leaders before acting. In 1958, when a crisis developed in relations between the United States and China over China's bombardment of the offshore island of Quemoy, Khrushchev warned President Eisenhower that 'an attack on the Chinese People's Republic, which is a great friend, ally and neighbour, is an attack on the Soviet Union.'

Up to the end of 1958, then, the Sino-Soviet alliance appeared to be unshaken. To the outside world, at least, the Russians and Chinese had no serious differences, and all public statements reinforced this impression. There were no obvious points of dispute between the two countries along their long common frontier, and each espoused the same atti-

tude towards the West. China was relatively underdeveloped and needed the expertise provided by the Soviets, and the USSR could only be relieved that the world's most populous nation was a member of the socialist camp.

In this latter area, however, lay the seeds for dispute and the eventual rupture of the alliance. The Soviet Union was happy to welcome China into partnership, and China was happy to accept Russian aid. But the precise relationship between the two nations was not defined. The Russians basically wanted China to develop according to the Soviet model, and to accept a subordinate position in the communist world.

Dominating the communist world

In effect, the Russians began to treat China, with its 800 million population, in much the same way as they had treated the relatively small countries of eastern Europe which they had overrun in 1945. They appeared to think they could make China into a 'satellite' of the Soviet Union, like Bulgaria or Czechoslovakia. As for the Chinese, much as they needed economic aid, they resented the way the Russians administered it, were disappointed in the quality of Soviet advice and workmanship, and disapproved of Soviet control of the 'joint companies' set up to exploit China's resources. The two countries were members of the same international revolutionary movement and were dedicated to the same end. But were the Russians really ready, as good communists and 'internationalists', to throw all their resources into the common pool and to share them and control over them, with the Chinese? The answer was that, in practice, the Russians were not ready to surrender their leading position, nor would they tolerate any encroachments on their dominant position in the communist world.

The Chinese could not accept the implication that they should be subordinate to the Russians. They believed that their model of communist revolution was as valid as that of the Soviets, and, in fact, was rather more applicable to much of the Third World, over which the struggle against colonialism was in full swing during the late 1950s. This was underpinned by a deeper cultural hostility. The Chinese felt themselves to be one of the world's great civilisations, and were not prepared to accept that they should

Above: Before relations broke down. Mao Tse-tung (second from left) and Liu Shao-ch'i (far left) in discussion with Nikita Khrushchev (second from right) and Mikhail Suslov (far right).

Soviet aid to China ranged from technical advice in processing plants (bottom, steel mills in Anshan province) to models for military hardware (below, Chinese Type 59 tanks, based on the Soviet T54).

take second place to any other nation. Just as the Soviet Union had inherited many of the traditional aspirations and areas of interest of Tsarist Russia, so the Chinese had their own historical attitudes and desires which were independent of anything the Soviet Union might wish.

Nevertheless, if the Chinese had their reasons for opposing Soviet aims in the late 1950s, the Russians too felt they had good reason to fear many of the aspirations of the new revolutionary state of China. Russia had had its revolution many years before; the Chinese victory was more recent, and, to the Russians, the Chinese manifested a foolhardy willingness to take risks in international affairs.

What appears to have alarmed the Russians most was the Chinese leaders' – and especially Mao Tse-tung's – eagerness to bring about a military confrontation with the West and their proclaimed lack of concern about the consequences of a nuclear war. Mao declared himself to be convinced that the communist East was now stronger than the capitalist West and that the time was ripe for the communist countries to press ahead with the revolution even at the risk of provoking a nuclear war. Mao dismissed the atomic bomb as a 'paper tiger', while admitting that hundreds of millions of people might perish in a nuclear war. The Chinese leaders declared that: 'On the ruins of destroyed imperialism the victorious peoples will create with tremendous speed a civilisation a thousand times better than the capitalist system and will build their bright future.' The Soviet leaders were not at all eager to bring about a nuclear conflict, however aggressive they might appear to the West. Khrushchev was presenting himself as a man of peace, preaching the impossibility of nuclear war and the need for detente – his avowed policy was that communism would be spread in the world by peaceful means.

In view of this fundamental difference of approach to grand strategy it was understandable that the Soviets were reluctant to provide China with a nuclear bomb or do anything to speed Chinese acquisition of nuclear weapons. By the middle of 1959 the Soviet leadership felt obliged to repudiate their 1957 agreement to supply China with the means of manufacturing nuclear weapons. This was the real turning-point in Sino-Soviet relations, though it was not revealed to the world until 1963. It meant that, whatever was said

about 'eternal friendship', the Russians did not trust the Chinese.

Although the full extent of the rift in Sino-Soviet relations was not apparent to outside observers in 1959 there were already some signs that the Chinese and Russian leaders were not seeing eye to eye. In August 1959 the Chinese provoked an incident on their frontier with India, occupying the frontier post of Longju and claiming it as Chinese territory. The Soviet government did no more than 'deplore' the incident without coming down firmly on China's side, a reaction which Teng Hsiao-P'ing (Deng Xia Ping), general secretary of the Chinese Communist Party, later declared had first 'revealed our differences to the world'.

Nevertheless, Soviet economic aid was continuing to flow to China; new agreements were signed in 1958 and 1959, increasing the number of plants to be built with Soviet aid to about 250. The Russians were said to have supplied some 10,800 technicians of their own and from eastern Europe and to have trained 13,600 Chinese in the Soviet Union. The total extent of Soviet loans to China was estimated to have reached $2200 million, of which $400 million were in the form of military aid.

Relations between Moscow and Peking had deteriorated to such a level by the middle of 1960, however, that the Soviet leadership took a step that brought the quarrel into the open for the world to see. In July 1960 they suddenly brought all their economic aid to a halt, withdrawing their 1390 experts and advisers from China, cancelling 343 contracts and stopping work on 257 projects connected with scientific and technical cooperation. The suddenness and the scale of this action was a major disaster for the Chinese who were already suffering from a number of natural catastrophes, including droughts and floods. It was an act which the Chinese leaders would never forget or forgive.

A rift between communists

The rift between Soviet and Chinese communists was now in practical terms complete and in the open. Naturally, the polemics between the two communist parties maintained great volume and heat. The argument touched on every possible major issue: war and peace in the nuclear age, Yugoslav 'revisionism', Stalinism, and especially the international revolutionary movement – whether it should have a 'leading centre' and whether that centre should be in Moscow or Peking.

The war of words between the Soviet and Chinese leaders continued unabated and unconcealed throughout the 1960s. In 1962 the Chinese were enraged by the Soviet decision to supply arms to India, which the Chinese attacked in October of that year. The Chinese denounced the Soviet attempt to place missiles on Cuba as 'gambling' and 'adventurism' and Khrushchev's withdrawal of the missiles as 'capitulationism'. At congresses of communist parties in various countries Russians and Chinese attacked each other in very strong language, with the result that the communist movement seemed likely to split into two warring camps. The 'Cultural Revolution' in China, with its attempt to revitalise the Chinese revolution, was further anathema to the Russians, who saw it as an heretical step further away from the Soviet model.

Up to the late 1960s, the war of words had not

become anything stronger, but after 1965 there were several incidents that threatened to escalate the conflict into something very serious for the peace of the world. Already in 1965, the Chinese had accused the Russians of expanding their territory at China's expense. Mao Tse-tung then proposed that the Soviet government should return the Kurile Islands to Japan and added: 'The Soviet Union has occupied too many places.' He went on to list Soviet territorial gains in Mongolia, Romania, Germany, Poland and Finland; the Soviet reply was that their frontiers were sacred, and they threatened a 'resolute rebuff' to any who violated them.

Chinese fulmination against the territorial gains of Soviet Russia was not mere rhetoric. Since the Chinese revolution of 1912, successive Chinese governments had denounced the so-called 'unequal treaties' which colonialist powers had forced upon the declining Manchu Empire in the 19th century, and China had already fought one border war, against India in 1962, which had arisen over the issue of borders drawn up in what the Chinese considered an unfair manner. The treaties of Aigun (1858), Peking (1860) and Ili (1881) between the expanding empire of Tsarist Russia and the Manchus, agreements that had ceded large areas of central Asia to the European power, were regarded by the Chinese as in need of revision. The most delicate point at issue concerned the precise borders along the Amur and Ussuri Rivers in the northeast of China. The treaties of Aigun and Peking had settled the borders as running along the Chinese bank of these rivers (thus giving the Russians some 600 small islands) but the Chinese insisted that the frontier should be in mid-stream.

Frontier incidents first took place in Central Asia, where the frontier runs between Chinese Sinkiang and the Soviet Tadzhik, Kirgiz and Kazakh republics. It was reported that tens of thousands of people had crossed into Soviet territory and that the Chinese had committed many frontier violations. But there appears to have been no serious fighting.

At the beginning of March 1969, however, Soviet and Chinese frontier guards fought each other over possession of a small uninhabited island, known as Damansky in Russian and Chenpao in Chinese, in the middle of the Ussuri River on the Far Eastern section of the frontier. Soviet troops fought a two-hour battle to expel 300 Chinese soldiers from the island, losing 31 men killed.

Fighting over frontiers

A much more serious engagement took place in the middle of March, involving a regiment of Chinese infantry (2000 men) and a full regiment of Soviet frontier troops (nearly 3000 men) using heavy artillery and tanks. The fighting lasted for 11 hours and resulted in heavy casualties. Between April and August 1969 there were further incidents on the Sinkiang border in which the Chinese suffered serious losses.

After much mutual recrimination on the frontier issue the Soviet and Chinese governments eventually agreed to hold talks intended to relax tension on the frontier and establish a mutually agreed border. The Chinese did not press their demand for a major revision of the frontier, declaring that 'even if it cannot be settled for the time being, the status quo on the border should be maintained and there should definitely be no resort to the use of force.'

Even though both sides had backed down from any

Border tensions between the Soviet Union and China came to a head over the sovereignty of Damansky Island on the Ussuri River, (top left). Some incidents were not militarily significant (left centre above, Soviet gunboats spray Chinese fishermen with waterhoses in the Ussuri River) but in March 1969, frontier guards clashed and Soviet troops successfully ejected Chinese occupiers (left centre below, Chinese guards warn off Soviet troops on an APC). Further incidents of open hostility soon followed (bottom left, scuffles between border guards in April 1979).

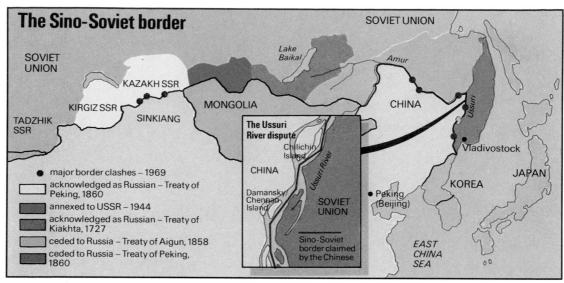

The Sino-Soviet border

- ● major border clashes – 1969
- acknowledged as Russian – Treaty of Peking, 1860
- annexed to USSR – 1944
- acknowledged as Russian – Treaty of Kiakhta, 1727
- ceded to Russia – Treaty of Aigun, 1858
- ceded to Russia – Treaty of Peking, 1860

SOVIET UNION
KAZAKH SSR
KIRGIZ SSR
TADZHIK SSR
SINKIANG
MONGOLIA
Lake Baikal
Amur
SOVIET UNION
CHINA
Ussuri
Vladivostock
KOREA
JAPAN
Peking (Beijing)
EAST CHINA SEA

The Ussuri River dispute
Chilichin Island
CHINA
Damansky Chennao Island
SOVIET UNION
Ussuri River
Sino-Soviet border claimed by the Chinese

Above: Jubilant Chinese border guards proudly display the remains of a Soviet helmet complete with bullet holes.

escalation of the fighting in 1969, and realised that they had no immediate reason to attack each other, tension remained high. The Soviet leadership went to great pains to woo many of the nations of Asia with offers of aid, and suggested (on 7 June 1969) that Asia needed a collective security system – a system that would obviously be aimed at isolating China.

The Sino-Soviet split did, however, contribute to an easing of international tension as well as adding to it by the threat of war. For the great disputes in the communist world were one of the most important background factors that enabled US President Richard Nixon to initiate the process known as detente, in which he used the mutual hostility of the two great communist powers to establish a more flexible world order. The fact that China was in direct opposition to the Soviet Union made the West more relaxed in its attitude to the communist world, for the Soviets were compelled to maintain over 40 divisions on the Chinese border. Over various parts of the world, the split within the communist bloc became the basis for local feuds – in Southeast Asia, for example, the victory of the communists in Indochina in 1975 was not followed by attacks on non-communist countries in the region, as many had feared, but by a breakdown in communist unity, with the Soviet-back Vietnamese invading Chinese-backed Kampuchea (Cambodia) and China conducting a punitive action against the Vietnamese. The communist split was part of a new complexity in international affairs. **David Floyd**

China in ferment
Red Guards and Cultural Revolution

The Cultural Revolution is one of the most puzzling, and yet one of the most important episodes in modern history. It is puzzling because we have so little information about what actually went on, and deciphering the statements of some of those who were involved is akin to interpreting the pronouncements of the oracle at Delphi. But it is important because China is the only great power to have undergone an upheaval of such magnitude in the modern period. Nor were the consequences confined to China itself, for one of the first steps that the Chinese Central Committee took when the revolution was nearing its end was to call for the normalisation of relations with the United States, a process which culminated in the visit of President Nixon to Peking in 1972, and opened the way for a realignment of international politics.

The Cultural Revolution is usually dated as having taken place between 1966 and 1968. Describing what happened between those two dates is another matter, however. The seeds were sown by Mao Tse-tung and those most closely associated with him in the Communist Party Central Committee – Lin Pao, Mao's wife Chiang Ch'ing and Ch'en Po-ta – who embarked upon an attempt to change the direction of the Chinese state. They wished to reduce the power of an entrenched bureaucracy, lessen the influence of established interest groups in the towns, and to press on with a specifically Chinese model of a continuing revolution, that owed little to the Soviet model of strong central party control and reliance on an urban industrial base.

The members of the Central Committee (or of the central organs of the army and state apparatus) who disagreed with this – politicians such as Liu Shao-ch'i, the formal head of state (the man always presumed to be Mao's natural successor) – were steadily purged, and there was a considerable loosening of central control. By 1971, it was estimated that the central government apparatus in Peking had fallen to one sixth of its former strength during the period of the Cultural Revolution.

If the Cultural Revolution had merely been the purging of some groups from the centre of power, then it would hardly have had the importance it did. What was so crucial was the method that Mao used to change the direction of the world's most populous nation. He decided to rely upon a mass movement among the youth of China, supplemented by the involvement of the army. The results were astonishing. Millions of young people, mainly students, were summoned to attend vast rallies – there were eight held in Peking between 18 August and 26 November 1966 – and these 'Red Guards' challenged traditional authority over the whole nation, allowing existing local tensions and antagonisms to come into the open. The movements and activities of these masses of young people disrupted politics all over China not merely because they attacked existing political institutions (usually accusing them of being

'bourgeois') but because Chinese culture had traditionally venerated age and experience. The fact that this revolution was being carried through by groups whose main binding factor was that they were young was a considerable shock to older generations.

Army involvement

As order began to break down down over wide areas of China, the army (known as the PLA – People's Liberation Army) was inevitably involved in the events. Lin Pao, as defence minister, had faith in the PLA acting as he and Mao wanted; and in January 1967, Mao made a public appeal to the army to come forward to support the radicalisation of Chinese society. Ever since the victory of the communist forces in the Civil War of 1946-49, there had been intense debate as to the direction that the armed forces of China should take. Many officers wished for a more stratified, conventional force, along traditional lines, but Mao had resisted attempts to make the PLA a mere mirror image of other states' forces. He had always believed that the army should reflect its revolutionary origins. In 1959, for example, there had been problems on the Central Committee when the then minister of defence, P'eng Te-huai, had demanded that Chinese industrial production be tailored to the creation of a more conventional force, while the chief of staff, Lo Jui-ch'ing, had been disgraced early in the Cultural Revolution because of his wish for a professional officer corps and conventional military appreciations of national security.

Yet the army that began to assume such a prominent position in 1967 was not at all the mass instrument of revolution that it had been in 1949. Commanders had built up considerable local influence, and had been at their posts for some time, while the troops, although they were subjected to considerable propaganda, were not the veterans of long guerrilla campaigns. The direct entry of the army into politics did not, therefore, have the effect of confirming the radicalisation of China; rather, it led to an even greater confusion than hitherto. Factions of Red Guards fought amongst themselves; the army tried to control revolution in some areas, while in others it accelerated it or even fought against it. With the bureaucracy in ruins and the obedience of the army uncertain, many of the provinces of China became virtually autonomous. There were even open clashes between the central government and some local military units: in July 1967, General Tsai-tao in Wu-han refused to obey orders to back a particular radical faction and imprisoned two representatives sent out from Peking to bring him into line. Only by astute manoeuvring and the use of obedient air force units could Chou En-lai, the prime minister, assert central authority.

Political procedures

The actual methods by which the Cultural Revolution was transmitted, and the language in which disputes were couched are difficult for most Westerners to understand. The 'big character posters' (wall newspapers) on which orders and ideas were transmitted; the ritual denunciation of certain members of the central government, who might be in favour one month and then disappear to be reviled the next; the imprisonment or internal exile of intellectual or cultural figures who had been pronounced 'bourgeois'; the Maoist study groups in which political discussion took place – all this adds up to a set of procedures that was distinctively Chinese. The actual meaning of terms such as 'leftist' or 'bourgeois' is very difficult for outsiders to comprehend, while the political thought processes behind the descriptions of political action (one of Chiang Ch'ing's last political campaigns was entitled 'Criticise Lin Pao and Confucius') are even more obscure.

The Cultural Revolution affected all sections of Chinese society. The Chinese armed forces (left, PLA troops) were to play a key role – with some factions fighting against and others supporting the Revolution (below, air force troops receive revolutionary indoctrination) – while young people denounced their elders (above, a young girl demands action). The whole process was begun by communist leaders, notably Mao Tse-tung and Lin Pao (below right, centre and right).

Although there were bitter disputes and violent public attitudes, the Cultural Revolution saw none of the mass executions that had marked the Stalinist period in the Soviet Union. The deaths (which are put at anything from tens of thousands – the official government figure, given in the 1980s, was 34,800 – to over 100,000) came from the street fighting of various factions, and the deaths of individuals held in bad conditions or roughly treated, rather than from a policy of slaughtering political opponents. But for many Chinese this was a period of terror, during which they might be denounced and ruined, particularly if they held any kind of official post or had any authority in the educational system.

Breakdown of central control

By the summer of 1967 the future of China was uncertain, and it was impossible to predict which way events would turn. The government of the country outside Peking was largely in the hands of so-called 'revolutionary committees' that had been called into being earlier in the year to replace the existing local authorities; and on these a mixture of army personnel and Red Guards vied for control. But by the autumn of 1967, the central government seems to have decided that things had gone far enough. How and why this decision was taken will probably always remain a mystery; it may well have been because the threat of outside intervention – by the Soviet Union – was perceived as imminent (certainly, in 1968 there were feverish preparations to resist outside attack); or perhaps the moderates, such as Chou En-lai, managed to make their influence more pronounced, particularly after the near breakdown of central control during the summer. For whatever reason, the Central Committee issued an 'urgent notice' in October 1967, telling the Red Guards to leave the towns and to go to the countryside and mountainous areas for service, and in July 1968 Mao himself issued a 'latest instruction' to all graduates to return to production.

By the autumn of 1968 the army personnel and Maoist groups that had control of most of the regions of north and east China had begun to lose whatever revolutionary fervour they had possessed in the previous year, while in the west and the more sparsely

populated areas, separatism was stronger than radicalism. The meeting of the Central Committee in October 1968 is generally taken as the end of the active phase of the Cultural Revolution; from now, the government would attempt to recoup its position over the nation. But the changes in Chinese politics were not to be reversed easily. At the 9th Party Congress, in April 1969, army officers and representatives of the 'revolutionary masses' had far more prominence than in previous congresses.

Perhaps as important as the changes within China were the effects of the Cultural Revolution on world politics. For the upheaval and violence marked the absolute break with the Soviet Union. China had chosen its own path of socialist development, and this was now clear to the rest of the world. The Cultural Revolution may have been a convulsion during which China was forced in on itself, but its result was the emergence of a new force on the world stage.

Ashley Brown

Above: Straw man or paper tiger? A young Chinese girl attacks a dummy representing the evils of US capitalism. Vigorous slogans and theatrical displays were all part of the political world of the Cultural Revolution.

Below: Young Chinese read street newspapers, the 'big character posters' on which political directives appeared and which were one of the main organs of political expression in the vociferous ideological debates of the mid-1960s in China.

Detente

A new view of world affairs

Detente is a term that was employed so frequently and so casually by such a host of world statesmen that it requires careful definition. One of the clearest was given by Henry Kissinger, one of the leading politicians of the early 1970s. 'Detente is not rooted in agreement on values; it becomes above all necessary because each side recognizes that the other is a potential adversary in a nuclear war,' he told the US Senate Finance Committee in April 1974. He continued: 'To us detente is a process of managing relations with a potentially hostile country in order to preserve peace while maintaining our vital interests.' The Soviet translation of 'detente' was *razryadka napryazhennosti* – literally, 'relaxation of tension'. And Soviet leader Leonid Brezhnev claimed that: 'Detente means a certain degree of trust and the ability to reckon with each others' interests.'

Detente was, then, fundamentally a policy of reducing tension between powers with differing ideologies and aims. It was a style of diplomacy; a way of managing relationships in such a way that these differences were subsumed by a desire on the part of both (or all) parties that open conflict should be avoided, though differences remained and conflicting policies might be pursued by a variety of means.

From the violent rhetoric of the Cold War to the comparatively restrained comments of the period of detente is quite a long step, and the acceptance of the interests and aspirations of competing powers which detente implied was also far from the attitudes of the Cold War. Some of the reasons for this change must continue to be difficult to analyse – exactly how the USA began to rethink its attitude towards the USSR after the Cuban missile crisis, for example, or the changes in American mood during the Vietnam War, can never really be accurately defined. Nor is it possible to examine the decisions taken by the Soviet politbureau except in the very broadest terms. It may well be that the installation in the White House of a ruthless right-wing politician like Richard Nixon and the importance then given to the conservative pessimism of Henry Kissinger made relations with the communist powers easier than had been the case when the more idealistic regimes of Kennedy and Johnson were in power. Or it may even be that the growing age of the Soviet leadership made them far more conservative, and more inclined to seek a stabilisation of the world order. As detente was so fundamentally concerned with attitudes rather than concrete actions, these factors may all have been important.

Be that as it may it is clear that the shift in attitudes was preceded by fundamental changes in the situation of world politics at the extremes of the Eurasian land mass. By 1969, the situations of both China and western Europe vis-à-vis the USA and the Soviet Union had changed greatly from what they had been 10 years previously; and these changes underlay much of what happened during the period of detente.

In Europe, the main change was one of greater stabilisation and acceptance of the status quo. Relaxation of tension in Europe had begun as early as 1955, when Allied and Soviet troops withdrew from Austria, and the country was declared neutral. Although there were several incidents over the next few years which stoked up tension (the rearming of West Germany in 1955, the Hungarian uprising in 1956, the Berlin crisis of the early 1960s, for example), none of these resulted in a change in the existing balance of power. During the mid 1960s, relationships in Europe began to change. Ceausescu's Romania in the Eastern bloc and de Gaulle's France in the West made clear their independence within the general scheme of an East-West split; West Germany, under Chancellor Willy Brandt, adopted the formula 'two states in one nation' as the basis of an *Ostpolitik* that accepted the existence of a communist East Germany. The events of 1968 were perhaps crucial in a general acceptance of existing frontiers, for the West did little to help the Czech regime when the Soviet Union applied pressure and then invaded; and nor was there widespread official Western condemnation of the 'Brezhnev Doctrine', by which the Soviet leader sought to justify any future Soviet actions in bringing recalcitrant eastern European nations back into the socialist fold.

Living with the Soviets

The Soviet Union wanted Western technology and goods, and desperately needed to give the economies of its satellites a boost by giving them new opportunities. In its turn, western Europe wanted to feel secure, and was looking to its own future. Great Britain and France had abandoned their empires, and were seeing their future in more regional terms – terms which implied a Europe that had to learn to live with the Soviet presence. The end result was perhaps inevitable; at the Conference on Security and Cooperation in Europe, held at Helsinki in 1975, a set of declarations was signed in which, in return for a rather nebulous undertaking to maintain certain human rights, the Soviet Union obtained its greatest desire; a firm commitment by the European powers to the maintenance of existing frontiers, including, of course, those established by the Soviet Union in eastern Europe after World War II.

The second major change in the international order that prefigured detente was the Sino-Soviet split, which had become an accepted part of international relations by 1969 – the year in which there was fighting between Soviet and Chinese troops along the Ussuri River, and when Soviet aircraft made 'dummy runs' over Chinese cities. It was clear that there was no longer a monolithic communist bloc bent on world domination; instead, China and the Soviet Union were regarding each other with little-disguised hostility.

It was the administration of Richard Nixon, US vice-president under Eisenhower in the 1950s and elected president in his own right in 1968, that acted upon these possibilities to produce the situation that became known as detente. 'You're not going to believe this,' observed an insider at the White House in 1969, 'but Nixon wants to recognize China.' Although Nixon had made his reputation as a hard-line anti-communist, he had a passionate desire to see himself viewed as a great constructive statesman able to undertake dramatic strokes that would far outshine the timid initiatives of Kennedy and Johnson; they would also form a springboard for a second Nixon term in 1972. Nixon's then agent in this process was Henry Kissinger. Initially Kissinger was to be nothing more than a 'brains truster' available for consultation. But he transformed the National Security Council into a formidable instrument for his designs, and the State Department was relegated to a very subordinate position in the evolution of policy, leaving initiative with the president and his national security advisor – two ruthless and single-minded men who were not above overriding legal niceties in pursuit of their conception of 'national security' which above all required secrecy and guile.

Keeping international order

Nixon and Kissinger were at one in the belief that the United States unaided could no longer maintain the burdens of keeping international order. 'America cannot – and will not – conceive *all* the plans, design *all* the progress, execute *all* the decisions and undertake *all* the defense of the free nations of the world,' Nixon declared in his first 'State of the World' address in February 1970. In 1971 he announced the first visit of an incumbent American president to Peking, 'to seek the normalization of relations' between the United States and China. In October 1971 Nixon announced a forthcoming visit to Moscow, and two minor (though significant) agreements on the prevention of nuclear accidents and the modernising of the Washington-Moscow 'hot-line'.

The historic visit to Peking in February 1972 was notable more for its symbolic significance than for any concrete achievement. Nixon was entertained in the Great Hall of the People and even brandished chopsticks, but discussions revealed little substantial progress. Both sides recognised that the position of Taiwan was a stumbling block and the US went so far as to promise eventual withdrawal of American forces from the island. Increased bilateral trade and more cultural and sporting contacts were agreed upon. The US supported China's demand for a seat at the United Nations but outright recognition of the communist regime had to wait another five years.

The high-water mark of detente was reached in May 1972 when President Nixon travelled to Moscow. The Vietnam War still cast its shadow over American policy, and on 8 May Nixon had announced a resumption of the bombing of North Vietnam and the mining of Haiphong harbour. Mos-

cow chose to ignore this escalation, and at the talks, the series of agreements reached indicated that the United States accepted the Soviet Union as an equal superpower. Four notable agreements were signed under the general rubric of SALT I: the Anti-Ballistic Missile (ABM) Treaty, limiting developments in this area to existing installations; the limitation of offensive strategic missiles for the next five years; a protocol defining the effects of these limitations on submarine-launched ballistic missiles (SLBMs); and a memorandum on interpretations and understandings initialled at the Strategic Arms Limitation Talks held at Helsinki where the details had been worked out. A number of other agreements, including such matters as protection of the environment, the ending of mutual harassment at sea, a joint space flight, and a major trade deal involving the sale of $750 million of US wheat were also concluded. It was optimistically hoped that this wide-ranging and virtually unprecedented series of agreements would secure a community of interest between the United States and the Soviet Union which would filter through into other areas of more marked disagreement. In June 1973 Brezhnev visited Washington and signed a declaration designed to accelerate the SALT process and to produce a second treaty by the end of 1974.

The first test of this 'community of interest' came with the Arab-Israeli War of October 1973. United States forces were placed on a 'precautionary alert' when it seemed that the Soviet Union would intervene on the side of the Arabs. Kissinger flew to Moscow and a ceasefire agreement was imposed by the superpowers on Israel and the Arabs. But arms control progress was slow. This was in part due to the tide of Watergate revelations that swept over the Nixon administration, triumphantly re-elected in 1972, during the following year. Nixon's successor in August 1974, Gerald Ford, was identified with the detente policy, but he was in a weak political position, and the word 'detente' was rarely heard to fall from his lips,

Above: President Jimmy Carter who was elected to the White House in 1976. Carter's reaction to the Soviet invasion of Afghanistan signalled the end of detente.

Above: Chancellor Willy Brandt, the West German leader, whose *Ostpolitik* was a major factor in the relaxation of East-West relations.

Right: Nixon and Mao meet in Peking in February 1972, during the visit that symbolised a fundamental change in international relations. Below: Henry Kissinger, national security advisor to Nixon, who is credited with the most influential role in Nixon's foreign policy.

Below: Nixon and Brezhnev prepare to sign the SALT I agreements after talks in Helsinki and Moscow. The SALT agreements, which recognised nuclear equilibrium between the US and the Soviet Union, formed the core of Nixon's proposed 'community of interest.'

especially during the electoral campaign of 1974-75. July 1974 produced a number of minor agreements; and a notable advance seemed imminent when Ford and Brezhnev met at Vladivostok in a convivial atmosphere in November of that year.

Detente had essentially developed, therefore, as a triangular relationship in world politics with the United States as the most important motive factor. All three major powers realised that their vital interests were not directly under threat from the others; but all wished to angle the balance of diplomatic manoeuvring in their favour. The Chinese, for example, pursued detente with the United States as the less dangerous of their strategic rivals, considering the Soviet Union to be their main antagonists. The Soviet Union on the other hand, pursued detente with the more dangerous of her rivals – the United States. The Americans themselves, less hemmed in by ideological pressures than they had been in the 1950s and early 1960s were able to pursue a policy of relaxing tension with both the communist heavyweights. It was within this framework that detente provided the means by which peace could be maintained.

The motives of the three major powers involved in this process differed widely. The Soviet Union sought economic advantages and the benefits of western technology. In this respect detente with western Europe was almost as important as with the United States itself. China sought an improvement in her weak strategic position. And the United States attempted to find ways of increasing her diplomatic influence while simultaneously reducing her staggering burdens in maintaining the status quo.

Unfortunately for the prospects for a lasting world peace, however, the essential differences between the superpowers had been masked rather than resolved by detente. Each side interpreted detente as it thought fit: in February 1976, President Brezhnev declared, for example, that: 'Detente does not in the slightest abolish, nor can it alter, the laws of the class struggle. . . . We make no secret of the fact that we see detente as the way to create more favourable conditions for peaceful socialist and communist construction. . . .' In the United States, too, it was difficult, after years of bitter rhetoric, to accept the USSR as an equal superpower. A strong president, like Nixon, with a firm right-wing constituency could manage it, but weaker politicians were unable to.

Souring relations

Strains were beginning to appear in American-Soviet relations before the election of Jimmy Carter in 1976. Ford had already felt the domestic pressure arising from what actually constituted 'parity' in strategic nuclear weapons, in that the American right was convinced that the Soviet Union was actually pulling ahead. Carter, moreover, placed great emphasis in his initial policy statements on 'human rights'. The Soviet Union had paid mere lip service to these in the Helsinki Declaration of 1975 which confirmed the status quo in Europe, and Carter's outspoken support for Soviet dissidents only served to sour relations, which had already been jeopardised by his clumsy suggestion in March 1977 that the SALT process be scrapped and replaced with proposals of his own. Attacks on the 'grain drain' by domestic critics of the administration highlighted the political muddle in which detente had become entangled. The longer Carter dallied over SALT the stronger became the domestic opponents of the whole process. The tactics employed by Carter undercut his chances of gaining ratification of any agreements he secured. The ratification of SALT II was rendered virtually an impossibility by 1978, and a dead letter after the Soviet invasion of Afghanistan a year later.

This latter event was a turning point in the relations between the superpowers, followed as it was by an increase in the American defence budget and the bitter disputes over Carter's attempt to mobilise a world boycott of the 1980 Moscow Olympics. When Ronald Reagan swept into the White House in 1981 with a massive mandate to rebuild American strength, detente was dead and the Reagan administration returned to the language of the Eisenhower years with reference to the 'empire of evil'.

Perhaps the most enduring result of detente is that relations between the superpowers are now almost exclusively gauged by the state of their arms control negotiations, placing unbearable strains upon them. Mutual suspicions engendered since the election of President Reagan will surely demonstrate that an improvement in superpower relations, as before, must be preceded by changes in style as well as substance. Hopes placed in the detente process will have to be deferred. **Brian Holden Reid**

Controlling the bomb

Nuclear proliferation and arms limitation

The danger that nuclear weapons pose to the survival of civilisation, and to the very existence of life on this planet, is one of the greatest challenges that mankind has ever faced. Since 1945 a great deal of energy and thought has been devoted to the issue of nuclear weapons, but the question of how to limit their use and deployment has never been satisfactorily answered.

During the 1950s, the nuclear powers (the USA, Soviet Union and Great Britain) were locked in the Cold War, in which mutual antagonism and fear built up the pressures for more rather than less nuclear weaponry. There were calls for disarmament from various quarters – for example the Campaign for Nuclear Disarmament in Great Britain – but the possibilities of either superpower undertaking such a course were remote.

In the 1960s, however, various forces came together to permit a certain kind of agreement on the deployment and construction of

weapons. As the decade opened, both the United States and the Soviet Union were moving towards a position whereby deterrence hung on the existence of mutual assured destruction (MAD), in which both sides possessed a sufficient number of invulnerable nuclear weapons to inflict on the other side an unacceptable degree of damage in retaliation to a first strike. A certain stability had, therefore, developed in the nuclear arms race, giving rise to the description 'the balance of terror'.

The stability of the balance of terror was always threatened by the relentless progress made in the field of weapon technology, and the survival of stable deterrence in the face of this challenge soon became an objective of both superpowers, encouraging them to pursue their mutual interests through arms

Above: Brezhnev (far right) and Ford (far left) meet in a train carriage at Vladivostok in November 1974 where the two leaders agreed, as part of the SALT II talks, on ceilings of 2400 strategic delivery vehicles. These Vladivostock accords marked the high point of the whole process of arms limitation.

Above: India's largest nuclear reactor at Trombay. India refused to sign the Nuclear Non-Proliferation Treaty of 1968.

Above centre: Although an Outer Space Treaty was signed between the US and the Soviet Union in 1967, prohibiting the deployment of weapons in space, the agreement did not preclude the use of military communications and intelligence satellites such as the Salyut 7 (shown here). Left: Amid a proliferation of missiles on transporters lies the Soviet Union's only ABM, the conspicuously large 'Galosh'. The arms limitations talks of the 1970s placed particular emphasis on reducing the deployment of these technologically advanced missiles which, if used, would substantially reduce the effectiveness of the nuclear deterrence policies.

control agreements. It was also becoming apparent that an uncontrolled arms race would be economically ruinous if both sides attempted to develop and deploy the whole range of weapon systems that technology was making available. The coalescence of these mutual interests in the defence field in the early 1960s coincided with political developments which made negotiations on these issues viable. The Cold War was giving way to increased contact between East and West, and some negotiation on armament levels was possible as a result of this detente.

Arms control emerged in the early 1960s as a specific theory which attempted to restrain armaments policy through negotiations and to limit the deployment of weapons to an agreed level. The danger of an uncontrolled nuclear arms race was recognised and it was accepted that disarmament negotiations were unlikely to be successful. Disarmament – a much older and more ambitious concept than arms control – had aimed at the reduction or abolition of armaments, whereas arms control was an attempt to slow down the planned rate of weapons acquisition by establishing mutually acceptable limits.

After the false starts of the 1950s, in which some progress had been made – for example, the Antarctic Treaty of 1959 (which stated that the continent should be used 'for peaceful purposes only') – detente began in earnest after October 1962, the month when the Cuban missile crisis had brought the world face-to-face with the possibility of nuclear disaster. Indeed, the following year marked the beginning of a whole series of agreements, some of which were between the superpowers alone, but others of which were multilateral. All, however, can be considered to be part of a broad interpretation of arms control.

In August 1963 the Partial Nuclear Test Ban Treaty, negotiated by the United States, Great Britain and the Soviet Union, was signed by over 100 states. The Treaty prohibits nuclear explosions in the atmosphere, in outer space and under water, thus making it more expensive and more difficult for any prospective nuclear power to test a weapon than it would otherwise have been. Some states did not sign and so are not committed to the undertaking, but the Treaty certainly has contributed a major environmental service to humanity in limiting the escape of radioactive parti-

cles into the atmosphere. The Test Ban Treaty has been resented in some quarters as an attempt by the small and exclusive club of nuclear states to preserve their nuclear monopoly by preventing other states acquiring the same power. For all its limitations, however, the Treaty did tackle a real problem and was symbolic in proving that East and West could work together on matters of mutual interest and global importance. Also in 1963 the Geneva Disarmament Conference produced an agreement which was intended to reduce the danger of accidental nuclear war. Known as the 'Hot Line' Agreement it established for the first time a permanent and direct communications link between the governments of the United States and the Soviet Union.

Exploiting celestial bodies

In 1967 the Outer Space Treaty prohibited the deployment of weapons of mass destruction in space or on the moon or in orbit around the earth. It also prevents the exploitation of the moon and other celestial bodies for military purposes, although it does not cover military communication and intelligence satellites. In 1967 too, the Latin America Nuclear Free Zone Treaty was signed to prevent the manufacture, deployment or use of nuclear weapons in Latin America and binding the states there to use any nuclear material and facilities in their control for peaceful purposes only.

One of the prime objectives of superpower diplomacy at this time was the prevention of the spread of nuclear weapons in the belief that the world would be a more dangerous place if more and more states joined the nuclear club. After six years of debate, the Nuclear Non-Proliferation Treaty was signed in 1968. By its terms, non-nuclear powers undertook not to acquire nuclear weapons and nuclear powers agreed not to transfer control of nuclear weapons nor to assist or encourage non-nuclear weapon states to manufacture nuclear weapons. Some states (most notably, France, China, India and Brazil) opposed the Treaty, but the increase in the number of states with nuclear capacity has not proceeded at the pace that was anticipated in 1968. Whether this can be attributed to the Treaty is, of course, an open question. Since the Indian nuclear explosion in 1974, the

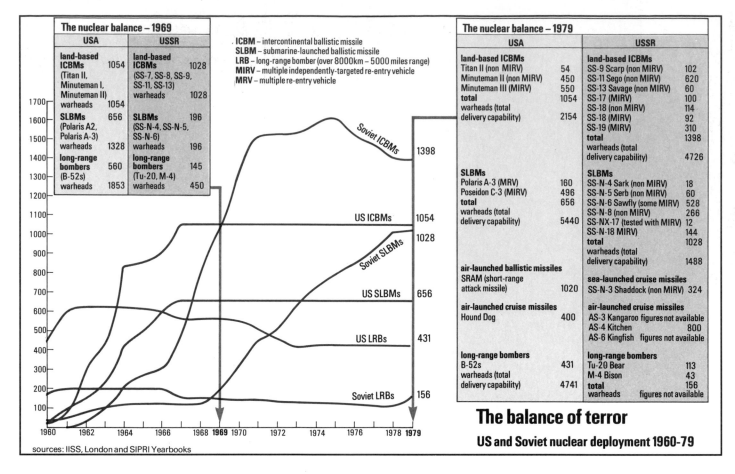

The nuclear balance – 1969

	USA		USSR	
land-based ICBMs (Titan II, Minuteman I, Minuteman II)	1054	**land-based ICBMs** (SS-7, SS-8, SS-9, SS-11, SS-13)	1028	
warheads	1054	warheads	1028	
SLBMs (Polaris A2, Polaris A-3)	656	**SLBMs** (SS-N-4, SS-N-5, SS-N-6)	196	
warheads	1328	warheads	196	
long-range bombers (B-52s)	560	**long-range bombers** (Tu-20, M-4)	145	
warheads	1853	warheads	450	

ICBM – intercontinental ballistic missile
SLBM – submarine-launched ballistic missile
LRB – long-range bomber (over 8000km – 5000 miles range)
MIRV – multiple independently-targeted re-entry vehicle
MRV – multiple re-entry vehicle

The nuclear balance – 1979

USA		USSR	
land-based ICBMs		**land-based ICBMs**	
Titan II (non MIRV)	54	SS-9 Scarp (non MIRV)	102
Minuteman II (non MIRV)	450	SS-11 Sego (non MIRV)	620
Minuteman III (MIRV)	550	SS-13 Savage (non MIRV)	60
total	1054	SS-17 (MIRV)	100
warheads (total delivery capability)	2154	SS-18 (non MIRV)	114
		SS-18 (MIRV)	92
		SS-19 (MIRV)	310
		total	1398
		warheads (total delivery capability)	4726
SLBMs		**SLBMs**	
Polaris A-3 (MRV)	160	SS-N-4 Sark (non MIRV)	18
Poseidon C-3 (MIRV)	496	SS-N-5 Serb (non MIRV)	60
total	656	SS-N-6 Sawfly (some MIRV)	528
warheads (total delivery capability)	5440	SS-N-8 (non MIRV)	266
		SS-NX-17 (tested with MIRV)	12
		SS-N-18 (MIRV)	144
		total	1028
		warheads (total delivery capability)	1488
air-launched ballistic missiles		**sea-launched cruise missiles**	
SRAM (short-range attack missile)	1020	SS-N-3 Shaddock (non MIRV)	324
air-launched cruise missiles		**air-launched cruise missiles**	
Hound Dog	400	AS-3 Kangaroo figures not available	
		AS-4 Kitchen	800
		AS-6 Kingfish figures not available	
long-range bombers		**long-range bombers**	
B-52s	431	Tu-20 Bear	113
warheads (total delivery capability)	4741	M-4 Bison	43
		total	156
		warheads figures not available	

Soviet ICBMs 1398
US ICBMs 1054
Soviet SLBMs 1028
US SLBMs 656
US LRBs 431
Soviet LRBs 156

sources: IISS, London and SIPRI Yearbooks

The balance of terror

US and Soviet nuclear deployment 1960-79

nuclear club has remained static and ostensibly includes only the United States, the Soviet Union, Great Britain, France, China and India, although some believe that Israel and South Africa also have a nuclear capability.

The Nuclear Non-Proliferation Treaty was followed by other international agreements: the 1971 Seabed Treaty, which bans the placing of nuclear weapons on the seabed, and the Biological Weapons Convention of 1972 in which signatories agree not to possess or use biological weapons in warfare.

It was in November 1969 that the most significant arms control negotiations between the United States and the Soviet Union began. These were the Strategic Arms Limitation Talks (SALT), which tried to put a brake on the increasing number of long-range offensive missiles (ICBMs and SLBMs) that were considered strategic by both sides. They also tried to prevent the deployment of defensive anti-ballistic missiles (ABMs) on a widespread scale since this technical innovation threatened to challenge the very basis of deterrence by negating the value of second-strike weapons. The resulting ABM Treaty signed in Moscow in May 1972 by Nixon and Brezhnev effectively prevented both sides deploying ABMs for the defence of their respective states – they were each limited to two sites only. In addition, the Interim Agreement on Offensive Strategic Nuclear Arms limited both sides to the number of land-based missiles that they possessed on 1 July 1972; a protocol attached to the agreement placed similar limitations on submarine-launched ballistic missiles.

SALT I, therefore, tried to preserve deterrence by eliminating defensive strategies and preventing the escalation of the arms race by freezing the numbers of strategic missiles. The signature of the SALT I agreements was considered to be a significant step forward in arms control – especially since it had been agreed that in November 1972 the second stage of the SALT process would begin in Geneva.

The SALT II negotiations were the principal focus of the superpowers in the arms control field for the rest of the decade. The basic principles of the negotiations were set out during Brezhnev's visit to Washington in June 1973, but progress was to prove agonisingly slow. The summit meeting of Nixon and Brezhnev in Moscow in July 1974 assisted both sides to find solutions to the problems faced and it also resulted in an agreement that each side would only build one ABM complex instead of the two allowed for in SALT I.

In November 1974 the new US president, Gerald Ford, met Brezhnev in Vladivostok where the two leaders agreed to ceilings of 2400 strategic delivery vehicles (ICBMs, SLBMs and heavy bombers), with sub-ceilings beneath that figure to cover multiple independently-targeted re-entry vehicles (MIRVs). Discussions continued in 1974 in the Mutual and Balanced Force Reduction (MBFR) Talks in Vienna, and in the Conference on Security and Cooperation in Europe in Helsinki.

The progress of arms control by 1974 seemed to indicate a willingness in both East and West to try to regulate the arms race. The concrete achievements might have been less than had been hoped for, but communication had been established between the superpowers which in itself many considered to be a crucially important contribution to the attempt to build confidence and understanding and thus help to avoid war. It was this, more than anything else, which made the mid-1970s an era of measured optimism.

David Johnson

Key Weapons
MODERN SMGs
part 1

Although a handful of sub-machine guns had been in military use before 1939, it was World War II which brought this type of weapon into prominence, and by 1945 there were several millions in existence. Most of these weapons were hurriedly designed and roughly made; the British Sten, the Soviet PPS-43 and PPSh-41, and the American M3 'Grease Gun' were indisputably effective military weapons but mass-produced at short notice they were strictly utilitarian guns lacking refinement and finish. While many war-time sub-machine guns were discarded after the conflict, a significant number had a quite extensive career post-1945.

The American Thompson sub-machine gun which had been developed in civilian form in the 1920s, saw extensive service during World War II and as the M1A1 has been used by guerrilla and terrorist groups to the present day. More significant was the US M3A1, a World War II development which was still in US Army service in the 1980s as a personal weapon for armoured vehicle crews. Although the magazine was often troublesome and tended to jam, the gun was all but immune to dirt, mud and water as it had no openings in the body, apart from the ejection opening which had a spring flap. The bolt operated on two steel rods providing it with a much smoother action. The cyclic rate of fire was kept down to a sensible 400 rpm which prevented the M3A1 from climbing upwards, enabling it to be held on target with reasonable ease. In addition, the slow rate of fire made the need for a

Previous page: A street fighter with sub-machine gun during a demonstration in Nicaragua. America has been a major manufacturer of sub-machine guns and the most famous designs are the M3A1 (above right) and the Thompson M1A1 (right). The Thompson was originally a civilian weapon but went on to have important military uses.

M3A1 Sub-machine gun

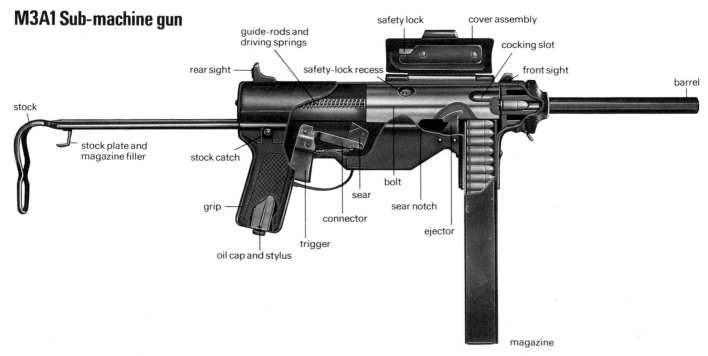

guide-rods and driving springs · safety lock · cover assembly · rear sight · safety-lock recess · cocking slot · front sight · barrel · stock · stock plate and magazine filler · stock catch · grip · oil cap and stylus · trigger · connector · sear · bolt · sear notch · ejector · magazine

Left: The M3A1 was still in use during the Vietnam War, although at the time this picture was taken in 1967 sub-machine guns were being replaced by the M16 in US Army service. Right: An IRA checkpoint in Londonderry, 1972. The IRA man on the left is armed with a Thompson M1928A1, a predecessor of the more utilitarian M1A1.

single-shot selector unnecessary, as even a raw recruit could squeeze off one shot and let the trigger go before firing another. The rugged qualities of the M3A1 ensured it a long life: it was used in Korea by the US Army, and since then has found favour with guerrilla forces around the world.

The first new designs to appear after World War II were from Scandinavia. Towards the end of the war the Swedes had decided to produce a sub-machine gun of their own design and manufacture and the Carl Gustav State Arsenal developed the Model 45 which has remained in use ever since. It has sold widely to other countries, has been manufactured in Egypt as the 'Port Said', and licence-built in America by Smith & Wesson for the US Navy. The mechanism was simple, a blowback system largely derived from the Sten gun while the body and barrel jacket were of stamped steel, rivetted together. The Model 45 featured a simple tubular butt, hinged to fold forward alongside the body and its 36-round magazine was carefully designed and manufactured to avoid the feed jams which plagued most wartime sub-machine guns.

The Madsen Company of Denmark produced an unorthodox sub-machine gun – also known as the Model 45 – which in most respects was an enlarged

Despite being a neutral country Sweden is an important arms manufacturer and the Carl Gustav Model 45 (left) is one of the more successful postwar sub-machine gun designs. The gun has been exported throughout the world as well as being used by peacekeeping units of the Swedish Army (above left, in the Sinai in 1976).

The MAT-49 (opposite page centre) was an interesting design that featured a magazine assembly that could be folded forwards underneath the barrel. Besides equipping the French Army the MAT-49 has found its way into the hands of Viet Cong guerrillas (opposite top – a VC surrendering to US troops). Below: A Chad government soldier armed with a MAT-49.

automatic pistol. The Model 45 was not popular, however, and it was soon replaced by the Model 46, a conventional blowback type which was an instant success, exported throughout the world, particularly to South America. A unique feature of the Model 46 was that the body was made in two halves, hinged at the rear and locked together by the barrel-retaining nut at the front. By unscrewing this nut the two halves could be hinged open like a book and the working parts exposed for cleaning and repair.

An interesting feature of the Madsen was the safety grip, positioned just behind the magazine housing, which with the magazine acted as the forward hand guard and ensured that the gun had to be fired two-handed. The Madsen was subsequently updated as the Model 50, and during firing demonstrations in 1950 it impressed the British delegation present sufficiently to recommend that it replace the Sten, although in the event, the British Sterling was the replacement.

The French produced a 7.65mm calibre sub-machine gun before World War II – the MAS-38 – but this weapon did not have a long service life as it was replaced by the MAT-49, although a number of examples were used by colonial forces in Indochina. The MAT-49, made by the National factory at Tulle.

Above: The Danish Madsen Model 50. This sub-machine gun works on the standard blowback principle and can fire single shots as well as full automatic. The Madsen has a similar folding stock to the Swedish Carl Gustav, although a rather unusual feature is the safety grip mounted just behind the magazine housing.

Below: The Owen was produced during World War II as a useful jungle warfare weapon for the Australian Army. The camouflage pattern shown here was typical for this type, most being camouflaged in some way or another. A highly reliable sub-machine gun, the Owen was widely used in the anti-insurgent campaigns after 1945.

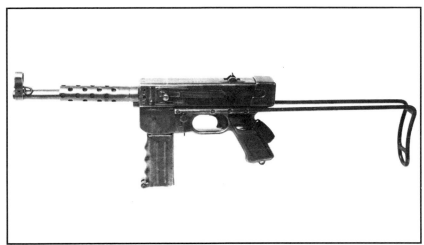

employed 9mm Parabellum ammunition which, by the late 1940s, had become the universal sub-machine gun round. It was a robust and well-made blowback gun, which was unusual in having a magazine and housing that could be unlocked and folded forward to lie underneath the barrel when being carried. It was quickly adopted by the French Army and saw widespread use in France's colonial wars in Indochina and Algeria.

The Australian Owen machine carbine was another wartime design that saw extensive combat service after World War II. Invented by a Lieutenant Owen in 1941 it went into immediate production for the hard-pressed Australian Army which needed a submachine gun for jungle fighting against the Japanese. Utilising a blowback system of operation the Owen was unusual in having a vertical top-mounted magazine which necessitated off-set sights. A rugged weapon, popular with combat troops, the Owen continued in service until the 1960s.

The Owen was eventually replaced by the F1, another Australian design intended to continue the Owen's reliability but which was of a lighter weight and would be easier to manufacture and maintain. The F1 has a straight-line stock which aids good shooting but calls for a high sight, which like the Owen is off-set because of the top-mounted magazine. This magazine is the same as that used with the British L2A3 Sterling sub-machine gun. The F1 was used by Australian troops in Vietnam, but some doubt was cast on its low-powered sub-machine gun round and it was dropped in favour of the American M16A1 assault rifle.

One feature which every designer has recognised as desirable in a sub-machine gun is small size, so as to make it convenient to carry and use. But the conventional blowback gun has its size set by certain physical constants: the body of the gun must be as long as the bolt and the compressed return spring behind it, otherwise the bolt will not have sufficient movement to load and extract. The size of the bolt is governed by the need to have a definite mass which will resist being blown open on firing, and with a given diameter or breadth of the gun body, this fixes the length of the bolt. Making the bolt too light means a too rapid opening of the breech and an over-fast rate of fire.

The first man to solve this dilemma was an Italian designer, Giovanni Oliani. In 1942 he broke new ground by producing a sub-machine gun which used an overhung or telescoping bolt. This development ensured that although the bolt had the necessary mass

Below: The successor to the Owen, the F1 utilised the same top-loading magazine but had an improved stock which necessitated a raised rear sight.

to resist opening, the actual length behind the breech was no more than an inch or two instead of the six or eight inches of a conventional bolt. Thus the space behind the chamber could be reduced and with it the overall length of the weapon.

Oliani had little success with his overhung bolt and it was not until 1948 that his system appeared in military use, embodied in the Czech CZ23. The CZ23 was a sensible design with a tubular gun body and with the barrel set back into the body for some distance. The bolt was just over eight inches long but was hollowed out, so that when it was closed about six inches of it surrounded the rear of the barrel; instead of being overhung the bolt was telescoped over the barrel. Slots were cut in the bolt to allow the incoming cartridges to be fed into the chamber and the empty cases to be ejected; and the design was arranged so that the ejection ports in the bolt and in the gun body only coincided as the cartridge case was ready to be thrown clear. At all other times the two were out of register so that dirt could not enter the weapon through the ejection port. The design of the trigger mechanism was unusual: for single shots the trigger was pressed lightly while harder pressure produced automatic fire.

Besides bringing the telescoping hollow bolt into general use the CZ23 introduced a further though related innovation, namely the magazine being housed inside the pistol grip. The construction of a weapon with a hollow or overhung bolt brings the chamber well back into the gun body, so that the bolt mass can surround it, and if the pistol grip is pushed slightly forward from its usual position at the back of the body then it is ideally placed for adapting it as the magazine housing. There is a practical advantage in this: changing a sub-machine gun magazine in the dark can be a clumsy business when the magazine housing is 'somewhere out in front'. But if it is in the pistol grip, which is already being firmly grasped, then, acting on the principle that 'hand finds hand', it becomes easy to change magazines.

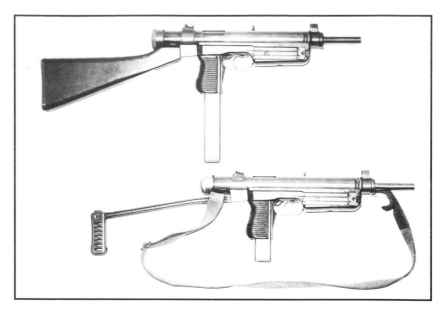

The CZ23 was fitted with a wooden stock but was followed by the CZ25 model which had a folding steel stock; both types were taken into Czech service use. The CZ was chambered for the 9mm Parabellum cartridge, but in 1952 the Soviet Union insisted on the use of their standard 7.62mm sub-machine gun cartridge throughout the Warsaw Pact, so the CZ23 and 25 were withdrawn. They were replaced by the CZ24 and 26 which were exactly the same designs but chambered for the Russian cartridge. The 9mm models were then sold off to various countries, notably Syria and Cuba. In recent years the design has appeared again, in South Africa, as the Sanna 77. In this version it is restricted to semi-automatic fire only and was sold in the late 1970s as a home defence weapon for farmers. These Sanna 77s appear to be the original Czech-built guns refurbished and with the mechanism altered to prevent automatic fire.

Above: The Czech CZ23 (top) with 40-round magazine, and the CZ25 with 24-round magazine. The CZ23 series was a major advance in sub-machine gun design as it made use of the telescoping hollow bolt; an innovation that was to be widely copied in future weapons.

Sub-machine guns

Type	Country	Calibre	Weight	Cyclic rate of fire	Muzzle velocity	Magazine
Thompson M1A1	USA	.45in	5.36kg (11.8lb) (loaded, 30 rounds)	700rpm	280mps (920fps)	20/30-round box 50-round drum
M3A1	USA	.45in	4.52kg (9.94lb) (loaded)	400rpm	280mps (920fps)	30-round box
Carl Gustav Model 45	Sweden	9mm	5kg (11lb) (loaded)	600rpm	360mps (1180fps)	36-round box
Madsen Model 50	Denmark	9mm	3.15kg (6.95lb) (empty)	550rpm	390mps (1280fps)	32-round box
MAT-49	France	9mm	4.76kg (10.59lb) (loaded)	600rpm	354mps (1160fps)	32-round box
MAS 38	France	7.65mm	2.85kg (6.3lb) (empty)	700rpm	350mps (1150fps)	32-round box
Owen	Australia	9mm	4.24kg (9.35lb) (empty)	700rpm	420mps (1375fps)	32-round box
F1	Australia	9mm	4.47kg (9.85lb) (loaded)	600rpm	360mps (1180fps)	34-round box
CZ25	Czechoslovakia	9mm	4.1kg (9.04lb) (loaded, 40 rounds)	650rpm	450mps (1475fps)	24/40-round box

Index